EL SER UNO VI

THE SIREN-LEMURIANOS – CITY OF LIGHT AND LOVE

EL SER UNO

VI

THE SIREN-LEMURIANOS
City of Light and Love

FRANCA ROSA CANONICO DE SCHRAMM

INTERNATIONAL DATA PUBLICATION CATALOGUE
REGISTRY COPYRIGHT / Peru - Lima
Franca Rosa Canonico de Schramm

**Book published originally by the author and channel:
Franca Rosa Canonico de Schramm**

We inform all persons of goodwill that EL SER UNO (Being One) is not associated with anyone who might use the name of the author or of the book to give conferences, form groups, sell printed copies, videos, advertisement and so on, or charge for services or ask for donations in the name of this knowledge.

The channel makes it known that she is not accountable for those who transmit and interpret the knowledge of EL SER UNO (Being One) in their own way, without being based on the original text. EL SER UNO (Being One) is free knowledge and it is not associated with any event or any person who may use it for personal gain.

ISBN: 9798773225157

Books:
EL SER UNO I – The Arcana of Thoth
EL SER UNO II – Planet 3.3.3 – The Guardians of Tera
EL SER UNO III – The Seramitas – The Long Path of Return
EL SER UNO IV – Cosmic Alignment – 7 Thousand Years of Preparation
EL SER UNO V – The Interanos – The City of Crystal
EL SER UNO VI – The Siren-Lemurianos – City of Light and Love

---

www.elseruno.com
www.elserunobooks.com

CONTENT

INTRODUCTION

EL SER UNO VI – The Siren-Lemurianos – City of Light and Love is a SELF-KNOWLEDGE book. It should be read consecutively. To read it out of sequence would be to no avail because it would not bring about the desired results. Reading this book will open up and connect the brain circuits of KNOWLEDGE, UNDERSTANDING and LOVE.

To help understand the contents and to aid you in grasping this knowledge, we suggest consulting the following dictionaries:

- English language and mother tongue
- Dream symbolism
- Esotericism
- Symbols
- Philosophy

Knowledge from *EL SER UNO VI – The Siren-Lemurianos – City of Light and Love* should never be used for profit, power, manipulation or personal gain. Those who do so will be responsible for forming their negative cause and effect. This book was received in order to help the being called Planet Earth become elevated and to do this, humanity will need Knowledge, Understanding and Universal Love.

We would like to make it clear that this book is being published exactly as it was received. The Arcana Masters of Thoth requested this in order to safeguard the original channeling of the book. The Masters said they had placed CODES between the lines and words so that through sequential reading, circuits and channels would be opened, which readers would activate in their minds as they progressed in their reading, because this book is *KNOWLEDGE OF HEALING*...

Readers should realize that this knowledge is not simple to read because it is not a story or a novel but it *is a channeling* based on questions and answers. We recommend that the book be read with an open mind, slowly, very patiently, and above all, following the SEQUENCE in which it was written. If you try to read it randomly you will feel very sleepy, you will have headaches and you will not understand anything at all. The codes inserted between the lines will make your circuits open slowly and due to this, understanding will help you assimilate the content.

We hope that through *EL SER UNO VI – The Siren-Lemurianos – City of Light and Love* you will discover your inner self and heal yourself. If you feel you cannot understand this book, keep on because the questions that may arise in you will be fully answered. Read it with interest. There is a reason for it having come to you. Do not dismiss it from your life. Analyze it, study it and make it part of your own knowledge, understanding and love.

Brothers, sisters and children of light and love

Through these books EL SER UNO, you have traveled with us on the Path of Return. The beings, who are making this journey, are doing it with an awake consciousness, a serious analysis, evaluation and an immense effort that come from the heart and soul. These books are for you; brothers, sisters and children of LIGHT AND LOVE because this is an ancestral knowledge that all of you carry in your thought-energies, in the soul of the ONE.

This is the last of the six books EL SER UNO that tried to transmit this knowledge in a straightforward and readable language. We intentionally have avoided going too much into particular fields of knowledge or abusing of sophisticated terminology as usually was done in the past. Nowadays, sincere and direct words from the heart, are the best way to transmit our message. When a great avatar said, let the children come to me, he meant that simplicity, the light of reason and a pure soul are the plenitude of the spirit.

The reason for our presence in these times, and you already knows about that, is that the Primary Dimension and planet Tera will move closer to higher realities during the Cosmic Alignment that occurs every 28000 and lasts 7000 years. This will approach Tera and other planets to the Star Sun and other more elevated dimensions helping them fill with thought-energies of outstanding quality. It will also contribute to the stabilization of the planetary system's electromagnetism and eliminate ill negative energy that seriously affects the elevation of souls.

We as your Elder Brothers Ayaplianos have transmitted these books via channeling out of the sixth, seventh, eighth and ninth grade of the electromagnetism and magnetism. This is our temporary habitat. Here we stayed when we arrived, and we will be during the 7 Thousand Years of The Cosmic Alignment. Once completed your rescue, that is, the cure and transmutation of the ill negative energy that so severely affected you, we are going to return to our planets of origin.

While evolution of the planet continues, many of you, not all, will settle in the magnetism and take responsibilities for the next generations turning them into the Guardians of Tera as we did. For this to occur, we will teach you everything related to the evolution and elevation of the energy. From this reality, you will teach to the new human-species such as we did it with all of you.

The universe is a very orderly place. Species develop and so do the Nimeos-Energy that become thought-energies. Thought-energies then turn souls, souls turn spirits and spirits finally ideas of the Universal Mind. This is the natural process of the human-species, it is the metamorphosis. That is how it was made the creativity of Tera and gave us the chance to rescue and take you with us to our home planets.

Now is the time of departure for all of us as brothers and spirits in fraternity, Light and Love. The Cosmic Alignment is going to work extraordinary changes for the Primary Dimension, the planet and you. This reality will be entirely different since future human-species will be nurturing themselves with higher and purer energy. The men in the future will transmute the energie and transform it into photons.

Nowadays, you are in a process of energetic immersion, which means to re-discover deep inside your souls the beings of LIGHT you are. Within the immersion process, we should distinguish the different levels. Younger souls apply the process to themselves by adjusting their Nimeos-Energy to the new understanding of the cosmos allowing them to accelerate transformation and comprehension. Consequently, human beings begin to nurture themselves from the flow of cosmic energy called Prana. In few words, the human-being in the future will only feed on the extraction of the universal fluid.

Advancing and turning ever stronger, the energetic immersion or spirit of the LIGHT's essence will be the Freedom of every human being. This spirit is the most elevated expression of the cosmological reality. It is the highest expression of life, sustained by the rest of the conscious universe; being It and part of It.

You as our brothers who having incarnated in these times, are taking the most difficult part of energy changes and therefore must procure to have patience and love in your hearts. Do not fear your innermost transformation, direct your thoughts toward the universe and open your minds to the vertical synchrony and expansion of the soul. Remember that the energy never stops moving because it needs to grow and express itself in a sublime way. This is the law of the cosmos and our creator: the One Origin.

We were always close to you and made us known in a thousand ways and forms. We adapted to beliefs, customs, idiosyncrasies and languages but always stayed the same. We are your vigilant, attentive, loving and dedicated Elder Brothers with an immense concern for your evolution and elevation. We will never leave you alone or adrift.

The universe moves as well with everything rotating around its center while the energy travels with it, manifesting and realizing what this permanent motion requires. Energy is the blood of the universe; it is the soul giving life and existence to the all and connects with the never-ending creativity of the Universal Mind. We all as beings of the universe realize the ideas of the creator. We revolve around its eternal existence, assimilating its wisdom that keeps us alive, dynamic, active and renewed. We live forever as the progeny of an eternal father to preserve the outstanding conditions of its creativity.

Beloved brothers, from the message of these books, you know how you became victims of the virus of distortion. All of you belong to the even (antimatter) reality but since you seem to have lost memory of it, you use terms such as angels, archangels and extraterrestrials to characterize its manifestations, the way you so often do with things you do not understand.

You therefore must learn to listen to yourself. Sometimes, the inner master does not teach or speak with words. It is very quiet and discreet. The silent voice of your heart and soul will always speak with a clear and sincere language to open your minds to the cosmic conscience with its universal message of LIGHT and LOVE. Finding deep inside you this illumination, you will be conscious of the eternity of existence.

Developing this broad vision will help all of you to think and act as authentic and free person and by right belong to you. Using it, will allow you a profound understanding of the Cause and Effect relationship. The conscience of those who comprehend existence separately, still suffers from fantasy. Thought-ideas throughout the universe represent the vast experience of all. Consequently, ILLUMINATION means a mind that finally contemplates the union of all that exists.

When you open your minds feeling certain of the place you hold in a universe consisting of atoms within atoms, your inner universe wakes and becomes very active with great respect and love for everything that surrounds you. This is when you feel to be a part of the cosmos knowing and recognizing that essence and origin of all are the same. This is where the divine DNA of the inner universe grows, evolves and elevates in unison with the principle of ONE.

Many of you stop walking or have great doubts about the Path of Return and spiritual knowledge because they do not notice immediate signs of illumination. Consequently, they perceive this path as one of illusion and fantasy or at least as a spiritual experience of little relevance. Henceforth, they return to the immediate satisfaction from the pleasures Materialism promises. It is very important to be brave, tenacious and to take true determination to persevere on the path of return.

May your inner force be the torch that never extinguishes. For this to occur, you must firmly insist on developing the inner vision necessary to understand the many mysteries of the universe and, above all, of human nature. Whatever your scientific and technological advance, life shows you there is still a lot of things to learn and understand. You must take the control of the unmanageable, beyond the beauty you can built from knowledge.

If you wish to find plenitude of the spirit, you have to think and feel about it in terms of merit. There is correlation between Plenitude and Merit. The Energy of Merit is a deeply rooted feeling in your hearts and souls. As you manage to rid yourselves of out-of-date beliefs and negative emotions, you gain this energy to concentrate on what truly matters...Joyfulness, Well-being and Love.

It is important to highlight that people who enter the real light will experience inner changes that those who are close clearly perceive. By gradually assimilating the teachings, people turn calmer, abandon negative habits and even look younger because they no longer overrate problems that eventually have a solution.

When they accept the knowledge, the light that fills their minds expands and they adopt a different view and better control of things. Gaining maturity, they start correcting and transmuting negative aspects into values that favor their social life and environment. Those who walk the path of spirituality will feel rewarded for having awaked to the cosmic message and grown with the search for LIGHT and LOVE receiving many unexpected answers.

You as a divine creation are beings of LIGHT and LOVE but do not remember this origin and have therefore become victims of control and manipulation by negative forces. You fail to recall your process of evolution and place of origin in the cosmos, to which you, sometime in a distant future, will return. You are a hidden treasure whose cosmic genes are the great fortune of creativity.

We are your Elder Brothers Ayaplianos-Volunteers of the Spacecraft called Brothers of Light, Elder Brothers Ayaplianos-Seramitas, Elder Brothers Ayaplianos-Elohim, Elder Brothers Ayaplianos-Interanos and Elder Brothers Ayaplianos-Siren-Lemurianos.

CHAPTER I

REVIEWING PREVIOUS BOOKS

After I finished the fifth book *EL SER UNO V – The Interanos – The City of Crystal,* I had been without communication from the Elder Brothers for about six months. However, yesterday, they made contact asking me to prepare for a new visit to the City of Crystal. I had been prepared for this new opportunity to deal with a number of pending topics from our previous encounter and, in addition, would take along a considerable list of questions from our readers.

They said, they would now give us further details on why and how the brothers Interanos offered unconditional support at all times and receive us at the Internal City of Atlantis after we disincarnate. The inconditional support that we have received from them in all the times. The foundation of Atlantis dates back to the moment, when Humans began to have conscience of themselves, their environment and the cosmos. The Masters of Atlantis are therefore working hard to prepare both incarnated and disincarnated souls for the return to their planetary and cosmic origin.

The books *EL SER UNO* contain guidelines and advice for our Path of Return. They should not be taken as a religion or as a bible. From all that, we are tired, and we expect that at this point of our existence, we have more answers and clarity, through which we have fall into lies, disappointments, and as a result, kept us blind, deaf and mute. This knowledge belongs to everyone but not for everyone. It is convenient to read the books when we feel calm and relaxed. It should be read them slowly and not desperately stuffed into the mind as a delicious treat for the spirit. It is also important making pauses between paragraphs for analysis using dictionaries of philosophy, symbols and dreams if necessary for better understanding. Reading them with other people is an interesting option to encourage a discussion about the message from different angles.

Considering the abundance and variety of information, we suggest that you take your TIME for reading each of the books. This will allow your soul to comprehend the message that your brain had been processing. If you go to fast, reading might become tiring and sometimes produce physical discomfort such as headaches, sleepiness, and indigestion or gluttony. In a direct and clear language, the books question and frequently disarm rigid and largely accepted concepts in religion and hermeticism of this and past lives.

The books EL SER UNO are knowledge that deals with philosophical, psychological and spiritual aspects. Regarding spirituality, they do not refer to it as defined by religion but as a spirituality based on Self-Knowledge and broad understanding of the Cause and Effect relationship through the active use of Thought-Energy. For this reason, the direct concepts used by EL SER UNO are not adapted to many people. It is important to analyze our soul because that way, we can see and feel what it is necessary for it. Many people prefer mysticism and even esotericism to seek to advance on the path of conscience and therefore need a different type of orientation.

We again insist that those who decide reading the books do so calmly and slowly to give their emotions a chance to experiment and, if possible, understand and accept what the books propose in their message. Since they seriously question deeply rooted structures, souls (people) suffer because they fear to give up beliefs strongly influenced by routine and superficiality. If they do, however could mean having to restructure their lives built on concepts taught and practiced for generations.

To walk that way, the soul must rid itself of a burden it carried for a long time. Leaving behind routine, automatism, inflexibility, fantasy and complacency with the whims of the Ego and the satisfaction of the external senses will demand determination, strength, perseverance, knowledge, understanding and much love.

Before my new visit to the Internal-Antimatter City of Atlantis, I had several conversations via telepathy with the Elder Brothers regarding pending questions from the fifth book. They say they would answer all of them and offered to teach us the procedure for Self-Healing that would keep us from depending on other means or people. They explain that this was also how they learned to be responsible and record it on their Nimeos-Energy. Consequently, wisdom passed from generation to generation nurturing the spirits so that they could join the cosmic reality of EL SER UNO.

On September 16th, 2013, the brothers Seramitas, Elohim and the brother and sister Interanos make contact as always. This time however, our conversations would not be in the previous hall room but at the wing of a large building, that according to the brothers Interanos is the access to the Internal Antimatter City of ATLANTIS and the nine grades of the electromagnetism.

We advance to a very large white and brightly lit oval hall room with chairs of Greek and Roman style similar to those ancient philosophers may have used, while teaching. Every detail of this place gives a sense of comfort, harmony and much peace. After we settle down, the brother Interano starts explaining the reason for being in this part of the Internal City. He addresses me while speaking but, in reality, what he would say from now on would be for all humans on the planet.

He begins by saying that in every one of the grades they would present live souls by affinity and merit. In all of them, there are instructors helping cure the defects that the Nimeos-Energy brought in from the odd (matter) reality, the anomalies of which we would be able to observe from a very short distance for the first time. He goes on explaining that in every grade of the electromagnetism there is a replicate of planet Tera. These replicates represent each of the Energy Centers of man and the cosmos and connect with their respective grade, plane and dimension of the universe.

This is how we establish contact with the Superior and Inferior universe – observes the brother Interano – without the need for space travel. We just pass from one grade to another. It is what you know as Wormholes – remarks the sister Interana.

There is a projection of every one's Nimeos-Energy on each of the nine Tera planet replicates – continues the brother Interano – what we say is that the energy of one human being occupies nine Teras at the same time. Let us show you an example about what would be the situation of our brother Charles. Each of Charles´ Energy Centers has its grade, plane and dimension. The Energy Centers 1 – 5 connect with the Physical and Psychical Bodies of the universe; the Energy Centers 6 – 9 connect with the magnetism of the universe, that is, the Spiritual Body of EL SER UNO.

Charles' Nimeos-Energy are thus present in the nine dimensions of creativity at the same time. Comparatively, this is the definition of the systems of material body, each one working within a whole, and each one forming a body. This is how the thousands of millions of Nimeos-Energies in the universe work for their preservation and the all called EL SER UNO.

You were made in the image and cosmic likeness – continues the brother Interano – you exist in the nine dimensions; however the problem is that you were not conscious of it for a very long time. With your awakening, you now are connecting with your Energy Centers and the Energy Centers of the Universe. Consequently, you are to have connected with your respective grades, planes and dimensions. Unfortunately, this is not the case. The reason is that distortion disconnected you from the source of EL SER UNO, that is, the Superior Energy Centers of the soul remained disconnected. This explains why you lack a global vision of EL SER UNO.

In that moment, I thought of the Kundalini Energy. The Sister Interana look at me and said: Yes, that is the way you elevate the soul and the spirit by allowing you to make a mental travel, enter and exit through the Energetic Centers of the universe – she stayed in silent for a moment and continues – for the time being, you can only make it mentally, but one day, when you form the spirit, you will do it energetically. This is the elevated body, The Ovni, who will transport you wherever your Desire of Creator is capable.

We therefore frequently mention the SUPERIOR SELF – remarks the brother Interano – what is the Superior Self? It is you living in a different grade, plane and dimension of a Replicate Tera, that is, in the Energy Centers of the sixth, seventh, eighth and ninth grade of the magnetism. When activating your INNER SELF (sixth grade), SUPERIOR SELF (seventh grade), DIVINE SELF (eighth grade) and SUBLIME SELF (ninth grade) you are living different and ever more elevated states of conscience. On the other hand, when activating the low grade Energy Centers (1 – 5), you live in these centers as replicates of low frequency energy. That is the ugly, monstrous and misshape image from yourself.

Every Energy Center is a world, a planet Tera with parallel realities – the sister Interana pauses, and the brother Interano continues – working the Energy Centers, your replicate energy of a higher reality will absorb that of an inferior reality. This way, the soul keeps gathering its Nimeos-Energy to form one single body, the Spiritual Body whose elevated vibration allows it to leave the electromagnetism and join the four grades (6 – 9) of the magnetism.

The other brothers and I have remained silent listening with attention. While the two Interanos are speaking, I remember Hell, Purgatory and Heaven of Dante Alighieri's *Divine Comedy,* thinking to myself that the author might have seen the different grades of the electromagnetism and magnetism during an Astral Walk depicting both in accordance with the religious beliefs of his time. Without interrupting my thoughts, the brother Interano looks at me and nods in agreement.

After this short introduction by the brothers Interanos, we all decide to begin the interview. I suggest starting our conversation with some of the pending issues from the fifth book, which all accept.

1. Some parts of the fifth book mention that the soul of people who did not manage to develop their Spirit through acts while incarnated will lose its individuality when disincarnating and turn a collective soul because its Nimeos-Energy disintegrate into the 9 grades of the electromagnetism. How can a soul incarnate again after it has disintegrated and lost its individuality? How could there

be consecutive acts, life after life, if we can receive anyone's Nimeos-Energy and the memory of a life we did not live, if we fail to preserve the same Nimeos-Energy?

Part of the Nimeos-Energy of this soul belong to the lower grades of the electromagnetism (collective-soul-electricity) – explains the sister Interana –. Its frequency, electricity, rhythm and colors will therefore determine the grades this energy will occupy. We may classify it as a material-collective-soul holding basic functions of the species such as instinct and sensations.

The lower grades of the electromagnetism characterize the material reality of the planet reflecting collective features of the souls (people) such as, for instance, culture, idiosyncrasy, language and habits. Their Nimeos-Energy are common to all individuals and will therefore be a part of any human-mold (physical body).

There are others Nimeos-Energy as the ill-negative and healthy-positive emotions related to the medium-grade electromagnetism. If ill-negative, they will disintegrate when disincarnating and occupy lower grades. If healthy-positive, they will disintegrate and occupy higher grades according to their vibration frequency, rhythm, color and electricity.

Higher Nimeos-Energy do not disintegrate, are individual and therefore join the superior grades of the magnetism. Consequently, we call them no longer collective souls but Spirits.

For a better understanding, we wish to point out that "disintegration" in the universe means classification according to characteristics, typology, etc. – explains the brother Interano – therefore, every grade of the electromagnetism and magnetism compares to the Energy Centers or Chakras of the human body. In fact, if we consider this, Nimeos-Energy of the soul will not disintegrate by losing them into the space. They just will be placed in order in the Energy Centers (Chakras) of the electromagnetism and magnetism.

The Energy Centers proceed to cure and prepare the Nimeos-Energy for the next incarnation where they will continue healing, learning and transmuting their lower and medium grade realities. After occupying a new human-mold, both grades gather in these Energy Centers taking up the learning process.

Since many of the Nimeos-Energy are collective souls, they incarnate by affinity of frequency, electricity, rhythm and colors. We call this process INCARNATION. From the fourth grade on, elevated souls and, of course, spirits are individual and therefore independent and always the same, life after life. This process we call REINCARNATION.

What is the purpose of the whole process? – observes the sister Interana – to eliminate the lower worlds by raising the Kundalini energy via the Energy Centers (Chakras) of the human-mold and electromagnetism to become MAGNETISM-SPIRITS. Consequently, superior realities working with the grades, planes and dimensions of Magnetic Vibration instead of Magnetic Electricity will attract the Kundalini energy. When this occurs, it will stop disintegrating into the electromagnetism via the Energy Centers because it now belongs to the eternal magnetism of the PINEAL GLAND of EL SER UNO.

2. How do we notice that the energy centers are becoming active?

When you work with your Energy Centers (Chakras) by using understanding, will, and inner senses, these Centers develop flexibility to open and close – remarks the brother Interano – this means that you can voluntarily open and close them for whatever needs you have. People, for instance, will no longer have sex to procreate driven by passion but always with the creative feeling of Love. This will cause the first Chakra or Center of Procreation to open allowing the energy of sincere love vigorously to flow.

3. I understand that people are not ready for the opening of their centers. However, when working with Reiki I have to connect with the universal energy. Consequently, the harmony gained carries the wisdom of the divine. Is this correct?

EL SER UNO says that: "Every individual is responsible for his/her universe and going to live in accordance with the energy of the thoughts" – observes the brother Elohim – reiki is certainly helpful because with the laying on of hands the healer does connect with the Universal Energy and deserves our appreciation for this effort. However, we have to understand that only the very patient is able to open the chakras or work the cure as this entirely depends on the merit of his/her inner work.

With the laying on of hands, in an act of affectionate intention, he/she is not healing but sending an energetic message from the cosmos to the patient. It is now the patient's turn to understand it and have the strength to work his/her alchemical transmutation. Reiki is therefore also help from the cosmos but again, neither the healer nor the universe will realize what only the individual with the desire for healing can do.

It now depends on the grade your thought-energies occupy in the electromagnetism or magnetism whether the Energy Centers or Chakras function in a more or less balanced way – remarks the brother Interano – if you concentrate on the material reality, you predominantly use the first three grades. If it is the astral (mental) reality, you will work with the first five grades. However, if it is the spiritual reality, the nine Chakras (grades) of existence will be active. It all is a question of the thought-energies' vibration frequency. Therefore, EL SER UNO says that: "Every soul has its grade that determines if your choice is to seek and find the dream of harmony and peace or run the risk to end up in a nightmare

4. Could we say that reaching complete illumination means joining all the replicates we are with our energetic being that occupies a different dimension?

Yes, this is correct – replies the brother Elohim – as you raise your thought-energy, the replicates keep joining and your soul enriches by assimilating higher Nimeos-Energy. These Nimeos keep rising via the Kundalini thus further strengthening the soul that sends positive energy to the right hemisphere of the brain. The brain then prepares the Pineal Gland for the conception of the Baby-Spirit.

When you consciously work an Energy Center and join one replicate to a previous one, – continues the brother Seramita – this Energy Center closes down because its transmuted needs have reached a higher grade and returns to cover the necessities of its grade. Illumination therefore means to raise all energy via the Kundalini and join the replicates until reaching the Energy Center in the Pineal Gland. Once completed the joining of all replicates, a person becomes ONE by forming the individual Spiritual Body.

This is why many of you transform the energy of their sexual needs into energy of a cosmic and universal need for love – observes the sister Interana – food suffers a change in priority as an object for refined taste and resumes its importance as healthy and tasteful sustenance of our physical lives. Our emotions change because, working and understanding them, we transform them into strong and active feelings. Deeds, acts and thoughts are early music, thinking is no longer just a mental exercise, performance is not about impressing the public and the action is by necessity and does not become an end – the brother Interano pauses and then continues – human beings turn to work on the transformation and refinement of their external senses. It is the long journey toward the Internal City, the realization of the species.

Not all are ready for this journey into the deep of their souls or to dive into the unreality of their lives. The truth of existence and the answers from our inner world are in every Energy Center or Chakra and they tell you the grade you occupy in the process. Therefore, communicate with your Chakras in a direct and clear dialogue and wait for the answer. If you feel you are addicted to one of the Centers, if the thought-energies live and work for them, you will understand what grade you occupy.

The desires of the Ego to procreate are the sensors of the centers – says the brother Elohim – these sensors clearly reflect your inclinations, desires, needs, positive emotions and those prisoners of the vices of materialism. Many of your reactions to the environment and interactions with people may cause emotional disorders that the Energy Centers will register. As a result, the creation of positive thought-energies will diminish. It is therefore of great importance to the health of your soul and mind that you deepen your understanding of how each of the centers works.

5. What can we do to harmonize reasoning and understanding with love? This should be the principle of a life of love that never will desist from looking for situations that give us happiness. While our emotions say thank you and I love you, our thoughts often do not.

There is much truth in what you say – agrees the brother Elohim – indeed, reasoning, understanding and love do not always meet because there are conflicting emotions and interests, exceeding expectations, the lack of knowledge of the Cause and Effect relationship and many others that often affect clear reasoning and understanding, which causes emotions to make decisions of the heart.

In general, reasoning starts decision-making by observing, examining and analyzing situations but, in the end, the emotions from a whimsical Ego take over by ignoring analysis and reason.

Reason is the principal voice of your mind. However, prisoners of the emotions that make your Ego jump with joy, you do not use the equanimity because that takes you away the pleasure of life – observes the sister Interana – consequently, you do not listen to the voice of the common sense. Instead, you prefer feeling and tasting the passion to the prudence words of love. Reason is therefore in the middle of a fight between the emotions and love, in which love will prevail if it manages to control, ordain and balance the emotions.

If this occurs, reason, thought and love will have vanquished and transmuted the pleasures of the Ego with a feeling of ecstasy that will forever reign in your souls. If not, the pleasures of passion will be greater than ever for some time until you realize that you again succumbed to the temptations of Ego and emotions.

The secret of happiness is not in your material lives but deep inside your minds. Its name is Thought-Energy because your thoughts create and transform whatever you can imagine. To give your minds the chance to project, design and execute in a correct way, your thoughts have to have order and equilibrium. The nine brain zones of the Lid Circuit must work in unison. Otherwise, creation turns procreation, there will be no reasoning, analysis and harmony as thoughts will move in a vicious circle. Love will have no chance because without continuity and correlation of the process of reasoning and understanding, the force of the emotions will reign and grow without the least control.

Consequently, for reasoning, understanding and love to work together, you must concentrate on the control, order of the emotions and place them where they belong – stresses the brother Interano – that is the only way to obtain real results. As long as, Emotions and Ego dominate, they will reign over your Thought-Energy. Thought-Energy-King will be no longer, but the Emotion-Ego-King and you will be unable to reason, understand and love.

6. What would you say about people who heal animals through laying on of hands?

Bearers of a higher-grade energy, these persons cannot use their energy on animals – remarks the sister Interana – since their vibration frequency is different from that of animals'. However, advanced the evolution of an animal, the difference is such that a healer with all the love for animals and good intentions would not succeed. The healer's function is that of a catalyst channeling cosmic energy for complementary medical treatment. Although, the moment this healer proceeds to use it on a sick animal, it will fail for a lack of affinity.

There are souls in the first two grades of the electromagnetism that not yet have incarnated in the human form. You call them Elementary souls or Spirits of Nature. These are the energies a healer must attract to work a cure on animals. However, it is not just the laying on of hands but the knowledge a healer needs to do a good job. This knowledge comes from astral advisors the moment the healer makes contact with the universal energy grades and adjusts to the particular need of each patient.

For the treatment of animals, the healer will receive advice on the type of energy to use – observes the brother Interano – this means that the advisors will indicate what energy from an elementary soul or spirit of nature a particular species needs for a successful treatment. Each one, vegetal, animal or human species have their own energies, in which they will be applied according to specific illness.

The many healers therefore must specialize in different areas, the way doctors in human and veterinary medicine do. This is the way to heal by the laying on of hands. Everyone has a specific field. Imagine a pediatrician would like to have the skills of a surgeon specializing in heart operations. They both are doctors, but they have different areas of study.

Advancing on your preparation for the Internal City, this is where you will gain the knowledge and wisdom about the energy – affirms the brother Elohim – the souls that succeed will receive our teachings to become the spiritual doctors of the future. Nevertheless, rather than the true healers who act with dedication and love, there are also those who practice the laying on of hands without this preparation, driven by ambition and the search for material well-being.

Those true healers generally preceded other life forms of a world ready to receive new inhabitants. Before these came to the planet, the healers tried to leave a legacy filling large libraries with the knowledge about immense cities of subterranean empires. These libraries built from small crystals hold the archives with the History of the Universe. A magnetic field protects them, which nowadays sometimes connects with sensitive people in the outside.

7. I never understood why animals have to suffer torture and some species to be food for humans. Nor do I comprehend why you, God or the One Origin have failed to care for them. They are defenseless and do not even speak. Why do they have to go through this? According to the books, we are in a process of evolution to advance to other dimensions, the poor beasts, however, are just entertainment, slaves and food for this species called human.

We understand your indignation because this is what people who are living the “Awakening of Conscience” deeply feel – starts saying the brother Interano – you call on Jehovah, the Energy of the Universe and many other entities that you consider the superior deity of the universe for human beings who are starving, in misery, sick and suffer so many other hardships of the primary reality. All human beings of conscience ask these questions and yearn from the deep of their hearts for Harmony, Peace and Love in this planet.

Nonetheless, what are your chances for the big change? Are you sure, you should ask other planets, realities or dimensions to face your egotism and lack of compassion, the manipulation and mistreatment of millions of human beings by those who have the power for the benefit of a minority and a legion of other vulgar abuses – questions the sister Interana – if this happens to human beings what are the animals’ chances for a decent treatment? Human-Specie is the biggest predator on earth. The most bloodthirsty, fierce and barbarian. However inhospitable and savage this primary reality might have been from the beginning, we immensely regret that humans failed to avert violence to invade their souls.

Compassion and love are qualities of beings who have awaked and are truly conscious of their condition and that of their environment – observes the brother Elohim – they are souls with the memory of great suffering and therefore incapable of making suffer others. Their feelings help them distinguish between good and evil and to make an appropriate use of their knowledge and the Spiritual Laws. How to ask a baby to take care of his toys or to put them in the closet? The baby will have to be taught and will grow up through the years becoming aware of the surrounding and when he reaches the adulthood.

In the other hand, we, as your Elder Brother, ask you this question: If you, for instance, lived with a tribe somewhere in Africa, in a place with very limited conditions for growing vegetables and fruit but with a reasonable number of animals for its sustenance, would you ask their members to become vegetarian or even vegan?

It is all relative. Living in a big city, you have all the possibilities for that choice – said the sister Interana – this means, that there is no need for the sacrifice of animals to feed the population and you should thank for the opportunity to be able to make a decision that will help your spirit grow. However, as students of a primary-planet-school like Earth, you cannot expect to be all in the same grade, plane and dimension of spiritual comprehension.

Life in this reality is slow. Therefore, try not to be radical in your judgement. Showing Compassion and Love means to understand that during the process of evolution and elevation, there is a moment for all Human Beings to Awake and the LIGHT of Knowledge, Understanding and LOVE for everything created turn essential for them. You will correct many errors from the early years of your lives related to a lack of compassion, a limited understanding of spirituality, errors of education, poor eating habits etc. This dialogue with your inner-self needs a good deal of patience – concludes the brother Elohim – those who have decided to walk this path of great responsibility nevertheless will realize that it is solitary, misunderstood and often criticized by people who resist to awake because they would have to face the ugly world they have created.

8. Will the study of new healing therapies such as cellular memory, Akashic record or Biodanza help us spiritually grow or is it just another desire of the Ego?

In all times on this planet, there have been rituals, chants, prayers and mantras, which in one way or another have influenced your understanding of spirituality – observes the sister Interana – there is also the legacy of beliefs from parents to children for generations that makes it difficult for you to decide what to do with everything you learned. However, you are so insecure about what spirituality means to you that you fear that dismissing something of importance from this inheritance might have you choose the wrong way in the process of illumination.

Then what? You study and study accumulating information, attend conferences of renowned “Masters and Gurus” who charge high fees, which supposedly guarantees that you are on the right way – remarks the brother Interano – you learn how to use the techniques and methods available in this market of spiritual instruction. You read, or rather, you eat all the books that come to your hands. You become members of groups that study metaphysics and esotericism and eventually end up with a SPIRITUAL CONGESTION. Besides this, you will be so fat for having eaten all this knowledge that you will not be able to walk backwards or forward.

This over-feeding with ideas and concepts will affect your thoughts, and could make you feel unable to decide which way to go – goes on saying the brother Interano – gaining knowledge is necessary but you have to proceed with EQUILIBRIUM. New knowledge is the desire and need of the Ego to define the meaning of a spiritual life, that is, you believe that advancing on metaphysical and esoteric concepts but also following inherited beliefs, your soul will give you the feeling to be on the right path. This idea is present in all incarnations.

The path of spirituality is one of QUALITY rather than QUANTITY. In physical terms, we would say it is not just eating but nurturing – observes the brother Elohim – it is extracting from what you hear and read what truly nurtures your soul. The market of spiritual orientation offers often delirious and useless ideas but also information worthwhile studying. You therefore have to detect what you consider of help for your process of illumination and to understand, there are useless information that will occupy important spaces of the brain. If you over-feed the brain with fattening concepts you will not be able to keep nutrients-knowledge. Those who accept any kind of concepts only fill their lives with provisions but fail to nurture their existence. In other words, the limited value of knowledge hampers the development of understanding.

Therefore, healers have to look for balance through useful knowledge instead of relying on methods and techniques. They will find this balance using the wisdom gained through great spiritual efforts life after life, where the healing circuits are clean and fat free or from useless elements. Thus, there will be a subtle and steady flow of sound elevated energy through their healing circuits toward the patient. He will be no longer feed but nourished with elevated, subtle, and correctly healthy elements.

Consequently, it is not just the laying on of hands that will start the healing process, but the ability healers developed in other lives gaining "Merit" through positive results – affirms the brother Elohim – true healers must heal their three bodies, before they use their hands on a patient because any kind of contamination in their circuits will make them responsible for a negative outcome.

Furthermore, healers' emotions have to show control and harmony. Their three bodies must be clean and their souls with sound positive thoughts. However, good intentions and love alone are not enough, only the convergence of Knowledge, Understanding and deep Love for Cause and Effect will produce Thoughts, Acts and Deeds.

9. About addictions: Do you also consider the pleasure we feel when we meditate absorbing the inner light an addiction?

There is no doubt about the meaning of addiction:

Addiction: A primary, in many cases, chronical pathology for whose development and manifestation genetic, psychosocial and environmental factors are responsible. The disease is often progressive and fatal. Its characteristics are temporary or continuous episodes with the lack of control over the use of drugs despite negative consequences and distorted reasoning, notably denial (Wikipedia).

As we can see – says the sister Interana – everything that is produced or practiced in excess, causing extreme excitation and anxiety has NEGATIVE consequences. That is NOT correct. You have grown a strong habit for techniques and methods, which you repeat over and again because, if you do not, you feel that something is missing. There are pleasures and addictions in those repetitions because you believe this to be the way your soul will find answers, harmony and peace. We therefore can say that you are addicts to what you understand as meditation. To begin with, you may not consider Meditation an "exercise" because it is synonymous of "reflection" on thoughts and acts – keeps explaining the sister Interana – meditation does not require a certain pose to be sure that you are meditating. In Eastern countries, many people used and still use poses to help their material bodies recycle the energy to allow it to circulate harmoniously through the energy centers (Chakras). Nowadays, – says the brother Interano – everything is less formal, your knowledge has extended and many of you, instead of using the old way, meditate by just using their Desire of Creation.

As humans' minds are working consciously, they have conceived their Baby-Spirit that helps them eliminate or change the old techniques. The energy of the spiritual body is fast and we could compare it to a modern universal program – observes the sister Interana – keep in mind that those who are gestating their spiritual body have no longer analogous mental-energy or low resolution but high definition Nimeos-Energy.

Imagine that this change to high-definition energy has favored all who activated their Pineal Gland with the insertion of new programs to make way for a new, mental Phase.

10. Why do we have to go through innumerable physical and mental transmutations and physical as well as mental suffering in this plane? Why do we have to repeat so many times the same process if according to EL SER UNO, we the human species hold all the knowledge for elevation? Why can we not go faster to reach the more elevated worlds? On reading the revelations of these books, I am asking myself why we have to stay so many years in an aging and declining physical body.

To take such a leap forward would mean to intend putting a child in university. That it would be impossible, right? – remarks the brother Interano – remember that planet Earth and its inhabitants are in the third grade, plane and dimension. EL SER UNO says that THE REASON FOR YOUR SUFFERING IS THE LACK OF UNDERSTANDING. Therefore, you all are students at the Earthly school with grades any school has.

Those who are studious really want to know (Conscience). Those who are idle show disdain, indifference and ignorance (Unconscious). Finally, those who have no interest at all in studying live in total darkness (Subconscious). Life is a school that gives you an opportunity to learn to grow with every true-to-life experience.

The reason you live is to know from where you come, whom you are and where you will go – keeps explaining the brother Elohim –. It is to get to know your inner self, learn to love others and yourselves, to know to forgive and share this process with other persons. You may make mistakes, reprove exams but always will have a chance to try again. Your goal must be to build a life of peace accepting and enjoying things as they are with the confidence that everything will be all right. This planet is a place for you to learn. Gaining Knowledge, deepening Understanding and having Love for yourselves occurs in the Primary Grades, for your environment in the Secondary Grades, for the planet at the University and finally turns Cosmic Wisdom in the doctorate in a process of Evolution and Elevation – ended by saying the sister Interana – your souls have to submit to this process because it is the only way for your energy to advance and gain the merit to transcend this world for the unlimited realities of universal existence.

11. What will be the human mind like in the New Age?

Human minds in the future will work guided by the waves of their brains – observes the brother Elohim – both the left and right hemisphere of the brain will produce them in a balanced way and without any difference since evolution and elevation will be a single expression. The acute vibration of particles traveling as sound waves across an infinite medium produce this perception by the inner senses – explains the brother Seramita – until now, this vibration has been horizontal through electricity. By turning vertical, the Nimeos-Energy will be moving back and forth and up and down, a characteristic we call: Spherical Waves.

Spherical Waves

They are tridimensional frequency sound waves, which means that they move in three directions at the same time and show radial spheres that the source of excitation produces. You so far have worked with the below listed type of waves.

Beta Waves

They are present when a person is awake and with full brain activity. The external senses concentrate on the exterior, that is, on the emotions causing the ill negative emotions to accompany a person in daily life.

Alpha Waves

They are active when you are about to fall asleep. They make you relax, produce a feeling of physical and mental well-being, and allow you to develop the stable harmony of Equanimity.

Theta Waves

They occur in dreams or profound meditation favoring memory, creativity, imagination and inspiration. You may start channeling thought-energies from other grades, planes and dimensions.

Delta Waves

They are responsible for the profound sleep without any perception or experience, which compares to deep hypnosis.

Gamma Waves

They are extraordinary activators of neurons during creative processes and in problem solving favoring the presence of Theta Waves. They are special neurons because they work with genius and creativity.

All these ***Spherical Waves*** will give human beings the exceptional condition to perceive themselves and their environment in a tri-dimensional way because the human mind will capture the frequency, amplitude and form of any of their vibrations at the same time – explains the brother Elohim – your minds will thus register harmonious expressions that produce stable vibratory waves but reject confuse sensations that fail to carry well-balanced thought-energies.

12. If we have the capacity of observing our thoughts, emotions, matter and environment but as some sort of witness are not part of what occurs, then who actually observes everything? Our conscience, soul, spirit?

EL SER UNO says that you have three bodies, the physical (Matter), psychical (Soul) and mental (Spirit) – remarks the brother Elohim – it also says that your thought-energies (soul) make your brains work and that these energies occupy the nine brain zones. The activity they will develop depends on the body to which they belong. The nine brain zones divide into the first five that belong to the grades, planes and dimensions of the Inferior Reality and the remaining four zones to the grades, planes and dimensions of the Superior Reality.

Consequences of thinking and acting relate to what thought-energies the brain uses. People, who work with the first three brain zones, have a predominant interest in material things (materiality) or, in a negative attitude, tend to materialism. If they work with the first four and five zones, they will go beyond materiality to cover their needs and therefore find shelter from materialism because their thought-energies are conscious of its dominating force. Having awaked, they will no longer be prisoners of dense and obscure thoughts. This means that they will concentrate on the elevation of their thought-energies. The maturity of their energy will help them gain the knowledge of existence and for the first time they will know that this planetary reality is a passage, a station on the long and infinite path

As you enter brain zones four and five, your thought-energies keep elevating and allow you to communicate or interact with disincarnated thought-energies (souls) of an equal grade of elevation. Consequently, your thought-energies turn the "Guides of Yourselves", this inner voice that helps you with the journey of return. We know it as MEDIUMSHIP

– continues the brother Interano – elevated thought-energies that communicate with you are THE SUPERIOR SELF, thought-energies (higher Souls and Spirits) that freely move in the superior brain zones. They may be elevated souls that disincarnated and entered the Internal City or Spirits in parallel realities, worlds of other planes and dimensions. If you continue elevating thought-energies, you will pass onto brain zone six and gain the vibration frequency of the grades and planes of the Superior Reality, where THE SUPERIOR SELF turns THE DIVINE SELF or THE VOICE OF THE CONSCIENCE. The Energetic Beings (Spirits) of this reality also become the "Guides of Yourselves", however, not in the quality of medium but as CHANNELING OR TELEPATHY.

The human brain is a recipient for thought-energies (souls) because the disincarnated souls need the electricity of the brain to continue existing – explains the sister Interana – you can compare it with the following: If you want to listen to music, you need a CD player to work an broadcast the music. The CD player is the matter-brain, the CD is the soul, and the music is the Spirit.

Thought-energy cannot function alone. It needs matter to do so. In a Thought-Energy's third, fourth and fifth plane and dimension, the "Electricity" will allow the thought to subsist. In the sixth, seventh, eighth and ninth grade, plane and dimension, "Vibration" will secure the continuity of the thought-idea that no longer needs a brain (CD player) for the generation of its frequency. Vibration as part of the cosmos' magnetism receives the continual and eternal energy of the Universal Mind.

13. What happens to those mediums who lose their ability for lack of confidence or look for some kind of evidence to restore it?

You sometimes see heavens without knowing it. We deeply regret that so many human beings listening to the advice from family members or other persons decide to shut down their medium channel – affirms the sister Interana – perhaps the lack of knowledge has affected their energy to the point of making them desist. A characteristic of channeling is that there is no proof by earthly parameters. We may, however, categorize it as Negative and Positive, of low and high frequency and recognize it by the Cause and Effect relationship it reveals. Another means of classification could be the form of the messages or teachings and therefore relate it to the Material, Inner, Superior, Divine and Sublime Self.

However, the thousands of people who realize channeling nowadays should not present it as a belief, religion or the one truth – keeps on the brother Interano – the messages they receive instead should serve for what the soul needs most. If they use them to help people learn to overcome their hardships, strive to be better persons, show them how to control and transmute ill negative emotions and thus lead them on the way to the Awakening of Conscience then channeling will have immensely served its purpose: Path of Return.

To know how to maintain channeling positive and stable is the work of channels who take utmost care of their physical and psychical bodies – reminds the brother Elohim – this means that their emotions must be in an advanced state of harmony and peace. They should live a retired life, away from vices. They always will try to do better and are aware that their mission demands great responsibility for what they receive and transmit as collaborators of the positive universal force in this planet. They must have a clear conscience and know well their earthly mission. As any human being, they have to satisfy material needs, however, without yielding to materialism and face the temptations of the Ego in the form of ambition for power and money successfully. If they failed, it would mean the end of their mission and darkness for their souls. At last, they must stand firm and unbreakable through the path of the Spirit Elevation.

True channels will therefore always procure to have elevated thought-energies and consequently never let dense and low frequency entities ridicule them. If they keep their energies in high frequencies, low entities could not live in the LIGHT that the soul emits. Channels who live by the canons of the universe striving to fulfill their mission will never doubt that their channelings carry the high frequency of BEINGS OF LIGHT AND LOVE.

14. I receive letters from people asking me if what they do is actually channeling and if their masters are real. They do not seem to understand the origin of those communications. What should I tell them?

If these persons trusted those "masters", they would not turn to EL SER UNO to be sure that they have chosen the correct path – observes the brother Elohim – the moment they ask this question, they seem to have doubts about it. When mediums or channels are truly conscious of their task, they do not vacillate since their "masters" will show them the way. People who want to embark on this work must know that the universe will ask them to follow certain rules strictly to guarantee the relevance required for this type of universal work. These are the rules.

- Those who decide on this work have to be very sure of themselves. They have to understand that before they start working for the benefit of "others", they must work on themselves. When they feel having gained the necessary physical, psychological and mental equilibrium, they will be ready to transmit in a correct way the teachings received from the "Spiritual Masters".
- Working with the energy of the universe does not mean that they may neglect their innermost personal work, which is an indispensable condition for their high quality universal activity.
- Channels have to be conscious and confident of the "Master or Masters" with whom they maintain contact. They must visualize them, that is, understand to which grade, plane and dimension they belong, what the knowledge they transmit would be and learn about the particular circumstances of the transmission.
- As long as there are no real answers, they may not start this work alone by using their intuition, good intention and determination to serve, nor because they think they just have to do it or because the emotions of their Ego seem to show them the way.
- True "Masters" do not present themselves without indicating their names, grades and hierarchies. The beings of more advanced realities are straightforward, clear and never would hide

information that could hamper transmissions and compromise this elevated contact.

- After accepting this universal task, channels gradually have to assume full responsibility for their work and correct any possible error never drawing a personal benefit that it might offer.
- Those who decide on this way have to be ready to face beliefs, habits, social pressures, confrontations etc. Nevertheless, knowing that their efforts will encourage the Awakening of Conscience, their inner strength will protect them against possible adversities.
- Dedication to the universal work is a lifetime decision. Channels must therefore look for equilibrium between the material and spiritual reality. This requires a stable physical condition as well as a balanced judgement to prevent that those human emotions affect their work with what could be a conflict between the material needs and the nature of cosmic teachings.
- Dealing with the negative part of their Ego is fundamental for channels. They should work on their character and personality which must be well founded. The Ego is prone to many subtle temptations and channels who fail to be aware may eventually fall for them.
- If channels meet with the above conditions having their "Masters" shown them the steps to take, have consciously worked with their innermost self in the present and past lives with proof of their ability, as mediums or channels, they will be able to initiate their cosmic work with LIGHT and LOVE.

WHAT DOES FULFILLING A COSMIC TASK MEAN? – Ask the brother Seramita – when channels begin this work, they have to feel sure about why and how they do it. They may not turn to the tarot, divination or other channels to make sure they are doing the right thing, as this would denote hesitation, insecurity and even irresponsibility. The very moment doubts make them worry, could mean that they do not know how to proceed or worse, distrust their inner voice and even their "masters". Therefore, we once again must stress that the cosmic task demands a firm compromise, balanced emotions and great responsibility.

The Channels must have courage, bravery, discernment, equilibrium, and the support of their "Masters", in order to be at the same level of the teachings received – says the sister Interana – those who lack these qualities will not succeed by just creating a site on the internet as spiritual consultants, giving conferences and forming groups of followers based on the knowledge from a number of courses they have attended or books they have read. Those who do spiritual work without the support from "Masters" must be aware that they are on their own. Theirs is not a universal but planetary work. As a result, they remain without the universal feelings that would assist them and instead rely on the Human Emotions in combination with "supposedly" cosmic guidance.

15. How can we recognize the presence of grade 1 or 2 thought-energy in messages and low vibrations we receive? I worry about those people who do not know how to protect themselves and could become prisoners easily.

To answer this question, we have to use planetary knowledge. We know or sense that there are universal and planetary canons as well as laws of creativity that watch over the energy and order of everything created – remarks the brother Interano – to tell ill negative from sound positive thought-energies, you must guide yourselves by these laws, many of which you have already known and recorded on the energy of your souls and others you still must accept and study.

You already live by the laws of the planet with their origin in religion, culture, education, beliefs and true-to-life-experience. The very energy of the soul emanates from the One Origin and carries inherent wisdom that will flourish in due time. The soul knew the moment the One Origin created it. As evolution and elevation advance, this wisdom will emerge and become a part of the human psyche.

However, there is planetary knowledge that each soul must gain through true-to-life experience, that is, via the Cause and Effect relationship during consecutive incarnations. On the other hand, the incarnated human souls still have to gather considerable cosmic and universal knowledge, to which they, so far, have no access owing to their current state of evolution.

To have a global understanding to differentiate between the ill negative and sound positive thought-energies of the more than 7 billion inhabitants of the planet, the human species still has to clear great barriers of idiosyncrasies, ideologies, laws, beliefs, customs etc. – ponders the brother Elohim – moral and social standards as well as legal practices differ considerably among a number of countries as, for instance, marriages between children and adults, polygamy and even such barbarian laws as the stoning of an adulterer. In the case of Western countries, many customs differ from the East or Africa because most of them would be condemned by the law.

To start this process of discernment, every single individual has to call on his/her conscience guided by Divine and Human Law – remarks the sister Interana – and assess how true-to-life experience and everything else learned and assimilated adjust to them. However, ignorance or poor education cause human beings to consider many of their distorted thoughts and acts as being correct. Likewise happens to ill negative emotions dominated by the desires of the Ego. In such circumstances, people do not have a clear mind and will find it difficult to judge what is negative and what is positive.

Therefore, knowing and strictly following the “Canons of the Spirit” of the planet and the cosmos demanding among others endeavor, perseverance and determination will help you mature and develop good judgement – affirms the brother Interano – even so, you will not be free of errors as long as your soul does not reach the highest possible expression of LIGHT and LOVE. Consequently, whatever knowledge and information you may receive you should welcome but have to discern to use of it what will actually help you find the “Path of Return” in your soul.

16. What will spiritual persons in the Age of Aquarius be like? Will they show particular characteristics?

Yes, there is a good number of them – remarks the brother Elohim – to begin with, these persons are free, responsible and no longer look for spiritual orientation from masters or gurus because they have formed their Spiritual personality. They have self-confidence and believe in their innermost work.

Practices such as bending the head, gentle talk, candlelight, quartz scattered everywhere, temples, chants etc. are NO LONGER NECESSARY. Nowadays, spiritual people are active and joyful, dress in a modern way, travel by air and are direct and clear when speaking. They accept severe but founded criticism and argue with empathy and wisdom and, most important, never seek to control other persons.

Humans are changing and entering a state of Mental Freedom – observes the sister Interana – they are no longer submitted by the sin and guilt. Those times of inner loneliness or regret took the humans to the extermination of their character and personality. They have freed themselves of the heavy burden of the original sin, the desperate search for redemption from supposedly sinful acts and the veneration of a God imposed and forced.

They are finally shaking off psychological ties and overcoming the consequences of brainwashing during their childhood, at least, in the Western world – says the brother Interano – they are leaving behind the limitations created by the fear for punishment in this and the life after death. Nevertheless, such or similar conditions survive in many parts of the globe representing a today's form of slavery.

In general, religious institutions have therefore been losing followers over decades. The solution of problems and acceptance of the challenges of our times are for people who reason, analyze and investigate. They keep their distance from demagogues and heavily question suspect or corrupt governments and private enterprises. Spiritual persons seek to explore their inner selves and the environment. They therefore are in search of an ideal: A Universal knowledge that would hold the answers they have been seeking for such a long time.

This knowledge would offer an understanding and its profound feelings of Moral and Ethics take them to the cosmos and the universes of LIGHT and LOVE. What we wish to say is – concludes the brother Elohim - that today's modern world does carry the idea of this knowledge and the revelation of its truth because it no longer trusts what largely appears as fabricated truths. It knows that the future of the human species lies in the inherent laws of nature and in the return to its origin.

17. You always say that we are slaves. Could you be more specific about this affirmation?

Nowadays, slavery is not an act where people capture and sell persons and entire communities to work the rest of their lives for their owners' gain – remarks the brother Elohim – in the past, people were enslaved through battles and war. In the current age, under the protection of international laws, slavery has been abolished.

Human people cannot be treated as slave or as an object to be sold to another person. Laws in many countries are clear about that. Even though modern law protects people against exploitation based on unconditional dependence, unscrupulous persons or organizations widely practice this type of slavery in a more or less sophisticated way.

Modern slavery – continues the brother Interano – goes unnoticed because it does not have the cruel overtones from the past. Although, if you pay attention and go over the global situation, you might realize that there is a bondage behind an apparent freedom. It is so subtle that the slave does not become aware of it. Nowadays, there are many people who live and work under conditions of slavery. It is illegal almost everywhere, but it still exists.

In current time, slavery hides in industries, farms and even private homes of rich and poor countries in the form of human trafficking, forced labor, child abuse and forced or early marriage, many times under the threat of punishment or with the use of physical violence. Today's world seems to have multiplied the terrible practices of past times, involving big corporations, financial system, and institutions who work under the same creator principle: power, ambition, manipulation, government, economy, companies and religious institutions. All of them, influence and direct their resources to obtain the highest profit and dominance possible. Humanity and environment wellness is not a profitable issue for them.

In addition, the armament industry, related to power, control and to the generation of huge foreign debts as well as the effects of compulsory consumerism keep modern society from escaping the vicious circle of dependence. The only way to free themselves of this kind of emotional slavery is basing education on the awakening and growth of conscience.

Unfortunately, this planet today is very short of true humanist leaders – affirms the sister Interana – those who dare speak up to encourage order, freedom and spiritual growth run the risk of suffering margination and even annihilation. Great avatars, at all times, left as a legacy the knowledge of LIGHT and LOVE saying that: "The meaning of life lies in striving to overcome egotism to get a good look at your fellow humans and your environment as a part of yourself".

18. In the fifth book, you say that the state of Alpha is the PEACE of the SPIRIT. What do we have to do to gain it in a world of controversy and problems, having to face particularly those of our homes?

Look for it deep inside your soul identifying and freeing repressed emotions; – advises the brother Interano – beneath those emotions lie Creativity, Intuition, Imagination and Wisdom. It is like discovering an inexhaustible flow of elevated energy. Your will and endeavor to find, accept and develop them is what it takes. The moment you do, you will be creating a harmonious state of LIGHT and LOVE in your souls.

If you wish to lead a life of plenitude, you have to look into your souls to attract what is good from the cosmos; – observes the sister Interana – feeling well with the Merit gained with your effort are an amazing pair. As you manage to transmute old beliefs and ill negative emotions, you will enjoy the energy you need to generate what has true significance, Joyfulness, Harmony, Peace and Love in your lives and all that surrounds you.

Use a moment of quietness to make contact with your souls. Deep inside them, there is Harmony, Peace, Love and Wisdom; – affirms the brother Elohim – use as much as you can from them for a new day. Concentrate on living them intense and positively from dawn to a good night's sleep to rest. Do not stay with yesterday, correct and learn from your errors because life is a never-ending today. Expect happily the daybreak, always shining with LIGHT and LOVE, the sun of all your mornings – the brother Elohim pauses for a moment.

In general, you analyze your ill negative emotions using logic from the left hemisphere of the brain; – observes the brother Seramita – emotions, however, should not be understood rationally. You have to look at them from your brain's right hemisphere to weigh them up with flexibility, gentleness and compassion. You thus will allow the elevated feeling of love to enter the soul and choose what the spirit needs most.

It is true that you may reach the Alpha State in your reality with great discipline only – observes the brother Elohim – however, discipline as we know is not an easy exercise to begin with. Techniques and methods are helpful, but indispensable are determination, perseverance as well as psychological and emotional equilibrium. If you succeed in joining these qualities, discipline will be in your nature. Therefore, the main idea of any technique and method to reach the Alpha State should not be their repetitive practice life after life but automatically function as a part of the soul.

Human beings in the Age of Aquarius handle their individuality and mental energy rather different from the way they did in the Age of Pisces – affirms the brother Interano – while during the Age of Pisces, government policies and religion seriously affected individual growth by using fear, threat, needs and fantasy, in the Age of Aquarius, there will be freedom for individual spiritual development.

All humans have the faculty of self-knowledge and the consciousness of a reality with multiple expressions. This knowledge is the driving force to deepen their understanding and help them gain maturity, freedom and wisdom – observes the sister Interana – unlike the knowledge about your external environment, self-knowledge emerges from your innermost self with revelations that occur when your conscience is ready to perceive them.

True understanding of life is not a consequence of the concepts or ideologies you have been adopting but stems from the comprehension you develop of yourselves with regard to the lives you live – adds the sister Interana – the ignorant is not who possess few concepts about life but who does not know himself.

This involves an important detachment from material things, which you should not confound with a lack of affection or indifference – observes the brother Interano – when you cannot change a situation, the wisest thing to do is to look at it in another way. Nevertheless, this detachment is something that takes time while you get a better understanding of the difference between Materiality and Materialism, that is, the material things to cover your needs and those that are superfluous. It is the moment to start working on yourself. If you love and need, let it free, if it returns to you with love and harmony, it belongs to you. If it´s not, don´t insist. It was not meant to be.

The adversities in your way will help you grow – continues the sister Interana – many are the challenges the universe poses because this is how you will become conscious of the need for changes. You must accept to deal with DETACHMENT because this is the way to rediscover your inner vision. Clinging to the material part of the world, you often fail to perceive how happy you could be seeing this world as it really is. You no longer should wait to leave a life of futile pleasures behind. The Age of Aquarius is the beginning of a new cycle where you will learn about detachment, as the path of plenitude to walk that freedom will grant you.

There are multiple universes with similar infinite realities – explains the brother Seramita – as you move away from the space-time coordinates, you will discover that those realities and worlds, in fact, are different showing environments of times and places that do not have any relationship with planet will be the differences you notice.

Would it not be a relief to free yourselves of all those ill negative emotions for good? – reminds the brother Elohim – this way, you would give your lives a good cleaning because what you would finally take with you after you disincarnate is the memory of this LIGHT and LOVE that you leave in the hearts of those who had been close. Finding the Innermost Peace here and now, however, is not a matter of techniques or methods but the state of conscience deep inside your souls because this is where you will find the answers you need. Therefore, listen to this inner voice that holds all the wisdom – concluded the brother Elohim – since you are of divine and universal origin, beings of love who deserve love.

When you cut a flower, you will be losing it because it will fade and be unable of producing seed for another springtime – observes the sister Interana – if you cage a bird, you will lose it because it no longer sings in the woods. When you fear risking freedom, you will start losing it because you have to risk it to be able to choose or decide. When you make your love a prisoner, you are about to lose it. Do not confine it and let it shine as the light of a candle that never will die. Open up doors in your lives and thank the universe for what you are...LIGHT and LOVE.

19. There are people who write me saying they have a contempt for the material life for being a world of lies and therefore decided on leading a spiritual life only. Are they right in doing so?

If you kept a distance from the daily material reality of the planet, who would satisfy the material needs of this world? Who would teach you right from wrong, the truth from a lie? What would Knowledge, Understanding and Love of what you procreated be like? – remarks the brother Elohim – you seem to feel safe contemplating your dreams from a world of make believe while keeping a good distance from the real world. If there however were not the process of awakening to help you vanquish a fantasy of millions of years, how would you manage to use your energies for the elevation of your Inner Self? Hiding in a place far from the problems of the real world, abandoning your loved ones, friends etc.

You therefore must transmute the information that your brain receives by taking it to a positive environment of creativity – observes the brother Interano – you thus produce elevated thoughts that will travel the planet and by nurturing other humans create a chain of healthy and strong cosmic thought-energies. This is how "humane" human beings may work for the benefit of other people, themselves and the planet.

Current thought-energies around the planet, nevertheless, are dense and dark because humans have only cared for themselves, chasing after visions of mysticism, astral walks, magic and miracles as well as channeling with other dimensions – explains the sister Interana – in general, humans by looking for extrasensory abilities largely create fantasies and enjoy the use of techniques, methods, chants and rites. They have done nothing for other people, for the planet or the system where they live.

If you feel the desire to work with determination and perseverance for the planet and yourselves, do so as spiritual beings by facing challenges as true warriors of LIGHT and LOVE – insists the brother Interano – real Spiritual Beings will confront themselves, their environment and face whatever adversities are in their way. They will do this every day with Harmony, Peace and Love. With a smile on their faces, they will change ugliness to whatever beauty there is in the universe. They accept their destiny because they know that it will help them walk the path, the way they will help others. They signed an agreement with themselves before they came to this reality, which is to stand any test with confidence, courage and intelligence. They are those whom nothing nor anyone can make desist from the course that will take them to the origin of an eternal existence.

To conquer the Matrix (this reality), you must live and change it from the inside out...

20. What is the reason for the imbalance of our emotions?

Most of you suffer from it; one day you enjoy peace, quietness and another feel uneasy and even anxious. Why? – observes the brother Elohim – you have to realize that there are factors of which you are not aware and therefore escape your control. These factors cause alterations of your emotions that you have trouble understanding and may affect your equanimity. These alterations could be worries about the fulfillment of a job or anxiety because of economic difficulties. You are a combination of chemical elements that are of great importance in nature. However, sometimes chemistry does not function the way it should causing considerable discomfort.

You often blame some unexpected problem for this discomfort but should realize that it may well originate from a serious eating habit disorder causing chemical imbalance or from uncontrolled emotions of your subconscious. You have to consider these possibilities to try finding the true origin of this unease.

Many people believe in yoga, meditation and respiratory exercises to help them get some relief from the hectic lives they lead – remarks the sister Interana – these techniques, no doubt, will produce positive effects but not the equilibrium, harmony and peace they try to find unless they self-analyze their emotions and particularly the ill negative, make permanent and intensive use of positive thought-energies and decide on an appropriate diet.

On the other hand, remember that you still live in a primary planet with considerable fluctuations of gravitational energy, electromagnetic waves and a severe climate crisis. Whatever your efforts, there will always be important variations of your, the environment's and the planet's energy.

"Equilibrium" is what humans need most – affirms the brother Interano – you must strive to create it wherever you go or live. You can if you sincerely try to study, accept and learn how to handle your emotions because this will make you physically, emotionally and mentally strong and allow you the control of thoughts, acts and deeds.

Otherwise, if you ignore or hide your emotions in the subconscious, you will have great repercussions both in the mind and in the physical body. A Conscience of LIGHT and LOVE will lead you on the way.

21. The book *EL SER UNO I – The Arcana of Thoth* tells us that there will be confusion and anxiety unless you open and close the dimensional passageways of knowledge and understanding correctly. What is the correct way to open and close these passageways?

Most humans live with the knowledge they have of an apparently real world – says the sister Interana – nevertheless, this knowledge only makes them feel basic emotions helping them build a life, a family etc. but leaves them without the conscience of a higher knowledge that would allow them to live a more advanced reality of existence. Living this way, it will make that your life be under these essential parameters, thinking and believing that is real life, without tearing the veil of other deeper realities. We therefore say that only the culture of spirituality, the work with their inner selves and the credibility of their souls will show them how to open and close the dimensional passageways of knowledge and understanding.

22. How can we mentally help counteract violence in this planet?

Violence: It is an act performed by a person or persons to submit any other person or group of persons intentionally to pressure, manipulation or other acts that threaten their physical, psychological and moral integrity. "Violence is mental torture or abuse of physical force to make persons yield to demands against their will" (Maternal Dictionary).

Violence is an ill negative emotion of humans' distorted nature that emerged millions of years ago – explains the brother Elohim – immense errors and the lack of understanding made it take deep roots in humans' souls shutting them off from true knowledge and comprehension and thus from living in harmony and peace. It therefore intimately relates to the preservation of the species. Very hard to understand and transmute, it will take humans many incarnations and great suffering to conquer it.

We say that the soul needs to suffer to understand violence – observes the brother Interano – this is true because violence connects with other emotions that make it grow. In fact, almost any uncontrolled ill negative emotion can cause persons to be violent because they feel impotent to face certain adverse situations. Let us have a look at the different types of violence.

Domestic violence

Psychological and physical violence on family members including child abuse.

Daily life violence

Disrespect for norms and rules. Indifference to fellow humans' suffering creates problems of public security and people perceive a threat to their rights for respect and protection in daily life.

Violence in politics and religion

Physical and psychological abuses by those who hold positions of power in society. Authorities use physical violence to control citizen who protest in public against decisions for which power denied them participation. Corruption and control from the military groups for domination and manipulation of the masses. The lack of justice for those who cannot defend themselves.

Social and economic violence

By governments, failing to create policies for the inclusion of marginalized populations and in particular programs of public health care and education.

Violence by discrimination

In societies that discriminate citizens of low-level incomes because of ethnicity, culture, language etc. affecting their feelings of identity and favoring an informal and deficient way of living.

Violence in unethical behavior

Resulting from illegitimate or illegal practices to obtain material things or other advantages ignoring established and generally accepted norms and laws for a practicable life in society. Those are expressions of the violence because it leads the society to the wrong way of no future or possibility and leads them to the goals that only can be gotten by out of law and order.

Violence in education

By inducing parents their young children to compete forcefully, in a fair or cvcn unfair way, with other family members, relatives and friends. Educational authorities tend to favor such attitude, which often is the beginning of discrimination among students. Humans as a universal species do not consider competition a "normal" activity since the energy of each soul; each spirit develops and advances in a particular way. This means that each energy has its creativity and need for spirituality. However, educational centers promote the dichotomy between the "strong" and the "weak" leaving early marks in students' souls by separating those who fail to adjust to the Matrix of the planetary canons such as intelligence, obedience, success, power etc.

Violence in spirituality

However strange it appears; this type of violence exists. It is the obligation of an incarnated soul to adopt a certain belief or religious credo without the chance to decide on it. Many families oblige their children to continue a traditional religion and deeply rooted customs without considering a violation of the soul's freedom of expression having to submit to those who control the denseness and dark force of the odd (matter) reality.

23. How can we turn economic hardship into economic abundance?

Humans feel confused by the dilemma of having to harmonize SPIRITUALITY with MONEY – replies the sister Interana – because in the past, you learned that wealth does not go along very well with humility and poverty is synonymous of spirituality. This way of looking at the Spirituality-Money relationship is in your soul's energy to the extent that many relate the simple fact of earning money for a decent living to Ambition or Avarice. The ugly truth, however, is that those who defend the above analogy do not follow it accepting whatever money people who do, in good faith, offer them.

What kind of relationship between spirituality and money should we establish to avoid feeling unease? – says the brother Interano – many persons start walking the path of spirituality feeling that it means to renounce drastically material things to the point that they quit a job, leave their families and give up a comfortable living. Their belief is that this way their spirituality will grow accelerated. Nevertheless, having to face the obligations of a material world, they will use spirituality to start charging for "spiritual services" and thus making it go together with money. Is this, however, the correct way?

EL SER UNO tells us that humans should seek "Equilibrium", that is, matter, soul and spirit must work together in harmony to avoid an energetic imbalance that might produce uneasiness, discomfort, anxiety etc. EL SER UNO reiterates that souls incarnating in this reality are responsible for making this a true and conscious world. This means that humans' mission is to have their souls energetically and mentally adjust to this dense reality. Souls need the "Material" world but not the world of "Materialism".

24. What does energetic and mental adjustment of the souls mean?

Material Reality (body)

It means to adjust to the canons established by a society, studies, professional skills and honest work to maintain a family. It also requires souls to gain the true-to-life experience this reality offers by overcoming daily adversities. Having learned to live on their own, humans will know how to enjoy with responsibility and equilibrium what they gained with great effort.

Astral Reality (soul)

To learn all about adjustment, flexibility and exchange of emotions. To distinguish negative from positive. To study human lessons and interactions for their positive assimilation forming sound thoughts to nourish the mind.

Spiritual Reality (mind)

To use all advanced Knowledge and Understanding you have about yourselves and your environment to feel the magnificence of Love. This way, the LIGHT of your Spirit and the ILLUMINATION of your Energetic Being will shine on your existence forever. When incarnating, the soul has come to learn about the SIGNIFICANCE OF LIFE and to understand why it is in this grade, plane and dimension – affirms the brother Elohim – and must adjust to the experience of this reality. It cannot refuse to do so because this is where it has to gain further knowledge and work on itself to grow.

The human soul cannot accelerate this process trying to save time and efforts nor live this life through the experience of just one of the three bodies. The one big step forward humans can take is to comprehend that their souls have to go through a learning process to be able to reach the higher realities of existence.

By living a material life, souls instill into it elevated positive Intentions with each thought, act and deed thus turning it an authentic expression of LIGHT and LOVE. Consequently, humans will register and experience the Spirituality of Knowledge (matter), the Spirituality of Understanding (soul) and the Spirituality of Universal Love (spirit).

What happens to so many of your ideas that fail to meet the necessary economic requirements? – remarks the sister Interana – will you give up on them? NO, you just postpone them until there are appropriate conditions for their realization. Not everybody has the ability for the fulfillment of great missions but may be ready to meet daily obligations with responsibility and competence. We do not say to that you should desist or renounce your dreams. You just need to start working on yourselves, then on your environment and finally embark on tasks you feel you can handle.

Therefore, instead of insisting to take big steps, you must LEARN to WALK first – observes the brother Interano – Another thing is that you have to define what "Abundance" means to you. For many, it is money and the accumulation of material goods; for others the love in what surrounds them. What is true Abundance then? Once you answer this question, you will be able to make a choice.

In the universe, "Abundance" means Plenitude of the Spirit – affirms the brother Interano – humans as a species of the universe do not go by the canons of planet Tera. An infinity of unnecessary material things you have created require dedication and abundance of resources to maintain them stable and secure but are only a part of the tools to handle this material reality. If those with global political, economic and religious influence emphasized the satisfaction of every single human being's real needs instead of preaching continual material growth as the only salvation of the planet's population, you would be truly able to focus on the human species' emotional and spiritual advance.

True-to-life experience, no doubt, is necessary but knowledge, responsibility for the environment etc. gained with endeavor must always accompany it to guarantee progress and favor the realization of ideas. When you perceive the positive effects of LIGHT and LOVE on both the work, you realize with your inner senses and in the exterior, your thoughts, acts and deeds will be a source of joyfulness and you will know that you are ready for the advance to a higher reality.

25. You suggest that we use our inner senses to transmute the burden we carry from past lives. How do we know what exactly we have to transmute? What would be the guideline to know that we have succeeded in fulfilling such a task correctly?

Since you have come a long way, have studied and learned, now is the time to relax and start using all the accumulated knowledge and experience in this reality – replies the brother Elohim – to do this, connect with your inner self in a peaceful, harmonious and loving way. If you feel confused believing that you must not fail and that all you have read and studied is to become a reality in no time do not worry because you now have the information for your daily routine and for the tranquility of your inner self.

Therefore, stop this hectic life of the exterior with no place to go – advises the sister Interana – instead, prepare for the quest that will take you to your soul, to the Internal City and, if possible, to your subconscious. During this internal journey, you will discover life and know how to control positive and negative emotions turning them into an oasis of harmony and peace as the reflection of a calm and mature soul. Learn to love one another because this is how you will transform what so very much troubles and confuses you...YOURSELVES.

26. How do we have to deal with family members, friends and relations who mock, attack or even insult us if we intend to discuss this message with them?

The day your vibration frequency is high enough to spare you a new incarnation in this grade and plane, you will not return to planet Earth – observes the brother Interano – nevertheless, you cannot continue on the path of spirituality in this material reality denying responsibilities prior to incarnation and greater in your new life on the planet.

It therefore would be an illusion to conceive a spiritual life characterized by prayers and hymns but far from obligations and temptations. If this were possible, every single soul would have this choice, but the world be more chaotic than it is already. People would hold on to idealistic contemplations and fantasies of a heavenly place without the need for reasoning and acting favoring their vision of a life of comfort and well-being, which is a fantasy since the universe does not work this way.

True spiritual life is only possible within this system as defined by the material reality. How do you know that you are spiritual beings without having had the negative true-to-life experience you need to overcome and transmute into a positive one? – continues the sister Interana – how would you know that you are growing without working that dark part of your soul? Spiritual growth means to feel stronger after having conquered adversities. Only with constant true-to-life experience, can your souls claim victory and turn Warriors of LIGHT and LOVE.

Therefore, never refuse learning this lesson life teaches you to avoid repeating an experience over and again that would slow down your traveling the Path of Return. Instead, thank life considering its obstacles opportunities that will encourage you to look for solutions and favor your spiritual advance. Trust the love of the universe for you and do not desist. The more it puts you to test, the more it loves you.

You may wonder about the very purpose of those tests – observes the brother Elohim – the answer is that the universe wants you to be souls that are able to open their chrysalis with determination and perseverance to become magnificent butterflies reaching out to the confines of the universe. This is how you will be a part of it. In this context, a term that frequently appears is BULLYING. We call it *Spiritual Bullying*. Here is what it means.

Spiritual Bullying

It is the psychological and sometimes physical mistreatment of people mocking and scaring or just ignoring them for some time aiming at making them feel miserable. This behavior may have serious consequences not only for these persons but also for their social environment.

Some types of *Spiritual Bullying* are speaking ill of or insulting people, mocking their religious faith, pushing them around or making them do something against their will – says the brother Interano – those who harass others lack respect, empathy and the capacity of understanding and accepting that people for particular reasons feel, think and act in different ways. They act aggressively and have great difficulty to apologize.

These kinds of people are selfish and unadaptable to the rules of co-existence. They do not accept any kind of limits. Their actions are impulsive and dictatorial. They often have problems with their behavior, even in the family context. Ignorance and the lack of a proper education and culture is the way they react. They live according to the emotions and pleasures that the Matrix offers.

People who practice spiritual bullying – continues the sister Interana – have little interest in topics of metaphysical nature because they fear the unknown or that these topics may affect their pleasant and comfortable routine life. Many are timid and insecure but also sad persons who suffer from eating and sleeping disorders, serious problems of communication and frequently are addictive to drugs.

They are what you call unsociable persons but more than feeling irritated those who have awaked should treat them with compassion – suggests the brother Elohim – there is, however, no doubt that both harasser and harassed have important behavioral problems. While the harassers' ill negative thought-energies trigger ill negative emotions, the harassed appear to have sound positive thought-energies but also a spiritual weakness because of misleading beliefs thus allowing harassment to affect them.

27. How can we fight Spiritual Bullying?

Strive to control your emotions trying to solve the problem via an active communication with all concerned – replies the brother Elohim – with true respect for people's otherness and understanding that there are different grades, planes and dimensions of teaching at this school called planet Tera. You should value these differences as true-to-life experience rather than as deficiencies. Having grown knowledge, understanding and love among all those persons, your answer will be cooperation and solidarity.

Face harassment openly but try to understand the reason and emotions that would make a person act this way. To live a life of respect and empathy in a community, the education people receive should therefore follow the canons of the universe by creating awareness about the need for opportunities for all and fighting insecurity and poverty. In other words, AWAKE, which is ELEVATING your CONSCIENCE to give the external world or material reality a chance to develop and advance with harmony and peace.

When awaking you remember that the world around you, is your deed because you created it – observes the sister Interana – you, however, have trouble remembering because while gaining true-to-life experience you moved away from the source of your existence. You are immortal souls and in spite of living a material life of illusion Love as the origin and driving force of this existence is in your memory.

28. How should a couple with different ideologies and beliefs act when one mocks or criticizes the other?

You should realize that often people who feel insecure because of a lack of arguments use irony or sarcasm in criticism but other persons also do so to make their interlocutor clarify or correct a statement – replies the sister Interana.

Those who feel insecure are afraid of losing their self-respect as well as status before other people. Many human beings (probably a majority) dislike changing their ideas or opening their minds to discussing new concepts that nevertheless would broaden the knowledge they have rather than affect the course of their spiritual growth. People, their families, friends and relations FEAR what they fail to understand and in a sort of self-defense react with mockery and irony – concludes the brother Interano.

On the other hand, many persons worry to create a mental distance with their loved ones. These persons have the following three options. First: They live with their beliefs without discussing them with anybody. Second: They base their way of living on them in a balanced way exchanging ideas with others. Third: They decide on strictly following these beliefs even if this would mean a separation from their usual social environment – says the brother Elohim – sharing your life with other people, in general, is not easy but you need to understand that spirituality is not an obligation and less an imposition. It is an exchange of knowledge that should occur in an atmosphere of patience and love.

In general, a difference in concepts should not be a reason for the separation of persons and rather the mutual assimilation of new energies via an exchange of knowledge. This way, people would expand concepts and enter the dominium of global and cosmic knowledge. Therefore, any belief must RESPECT other people's SPACE and FREE WILL as an expression of UNIVERSAL LOVE in the Age of Aquarius and Awakening of Conscience.

29. Why people cannot transmute negative emotions that every so often appear in spite of having read books, attended courses and practiced meditation and studied synonyms and antonyms of the emotions?

Most people identify with this experience – observes the sister Interana – EL SER UNO says staying awake is much harder than awaking because it makes you feel disoriented, sad, uneasy etc. leaving you worrisome and anxious.

Let us have a look at the EMOTIONS – suggests the brother Interano – first, we have to look at the negative emotions and try to understand why they continue negative. It is important to know the Origin of any emotion and when detecting a negative one asks where and why it appeared? In past lives? In childhood? In your present life? You may find answers with help from your parents or friends or through psychoanalysis, regression and others...

For every incarnation, you carry thought-energies recorded on your soul. These energies emerge at one time reminding you that there is still work for you to do. Each negative emotion has a dynamic of its own. – says the sister Interana – you must analyze, understand and transmute it. Sometimes, you will be able to do this alone but frequently will need professional help. However, you do not have to do so with every single negative emotion but only with the ones that are recurrent and seem to keep you from advancing on the positive path you have chosen to travel.

It is of great importance that you stop worrying for being unable to transmute whatever negative emotions there are – advices the brother Interano – as this might produce anxiety. You should not be so hard on yourselves because Love is also self-love and self-respect knowing that you are far from perfect and therefore living this reality to discover and understand your faults with the inspiration LIGHT and LOVE may give you.

Show yourselves as persons with qualities and limitations and learn to live without appearances, imitations and exaggerations. Be yourselves and accept others to do likewise using always discernment, equilibrium and good sense for your inner growth.

Until now, most inhabitants of Tera have concentrated on embellishing their home (material reality) with courses, techniques, methods, esotericism, metaphysics, trips to mystical places, supposed encounters of the third kind, etc. – observes the brother Elohim – quite a way to travel around! Nevertheless, they continue feeling an emptiness in their souls because "appearances" made them believe that all this would help them find answers.

There are furthermore family therapies, spiritual circles of certain masters or gurus and the market of "Spirituality" that offers what they think they need to feel spiritual and on the right way. You all look at your home, but you forget there is a basement where you sent those things you considered useless, old, broke or dirty. There is a big difference between having spiritual culture and being spiritual.

Desperate, they sometimes take to asking heaven, the universe and the Elder Brothers for help – affirms the sister Interana – now, do they not see that the universe is already giving them the knowledge they need, all the traveling and learning and the opportunity to read books and attend courses that many would appreciate but cannot for innumerable reasons. What else would they need?

Do you not agree that it is time for you to turn everything in your hearts and souls into realty in your material, psychical and spiritual lives? You do not seem to know the treasure that lies inside you, that the universe loves you and always will although you are doubtful believing that only through great realizations your souls will grow, which is not true because this would reflect the EGO. The moment you understand – continues the sister Interana – that in the little things, in nature surrounding you, in your daily routine lies what makes the universe great: the Plenitude of Contemplation, Humility, Joy, Satisfaction and Thankfulness for all it grants you. When you perceive that, your souls have turned a source of LIGHT and LOVE you will finally realize that you and only you are casting the light that illuminates this never-ending journey called Existence.

30. In the book *EL SER UNO I – The Arcana of Thoth* – question No. 123 is how does a catalyst work? The Elder Brothers' answer is that serving the universe, it works with love, altruism and great dedication. I appreciate your commenting on the following. Are there human beings who are catalysts? Is theirs an exclusive daily routine? How could we identify them?

Let us succinctly explain the meaning of the term catalyst in this context before answering your questions – proposes the brother Elohim.

Catalyst: A substance that changes or increases the rate of chemical reactions, but also a person who inspires important further events. It is an activator and facilitator for the transformation of elements with positive or negative results. With view to the importance of the energy in this process, we can understand it as the fast chemical.

Transmutation: Of ill negative into sound positive thought-energies affecting one way or another the reasoning of a person. An incarnating soul carries a series of genetic implements (tools) from the beginning of creation. Consequently, we must not only look at it as an ethereal, invisible and therefore impalpable entity but rather as an energy consisting of elements with correlated sequential formulas based on Chemistry and Mathematics. These formulas hold a spirit-form with infinite energy throughout the universe.

All Human Beings are catalysts of this energy and individually responsible for its preservation. Letting it corrode, oxidize and stagnate or maintaining it stable, flowing and in continuous transformation is anyone's choice – insists the brother Elohim – catalyzing thought-energies and universal ideas will grant you the renovation of this cosmic energy through elements that revitalize it and their frequent recycling during the Transmutation make you feel vigorous and dynamic. Catalyzing means allowing new standards of existence, that adjust to the situation of soul and spirit in each incarnation, to enter your hearts and souls. Opening thus your minds to elevated thoughts that nurture your souls' energy will offer you opportunities of cosmic growth. Therefore, you will recognize a Catalyst by these qualities no matter he/she is rich or poor, the language they speak, if they are young or old – concludes the brother Interano – catalyzing is an ability that every one of you has and may use with free will and the conscience for right and wrong.

Humans are the vivid reflection of EL SER UNO, with equal rights and opportunities but not all have the knowledge, determination and perseverance to learn how to make work LIGHT and LOVE that the creator gave them. The key to it is to initiate the CONSCIOUS RETURN to their origin, the source of their lives and existence.

31. There are persons who feel emptiness in their souls and are unhappy even though they are already traveling the path of spirituality. What seems to be their problem?

Most people on the planet believe that spiritual courses or the teachings of Ascended Masters will make them comprehend the message of LIGHT and LOVE because this way they avoid facing up to problems by hiding in sublime sensations to cover the shortcomings of their souls – observes the brother Elohim – they have their heads in the clouds dreaming their souls will take them to such elevated realities that everything on Earth appears vain and meaningless. No doubt, the higher realities will allow them to fly, work miracles and just do what they please because there is no need for intermediaries to talk with the Ascended Masters who are their friends and the beings of Light a part of their lives.

What is it then that makes them incarnate over and again in a world of madness and violence, a reality to which they feel they do not belong? Why do they have to live in this reality when their true reality is in a beyond of happiness where all are equal and real brothers? What is the reason for having to suffer here, working for the sustenance and having children who eventually will have to live the same experience? Who has created a cruel and merciless world where nothing seems to make sense?

Most people ask these questions feeling that the universe does not treat them right. They believe it to be a punishment having come to a world without compassion and beauty – affirms the sister Interana – others feel that malicious aliens abducted and use them for slave work. There are also those who blame the Anunnakis, Reptilian Grays and Grays, their parents, relatives and friends for this misfortune. However, all – and we mean all – will continue looking for those, they believe are truly responsible until they grow during their process of evolution and elevation and finally understand that if this world is what it is they are the ones who made it that way. At this point, you have to ask yourselves again what you actually understand by SPIRITUALITY. As long as you unconditionally trust in what you hear in those courses, striving to imitate Ascended Masters, you will continue living dreams and fantasies – affirms the sister Interana – you will spend your lives discovering cosmic names and dimensions, to which they possibly belong; you will look for fame by striving to stand out as healers, work miracles, would love to become spiritual leaders and grow a passion for trying time traveling. All this would keep you from living simple routine lives.

Nevertheless, however assiduously you repeat the magic words they taught you elevating them through chants, use mantras, practice respiration, call on the Ascended Masters and great Avatars, you are unable to see, feel or contact the beings of Light. What have I to do to find spirituality? – you then ask – while looking around, you feel desolate and impotent for not having experienced what they said you would; watch and feel.

Spirituality

Means a way of being, living and feeling every single moment of your lives, your endeavor to do the best you possibly can always – explains the brother Elohim – it means self-esteem and self-love to be able to love others. Spirituality is not Extrasensory Phenomenology to make you live emotional events. It is of such simplicity that it may appear dull to you and therefore require the adornment of a legion of experience. You have the habit of spiritual ceremonies with brilliant and eye-catching dresses, rites and chants, phenomena of the senses, emotionalism of the soul and expressions of the Ego and therefore fail to see and feel the very LIGHT and LOVE in your lives.

Souls incarnate over and again in this reality to learn how to overcome fantasy but need to dream wide-awake and re-record the thought-energy that thus will find the true path of return – observes the brother Interano – your thoughts have suffered from distortion and you have extolled the spiritual reality to the extent that your minds have produced dazzling hallucinations showing the soul as it IS and not as it should BE.

Spirituality means that you accept your reality but work positively to be conscious what spirituality truly signifies, that is: follow the universal canons of LIGHT and LOVE in daily life. Enjoy the simple things and be thankful for them. Love your family, friends and acquaintances the way they are. Get up in the morning thanking the universe for every detail, look and light. See and listen. Be authentic. Know where you stand and why. This knowledge will guide you and respond to your innermost concerns. Have the courage and strength to save souls from hell. Spirituality is what you ARE and not what you REPRESENT.

EL SER UNO says "when you stop believing in magic, miracles and divine entities to come to your rescue, cease living in an unreal world, leave to be children guided by a celestial father, turn responsible adults and you be aware that all what you believe is becoming on yourself, you will know that you have awaked and grown" ...

32. Can people's thought-energies do harm to other persons as an act of "sorcery"?

What you call sorcery is the malice in ill negative thought-energies – observes the sister Interana – if you believe in sorcery, you open your brain to receiving these energies, which will make you fear that sorcery is real. This fear opens a door to the emotions and the brain starts making it work by sending these thought-energies to the physical and psychical body. When believing you assimilate thought-energies and activate a process of response that works with both ill negative and sound positive thought-energies.

Electrical impulses make the brain function. These impulses carry Nimeos-thoughts (recorded crystals) and the brain will send out an appropriate impulse according to these recordings – says the brother Interano – these impulses are in the air and obviously invisible to the naked eye. However, sometimes they remain confined in the electromagnetism where they produce irregular flashes of light that you call Orbs (orbital phenomena) or believe them to be alien spacecraft.

People who accept the entry of uncontrolled thought-energy will leave their brains unprotected – continues the brother Interano – if their Gravitational Field (ethereal body) and Defense System of the soul (objectivity) fail, the brain will attract and assimilate both positive and negative thought-energies making them a part of its functions. Thought-energies travel the entire planet carrying Sounds, Images, Colors, Rhythms, Impressions, Symbols and Perceptions that nurture innumerable brains. These elements characterize the Collective Soul.

Everything starts when people feel general discomfort or pain – replies the sister Interana – they tend to hold some physical disease responsible for it and decide to see a doctor. On the way, they begin to doubt thinking that someone could have used “witchcraft”. By merely considering the possibility, they give witchcraft the chance to have an effect on them. Thinking of people who might have an interest of doing this, they remember persons they dislike or believe their enemies.

Visualizing their images, they will think about the persons for whom their emotions show the greatest aversion. They will then have the brain confirm that they are right and that there is no doubt about the presence of a malicious force. Since the brain has no protection, it will nurture dark and dense negative thoughts giving diseases a chance to attack the physical and psychical body – says the brother Elohim – microscopic agents such as virus and bacteria come then to your mind as the cause of the diseases, but you forget that your ill negative thought-energies have created and shaped them according to the creator of it. This is the form, in which these thought-energies will return to their origin where they have been made and embodied.

Under these conditions, the brain will lower its vibration frequency and rhythm and colors disappear. The resulting ill agents will become a part of the matter-energy and affect whatever is in their way but people believe that sorcery is what has caused the illness failing to understand that they have given life and form to the ill by believing in its presence.

This is why witchcraft works – observes the brother Interano – SUGGESTION is the greatest weapon that ill negative energy has to harm you. The moment you think it real, you re-program your brain for the ill to attack you. You have become a victim of AUTOSUGGESTION.

Do NOT BELIEVE in witchcraft and reject any type of suggestion by raising your vibration frequency. If you feel you cannot do it by yourself, the way is the hypnosis. Look for experienced psychologists and parapsychologists to help you concentrate on elevating your self-confidence. This is the way to oppose Autosuggestion and block ill negative thought-energies.

33. If we were creator and former of diseases what would be your comments on the Asperger syndrome?

Bearing the name of the discoverer, this syndrome as well as schizophrenia are mental disorders originating from inhabitants of the Northern countries. We call this syndrome Convex Energy – explains the brother Interano.

> ***Convex:*** Is of Latin origin (convexus) and relates to the exterior area of curved surfaces as in the case of spheres. A convex mirror is the fragment of a sphere reflecting a virtual (and therefore distorted) image on the outside of this spherical fragment, which is smaller than the object it reflects. Psychologists use the term *Convex* on patients who suffer from a distorted perception of themselves (Wikipedia).

When we talk about the Asperger Syndrome, we are referring to the PERCEPTION that these people have about themselves and their environment – continues the sister Interana – which characterizes because their thought-energies collide going in circles. This means that their energy mirrors fail to pass on the image to other areas of the brain, rebound and tend to repeat this procedure. However, people sometimes confuse low-grade autism with the Asperger syndrome because of similar symptoms. The difference is that Asperger patients manage to escape the vicious circle of repetition while autist do not. In reality, the distortion of the thoughts occurred when the species began to use reason to tell “right from wrong”. The existentialist concept of being, when he began to analyze the essence of thoughts and made the mistake of believing that what he thought was correct.

This distortion is very old and of genetic origin – affirms the brother Elohim – it started in the Northern-bound countries where tribes of dominant warriors conquered extensive areas enslaving their inhabitants. Thought-energy began to record erroneous concepts in an inflexible way and the mathematic sequence of the thoughts became stagnant over the time. This affected large populations turning them reserved and intolerant.

Under those conditions, human beings find it hard to develop subjective thinking and their thought-energy lacks the ability to understand an "illuminated" thought – adds the sister Interana – reason is a part of their minds but fails to understand the essence of thought. Their spirituality entirely founds in reason and, incapable of abstraction to turn it into an elevated subjective idea, has no room for illuminated thinking.

Illuminated thinking or intuition does not depend on comprehension. This is not anyone's condition because, as in the material world, unluckily most people have trouble to hear and see in the spiritual reality, too, and many of them show clear symptoms of the Asperger syndrome.

34. If the distortion of thoughts has its origin in Northern-bound populations giving rise to the Asperger syndrome, would the population of other continents be responsible for the appearance of similar diseases?

Yes, absolutely – agrees the brother Elohim – after the catastrophic fragmentation of Pangea into several continents, the human species in the exterior split and settled on these continents separating thus from their origin: Lemuria. Entirely on their own, the essence of their thoughts changed producing an adverse and negative form of thinking. Distorted energy invaded the material body triggering diseases that also affected their psyche – concludes the sister Interana – such as the Asperger syndrome, autism, depression and bipolar, panic, compulsive-obsessive and post-traumatic stress disorders that spread planet-wide with severe consequences throughout evolution. There are numerous factors producing physical and mental illness – continues the brother Interano

– genetics, diet, physical and mental traumas, bacteria and virus, air and water pollution, legal and illegal drugs play an important role.

35. Why do we always confuse falling in love with true love and its many expressions?

Sometimes you meet a person whose soul perfectly matches yours – observes the sister Interana – but both will NOT necessarily become a couple. Nevertheless, many times there is energetic compatibility with equal cosmic and universal vibration frequency of two souls who truly love each other. Many couples therefore have an entirely satisfactory relation. They may over the years, occasionally feel an attraction for other souls but should realize that this is only because of a similar energetic and spiritual elevation.

If there were confusion of emotions, you might feel having found your soul mate. This is not so because what you feel is the vibration of universal love beyond body and mind. It is a feeling that you may share not with one but with many souls thus helping shape this immense soul of the universe. Too often, you confuse this love with making love, characteristic of the human species.

Walking the path of spirituality, you may feel this type of emotions and meet with souls that vibrate in your frequency but not having analyzed and worked their emotions these souls tend to confuse and mix them with those intimately related to the material reality of Earth. You therefore have to separate them knowing that what you feel is not the desire of carnal love but the elevated and universal LOVE of the souls.

36. Could you explain what SOUL MATES are? Do we all have one?

There are many stories and tales about this topic inspiring the great writers of all times. The sublimation of love, the couple, the perfect relation between the masculine and feminine have idealized the meaning of LOVE – starts explaining the brother Interano.

The soul dreams of the ideal and perfect but suffers when these desires remain unsatisfied. Consequently, you are desperately looking for a loving soul to fill your heart and end your suffering. Emptiness is what makes you search for the Soul Mate and the urge of your soul to find what you feel is missing, the other part.

> ***Soul Mate:*** Means to find a person who besides physical attractiveness and a gentle character shares your interests. It is love that does not care about age, ethnicity and credo. Looking at each other, the couple feels a great need for caressing each other to extend the energy of their hearts. Both seek to grow intellectual and spiritually incentivizing their personal evolution and elevation mutually. They control egotism and individualism with the desire, though unconscious, of fulfilling their mission together.
> They complement each other in every way. Almost think alike. Soul mates attract each other more easily when both are good-humored, active, lively, good talkers, music-lovers etc. They seek and enjoy the ecstasy. Making love is for them an experience of extraordinary significance and in an indescribable instant of their union, their eyes recognize the soul they had been seeking and...know that this is the other half (Wikipedia).

This is the somewhat romantic definition of Soul Mates – observes the sister Interana – let us see now what it actually means in the third grade, plane and dimension. In this dimension, the chance to find a soul mate is remote because that half is not in the third plane but in a more elevated one and from there will act as the "Master" of the other one that remains in the planes of the material reality. This half or master will provide it continuously with the force, energy and enthusiasm necessary to fulfill its mission. We are you meaning are your souls as an expression of higher planes of existence.

Beyond all the romanticism of the term, the incarnated soul mate is a human being who has the two forces of the universe, the masculine and feminine. Soul mates do not have the same deficiencies. They will aid each other to work and light the darkness of their genetic, cultural, educational and whatever true-to-life experience they are confronting. This means that they cannot realize the necessary fusion by expanding the Light as a UNION and Soul Mates they are because they must transcend their reality to become ONE and not be TWO.

In reality, "Soul Mate" is not what you should seek in your world. It is not impossible to find the other half, but you have to be realistic to be able to adapt with flexibility to the situation in a time, in which "Soul Affinity" is more viable than "Soul Mate" – affirms the brother Elohim – modern times offer relationships between people with very similar energies characterizing "Soul Affinity". These souls are a blessing because you will find them in every incarnation as persons who are a part of your lives such as family members, friends or relations. They are easy to recognize because your heart will jump with their sole presence. If a soul with affinity incarnated in a family member, you would enjoy a happy and easy-going relationship with great support. People with "Soul Affinity" are very close to each other as they have been meeting and giving mutual assistance many times in past lives.

The school of life called Planet Earth, for the time being, is unable to offer you finding the "Soul Mate" – affirms the sister Interana – you are here to learn and gain true-to-life experience, positive and negative, to grow as human beings. For this to occur, you need to know and understand the essence of the soul transmuting and drawing from it the correct nourishment (knowledge) to form the Energetic Being (Spirit).

This requires your relating with the diversity of energies of many souls, the more different the better. If you accept a relationship with little or no affinity, you have to know the reason and the lesson it may be teaching you. You also will have to learn from your children, relations, friends and acquaintances. In fact, you are not to live this life looking for a "Soul Mate" just to be comfortable because both of you are alike. What would you learn from a person if he/she in almost every aspect were like you? What actually would impel you to go for the knowledge of this reality?

The best you can do is to look for "Soul Affinity" throughout your incarnations because, however, these similar souls may be different – observes the brother Interano – this is why in so many families, different personalities are happy to learn from one another. Therefore, when observing the relationship of other couples, families, friends and acquaintances, you should not criticize or judge it but look at it as if into a mirror to see what you could use from it for your own relationship. Once you have grown and become conscious adults, you are ready to attract the other half present in all of you because you will have joined into ONE, the feminine force that is the SOUL and the masculine force, the SPIRIT.

37. What are multiple universes?

If we say that the universe is a gigantic body – reminds the sister Interana – we say the same about you because the One Origin created you to the image of the universe. You have to remember that planet Tera has nine realities being every one of them a universe – continues brother Interano – after you disincarnate, your energy's degree of elevation will determine the Internal City to receive you as well as the corresponding reality. The nine realities of Tera connect through a spiral of nine independent rings. The first five realities are in the electromagnetism, the remaining four in the magnetism. Your disincarnated souls nevertheless are not to wander about. They need bodies or realities to continue their cycle of incarnations perhaps in different families but you may rest assured that there are realities in other grades and planes of existence than only those, dense or elevated, in the planet that appear in your dreams – affirms the brother Elohim.

If you, however, return to an inferior grade of planet Tera, it is because in all probability your emotions or not understood topics need more in-depth work. In case, you do feel that you no longer belong to this reality, you must have a deep look into your souls to understand why you have to come back over and again to this grade of the planet's vibration. While you don´t work your ill-negatives emotions, you will be attracted to incarnate.

Vibration quality, crystal color and frequency define thought-energy – observes the sister Interana – if that thought-energy has the frequency to qualify for grades of higher elevation, the soul will be ascending grade after grade and no longer feel attracted to an inferior frequency. If the soul has a percentage of elevation but still has a part not worked then it will be attracted to incarnate in a lower grade until this soul purify and vitalize its thought-energies.

38.Are there souls that incarnate for the first time? If so, what is their origin? If not, how is it possible that the population has grown to over 7 billion incarnated human souls?

EL SER UNO tells you that there are no "new" souls in the third grade, plane and dimension – answers the brother Interano – yours are the same, more or less advanced, souls ever since we came to this planet, souls whose thought-energies hold the recordings that determine their grade and plane. Yours is a particular reality because of your history, the distortion you suffered and the long path of return to your origin that the books depict in a comprehensive way.

Regarding the population growth, – continues the sister Interana – it is somewhat complicated to explain and understand from the steadily expanding number of human beings on the planet. To begin with, you will not be able to understand the situation by considering the number of disincarnating equal to the number of incarnating souls. A soul consists of thousands of thought-energies, which along with the cells form a human body. With the division of the thought-energies as of the creation of the human-mold in the planet, you needed more bodies to house them. This process continues resulting in a steadily growing population rate. We have to realize that the first thought-energies to occupy a human-mold were numerous, dark as coal and space-filling representing "Quantity". As they developed and elevated, the coal-like characteristics (the lack of knowledge, understanding and love) changed to crystals of "Quality". Through evolution and elevation, these crystals have broken down into diminutive particles without changing the very nature of the soul that carries an enormous number of crystals with a great capacity of recording Knowledge, Understanding and Love.

Here is a metaphor as another example of how thought-energies advance and elevate – says the brother Interano – fill up a cup with coffee grains. Empty it into a mixer and grind the grains at low speed. Putting the ground coffee back into the cup, you will notice that it fills only about half of it. Now, repeat the procedure pounding the ground coffee at high speed. When returning this fine and light coffee to the cup, it will only fill a quarter of it. Similar occurs with the soul. Any thought-energy that you work, understand and transform will produce a Big Bang in your mind with an explosion of thought-crystals that turn light, dynamic and fast thoughts. This work helps you form your Baby-Spirit, which assimilating the high quality thought-crystal-energies will allow you to create your Energetic Being.

The smaller the soul's thought-crystals the more elevated they are – concludes the brother Interano – in your third grade, plane and dimension, you will manage to reduce your crystals to a size that will make you advance to grades and planes of superior elevation. Nevertheless, the ideas-crystals of the Energetic Beings of the higher dimensions are so tiny that they could compare to diamond dust, which leaves you still with thought-energies of considerable size and volume. In reality, evolution and elevation among humans in the exterior vary widely. There are people with thought-energies resembling coal, others already discovered and started polishing their innermost crystals but there are those who sculpted and turned them into magnificent diamonds of LIGHT and LOVE.

39. What is your idea about sexual energy? Should one handle it individually and if so, would it not mean self-satisfaction? Many of us live alone...

Masturbation is the kind of satisfaction that involves the physical and psychical body and therefore a pleasure of the Ego – comments the brother Elohim – in the material reality, you enjoy sexual pleasure as a couple or in many other ways that you thought up to satisfy the senses but also often degenerate and take it to the deepest part of your soul. There is belief that sexual pleasure should rise through the Kundalini (spine) because by passing the chakras sexual energy is on its way to elevated realities of thoughts thus gaining the primacy of "Elevation and Illumination". This philosophy also associates it with the "Awakening" but demands an orgasm without ejaculation.

EL SER UNO nevertheless tells you that "Sexual pleasure in the primary reality is necessary in the process of procreation and therefore preservation of the species" – continues the brother Interano – in other realities of existence, however, the energy generated by what you know as sexuality is subject to transmutation into sensuality. This means that the energy works there for "Creativity" rather than for "Procreation" and the pleasure, it produces during the orgasm in the material world turns deep SATISFACTION and PLEASURE of the soul.

The energy that rises through the Kundalini, in reality, is not responsible for the pleasure of the orgasm, pleasure that you enjoy as a couple, with a partner of the same sex, alone etc. Its true function is: To rise from the inferior reality of the first four chakras to the five chakras of the superior worlds to turn elevated energy.

An orgasm can never work this transcendence. It takes the firm determination of your ACTS, DEEDS and ELEVATED THOUGHTS life after life in the physical, psychical and spiritual reality to produce it. You therefore have to raise the thought-energy your mind has worked, understood and transmuted. You have to understand that in the universe EVERITHING IS MENTAL. Remember that in this dense reality, your mind has trouble understanding it and you therefore must create solid external forms that you can see, touch and feel.

Complacency is natural in human beings. It is the pleasure to perceive, obtain, touch, taste, smell etc. but which, at the same time, has you accept a world of fantasy that produces the security of well-being – concludes the sister Interana – you have lived a long time using your external senses. Now, the universe asks you to awake, which means to wake your dormant inner senses.

You have to realize that by using your inner senses, you no longer depend on the "orgasm" of an ephemeral materialism. Humanity's future is the MIND of POSITIVE AND ELEVATED THINKING. The day you truly understand this, the material pleasures will be in the background because you will be transforming the unimaginable into the INFINITE DELIGHT of BEING.

40. How can we reach the deep of the soul? It is not easy for us to follow your teachings given the hectic life of emotions, ambition, money, and power we life.

This is a good question – observes the brother Elohim – we know that most question the way of living in a world of insanity and uncontrolled emotions. To manage, you have to learn to live in two realities simultaneously, that is, one in which you LIVE and another in which you EXIST. Many of you may think that this is schizophrenia, but we say you can because it is one of the most frequently used ways in the field of energetic elevation called: Intrinsic Dualism.

Intrinsic Dualism

Refers to what you desire and what is possible or what you desire and what you need. Between fantasy and reality – replies the brother Interano – it is also compromise and fulfillment as well as growth and relationships without establishing parameters for society and yourselves. There are some other factors to help you understand how humans must synchronize thoughts harmoniously. The more consistent your elevated thoughts are the sooner you can assume responsibilities and attain the Intrinsic Dualism. That will help you create conditions – remarks the sister Interana – to Live and to Exist establishing interpersonal relationships in which every one of you must arrive at conclusions to secure a permanent synchronism – She stays in silence and continues...

Consequently, we can say that Intrinsic Dualism is present in every human being but with individual characteristics. This means that body, soul and spirit join and understand one another following a harmonious course and enjoying the benefits of their union. Knowledge, Understanding and Love have become ONE from where the spirit will guide human beings to Living and Existing at the same time. Evolution of intelligence and great cognizance will make them accomplish this outstanding experience and finally reach illumination. Having humans the freedom to decide on their acts, deeds and thoughts, Intrinsic Dualism, however, implies great personal responsibility regarding the Cause and Effect relationship – concludes the brother Elohim.

Nowadays, concepts and understanding of metaphysics differ considerably from those of the 19th century – continues the brother Interano – favoring individual self-knowledge to make positive and correct Intrinsic Dualism become a reality and thus advance the development of the soul's energy.

While we, to this effect, are transmitting ancestral cosmic knowledge, we are helping you eliminate techniques and methods of repetition because once you record this knowledge on your energy you no longer need them – observes the sister Interana – nevertheless, as it often occurs you feel you need to believe that you are able to accomplish whatever is necessary, even work miracles and therefore have to be every day superheroes whom people entirely trust. However, what happens if you fail? Beloved brothers, if there is something you cannot handle, do not despair and with a smile remember that "The Master Time and The Master Life" are on your side building and organizing your Desires of Creation.

Time and Life are busy using the energy of creation to find the solution in the higher realities of LIGHT and LOVE. Therefore, be patient since the cosmic book of life and immortal souls holds this solution for a long time but souls incarnating at the wrong time suffer, in particular when it involves people who love one another most. The path of spirituality is not the same for everyone as every human being has a rhythm of his/her own. All of you awake at different moments – says the sister Interana – we have to consider that there are both very young and old souls. This may explain why the souls of those who are close to you do not have a rhythm of equal development and maturity. Some will always be ahead of you, others behind. Only Love will make you understand this difference giving you the strength to support and aid one another on the path of return to the origin of existence. You cannot open a rose bud without ruining its delicate petals. You have to let nature determine when. The soul is intimateness, a place where you visualize the deepest truth and connect with your most elevated being.

This is where the Masters of Light will teach and prepare you for a new incarnation. Your soul is the door that connects you with what you were, are and will be in each life and which finally have you join your divine being. The source ONE, the true place of the soul and heart's authentic feeling and specific reference to UNIVERSAL LOVE – affirms the sister Interana – to which all have to awake in the presence of the beloved universe of themselves and their children. It is living in the ALL enjoying the plenitude of its harmony.

41. Does one live in the Antimatter Reality according to the Intrinsic Dualism?

In some grades, in a way souls continue in this condition because they still have to work on the transmutation of the emotions – replies the brother Elohim – the antimatter world adjusts to the characteristics of their energy and those grades therefore are the effects that the souls' thought-energies produce. The moment, human beings discover and start developing the potential of their inner senses, they will have the unconditional support of the universe to find and establish their personal spiritual connection. This spurs humans to combine the abilities of their inner senses to envisage the realization of important goals the way they never imagined before. Their self-knowledge is the faculty they have to broaden the awareness of whom they are and what the reality of their lives in all areas is. This knowledge will lead to understanding, maturity, psychological freedom and wisdom.

Unlike the knowledge about the external world, self-knowledge emerges from the inner world, from revelations that occur when the conscience has great receptivity for internal or external events – continues the brother Elohim – true understanding of life does not come from concepts or ideologies people might have adopted but from the comprehension of true-to-life experience.

Parents by their way of living must teach their children values as well as the development of body, psyche and the relations in society – continues the brother Elohim – children's souls are ductile but their pureness and innocence may make parents change certain beliefs and decide on walking the path of spirituality with them. Communication is of great importance as questions and answers from both sides will nourish souls that have come to learn and teach at the school of this reality.

Dualism: The following are considerations regarding dualism as found in philosophy and religion. The Latin word "Dualitas" refers to the existence of two opposing phenomena in a person or event. Dualism is the doctrine that postulates the existence of two supreme, independent and antagonistic principles. In this sense, the idea of good and evil is an example of dualism as both are of an entirely different essence. Matter-Spirit and Realism-Idealism are further examples. Contrary to Dualism is the concept of Monism that considers, for example, Matter-Mind undifferentiated.

In Chinese philosophy, the idea of yin and yang refers to the dualism of all that exists in the universe. This concept is valid for any situation or object under the premise that in all good there is something bad and vice-versa. In theology, dualism defines the existence of the divine principle of good (associated with the Light) and the divine principle of evil (Darkness). In this context, God is responsible for the creation of good while the creator of evil is the devil. Consequently, this dualism exonerates humans from the responsibility for evil in the world (Esoteric Dictionary).

Intrinsic: Philosophy frequently uses the term to designate something that corresponds to an object by nature and not because of its relation with another object. There is intrinsic certainty and evidence, intrinsic possibility, intrinsic glory of God etc. Intrinsic is what is essential (Wikipedia).

Intrinsic Dualism is a way of existing and living that should be a part of you – concludes the sister Interana – it means the need for LIVING but the true belief in EXISTING, to be in different places at the same time. It is also the presence in different grades, planes and dimensions of YOURSELF. Intrinsic Dualism occurs – continues the brother Interano – when you have a direct perception of Knowing, Understanding and Loving, that is, without using your mind. Everything just...IS.

You know by intuition that sound positive emotions will keep your spirits up. This is why we say that you must procure to have positive thought-energies. Did you notice that while showing positive emotions negative emotions do not appear? – says the sister Interana – having positive emotions is healthy for body and mind and makes you truly conscious of yourselves and the environment. Positive emotions will help find the way to prosperity and happiness. This is the true meaning of...EXISTING.

42. If EL SER UNO says that we are souls studying third and fourth grade at school just as children do, what are souls in these grades to study at a school called Earth?

Both souls and children in these grades have to respond to higher levels of learning but what distinguishes them is the true-to-life experience regarding family and social ties of the present and past. The Master Time and the Master Life are therefore educators to help all souls of these grades gain knowledge about evolution and elevation related to the satisfaction of basic needs and interests with growing conscience thus balancing their emotions – observes the sister Interana.

True-to-Life experience

Incarnated souls of these grades highly value sensations and perceptions, which become more intense owing to the acuteness of the external senses. They know the importance of forms and colors and react to the stimuli from those senses – explains the brother Interano – growing perception gradually lowers their emotiveness turning them beings of major objectivity. Consequently, they start observing themselves and their environment. They use the external senses in a more conscious way thus obtaining detailed knowledge of the forms and their relation with them. It is what we call the relationship of thought and intuitive perception of their reality. Appreciation of their innermost self and the understanding of objective forms develop extraordinarily as they realize that this process is creating parameters that help them establish relations with other souls, an interaction that largely depends on an exact perception via the external senses.

Thus, incarnated souls (persons) succeed in identifying and interpreting their existence. However, to secure a correct vision of the perception, they need to classify and register everything they perceive using techniques, methods, rites and chants. This means they will have to contemplate, analyze and ponder carefully situations to know, in which way these will contribute to the elevation of their energy.

Recording the energy

Recording of a soul's energy depends entirely on good intentions and free will – reminds the brother Elohim – while traveling the vastness of their existence souls, life after life, keep recording and creating superior conditions of shaping their energy. Whatever they experience during an incarnation, their memory will register. Nevertheless, it is not only recording but also fixing it on the energy to preserve the memory of what is positive of an experience in a language of understandable universal concepts.

Souls have to use their memory, as this is the way to establish communication with other souls. For this to occur, they must use concepts they "understood" and therefore look for a learning material not based on logic or some other kind of formal reasoning.

Imagination, an important quality

Imagination is of great importance for the correct recording of thought-energies – continues the brother Interano – because it connects the mind with verbalized concepts. This enriches the thoughts' Desire of Creation. Souls that develop imagination help conceive this objective constructively and thus create particular cognitive concepts. Imagination develops from life to life and unfolds through cause and effect because it determines situations of personal and environmental objectivity. The souls' cognitive process registers the reality, in which it lives and acts. Even though souls see themselves surrounded by a reality of fantasy, they recognize their particular reality, which allows them to develop the ability to imagine.

What motivates souls?

As they advance on their cognitive process, souls stimulate the thought-crystals enriching thus their concepts about knowledge – observes the sister Interana – in fact, this process is responsible for their orientation because they will not only receive this orientation from other souls but also start obtaining means of development of their own, which is indispensable for the formation of their spiritual character and personality. Knowledge and Understanding are therefore of immense importance. Without them, they would not be aware of the concepts recorded on their thought-energies and losing their way.

Emotions and feelings

Stimulated as they now are, incarnated souls (persons) will have better control of their emotions and physical responses – observes the brother Elohim – they will develop qualities such as morality, friendship, self-respect, respect and affection for others. Emotional true-to-life experience begins to produce the kind of success that spurs them to reach goals that are more demanding. Emotions and feelings become an inexhaustible source of sensations with parameters for the growth not only of knowledge but also of understanding. This will make them perceive major progress of energetic elevation and give them a feeling of harmony, peace and general well-being.

The thought-energies of the soul

Souls of the third and fourth grade are highly deliberative, driven by the desire for a deeper understanding of the world around them – affirms the sister Interana – however, they are not only eager to learn but want to know the reason of the teachings. At this point, techniques and methods of meditation and reflection may ease the task of the inner senses.

This inner work includes the discipline of analysis that souls impose on themselves for the comprehension of their acts, deeds and thoughts. In addition, their inner language will express everything so consistently that it will help them understand the very message of their emotions that they then will share with other souls.

The kinetic characteristics of the soul

When souls' development advances in a correct way, possible perturbed movements will vanish, which means that the process is reaching a state of peace and harmony – affirms the brother Interano – both physical and psychical movements are calm, and their language expresses an increasing comprehension of the environment. Patience is an important quality helping avoid the stimulation of emotional thought-energies that would lead to distraction and a slow-down of attention.

We realize – concluded the sister Interana – that incarnated souls' development needs the important support of their social environment as well as true-to-life experience they gain on the planet to aid their process of evolution and elevation. This is the so-called Earth school's principal function. Nevertheless, in this process, play an important role their intelligence and great curiosity for a knowledge, for which they receive first vigorous stimuli from their families but which reaches way beyond the limits of social ties, communities, society and the multi-media, however indispensable for their advance.

43. How can we find steadiness in a life replete with controversy?

People who have awaked – observes the brother Interano – know that they live in a planet run and controlled by a Matrix that provides food, clothing, medical drugs, technology etc. but are conscious that they have to decide using discernment and common sense on what is necessary to cover real needs and what seeks to satisfy fantasies. We call the possibility to make this choice FREE WILL.

Given this faculty, you stay with the challenge to look for balanced solutions – continues the sister Interana – if you do not, you might find yourselves declining the use of computers and cellphones. Your children would not be in good, although expensive private schools nor would your wife, husband or other family members work for some company.

In the middle of a considerably negative social environment, you must not forget that every one of you has to decide on what he/she feels is necessary for the spiritual elevation. You therefore should avoid making radical decisions and live as free as possible in a world of important limitations. A reality of LIGHT and LOVE – says the brother Elohim – without massive controls is every conscious human being's dream. While seeking the realization of your innermost desires, however much to our regret, you are not yet in a condition to ignore the rules of this material reality.

It takes common sense and good reasoning to try to achieve what is possible in a world full of contradictions, but you have to act as positively as you can to give your soul the chance to transcend and advance on the Path of Return. Therefore, let your intelligence guide you in this process of EVOLUTION without compromising ELEVATION. For that, you will need... a good pulse.

44. Would reading about metaphysics help our elevation or should we raise prayers to EL SER UNO?

Your reality are the third grade, plane and dimension. You are incarnated souls that depend on terminology, studies, knowledge, perception through the five external senses etc. to prove to yourselves that you are on the right way to advancement and elevation – observes the sister

Interana – it is, however, amazing to see that the greater the difficulties you feel walking this path and the more you pay for courses and conferences of spiritual leaders and gurus, the more you believe and reaffirm having found the truth – ponders the brother Interano.

Spirituality

Continues the brother Elohim – what is behind the term is of such simplicity that you might find it uninteresting or even boring. As you feel that you are lacking something, you start looking for it at institutions in far-away places that use techniques so complicated that you feel never be able to come even close to your goals. This way, you become addictive to "Spiritual Leaders and Gurus" who bend over backwards to satisfy doubts about your search for spirituality by looking for psychological-ancestral references regarding your descent during past generations. However, this is not what you need. EL SER UNO says "In the simplicity you live, do the best as you can. Use what is the most elevated feeling in yourselves on all your ACTS, DEEDS and THOUGHTS. Lead a life following the canons of the universe, be AUTHENTIC HUMAN BEINGS, without thinking...just BE. You do not need to try magic and miracles or jumping like clowns to be sure to walk the correct path because your way of acting will produce the hoped-for results.

Look for harmony and peace in your daily routine. Work on your ill negative emotions controlling them with knowledge, understanding and love; discover your origin and the reason for being in this reality. Gradually, this inner work will turn the essence of your soul. When this occurs, you will have attained what we call spirituality.

45. Should we pray to EL SER UNO?

We are sure that EL SER UNO does not want you to venerate it – affirms the brother Elohim – instead of raising prayers, you should start analyzing deep inside your hearts and souls the way you live this reality. Consciously, ask your soul to make you understand how to discover along the path to spirituality the deep of your subconscious replete with old concepts of little use lost in your memory but being an important part of your reality. Nevertheless, do elevate your thoughts asking the universe to give you the LIGHT to transmute the great burden that you carry from past lives.

Finding the way to spirituality in our times means gradually leaving behind this heavy burden and turning lighter and more subtle persons – concludes the brother Interano – one of the most inhumane treatments you have ever received is that they have made you believers of GUILT enslaving you thus for generations. Time has come for you to gain more self-confidence and be aware that you are BEINGS OF DIVINE ORIGIN who belong to an ALL of wisdom. When everything you have learned becomes a part of yourselves, you will be free of prayers, chants, religious beliefs, temples etc. and turn AUTHENTIC BEINGS of LIGHT and LOVE who without THINKING, ASKING and PRAYING...ARE.

46. In the first book *EL SER UNO I – Los Arcanos de Thoth* we learn that we are dwellers of El Ser Uno's subconscious. Does this mean there is a god who listens? Do we receive answers when we raise prayers? Whom do we address when thanking for what we receive in life?

This, indeed, is a very important question to ask because it contains the deep concern of all human beings with a thinking mind in this planet – remarks the sister Interana – in fact, the book says that you are a Planet-Cell of the Digestive System in the Primary Dimension of the Inferior Worlds and, as such, live in the Subconscious of EL SER UNO. Remember that you are thought-energies (souls) dwelling in the First, Second and Third Zone of the Universal Mind (EL SER UNO), the most conflictive and controversial of all. At present, about 30 percent awaked thought-energies (souls) live in the Third Zone and beyond, while about 70 percent are still dormant in the First and Second Zones classified as not having conscience of themselves. They incarnate, procreate and disincarnate without understanding their situation in this reality. However, the universe considers souls living between the Third, Fourth and some even in the Fifth Zone souls with full awareness of themselves and their environment. Consequently, EL SER UNO will listen to all human beings who meet these conditions.

The subconscious part in the brain of all human beings holds positive but predominantly such ill negative thought-energies and emotions as complexes, envy, anxiety, fear, hate, violence and others – observes the brother Interano – the latter are responsible for great uneasiness, but you seem to ignore them because of your concern to satisfy material needs, are almost indifferent to their claiming for help. As these thought-energies mark your character and personality, you would need to practice a sincere self-psychoanalysis about your lives. Do you listen to, observe, examine, analyze, discover and know that they exist? neither does EL SER UNO.

Declining to deal with these thought-energies, in practice means to deny their existence and therefore the need to LISTEN to them – observes the brother Elohim – if you made a careful and detailed analysis of your lives, you would discover the numerous negative thought-energies in your subconscious. You, however, ignore them and open thus the door to physical and mental disorders for whose origin you have no explanation.

Perceiving a serious malfunction, the Universal Mind of EL SER UNO had sent ideas (spirits) to the confines of the universe and the Elder Brothers Ayaplianos in their "Ideas-Spacecraft" to a cell called Tera to heal it. After leaving their spacecraft, they found themselves with a dark and threatening reality suffering from a distortion that turned their ideas into millions of thoughts without Light. When finally recovering, they realized having penetrated a reality even unknown to EL SER UNO that after thorough investigation they called Subconscious.

Nowadays, the Universal Mind of EL SER UNO knowing that there are conscious thought-energies (souls), analyzes, heals and returns them to their true reality. The messages with information, knowledge and manifestations of the awakening we are sending you is EL SER UNO working the thought-energies of its subconscious, that is, you.

When you elevate prayers to "God" - "HE" IS LISTENING TO YOU – only if your Awakening of Conscience has occurred. However, if you continue dormant, as a sleepwalker, in a life marked by the absence of light, a dialog would be impossible because "God, the One Origin, EL SER UNO or whatever you may call it only exists in Light and Love and to communicate with it you must be: IT AND PART OF IT"

47. I recently read about a foundation for the development of advanced technology with important benefits for humanity. When asked how his organization would obtain this technology, the founder says that he receives support from different parts. It seems that this also includes channeling with Elder Brothers. Is it you, our Elder Brothers, who are intervening?

EL SER UNO says that you have come from the future and will return there – comments the brother Interano – we all have souls created by the One Origin. They are very old and carry therefore important knowledge recorded in the Akashic Register, that is, in the Thought-Nimeos of the universal and our individual souls.

Souls accumulate wisdom whose energy, that you call "God", gives life to everything ever created. Souls incarnate in thousands of different molds adjusting to the stimuli they receive and the information they register. Consequently, the human species dwelling in many grades, planes and dimensions of the universe shelters souls the Life-Energy of which is forever part of its existence.

As dwellers of the third grade, plane and dimension – explains the sister Interana – your souls do not only mean LIFE but knowledge, understanding and love. They carry ancestral wisdom that emerges sometime during incarnations. In most cases, however, this wisdom remains hidden while your souls keep incarnating without any notion of its existence. Nevertheless, there are souls that awake and start remembering the accumulated knowledge through natural activators such as dreams, visions, extrasensory perceptions of parallel realities and contacts of the third kind.

When this occurs, many humans consider this knowledge a supernatural experience, which they do not seem to understand – continues the brother Elohim – their reactions range from comprehension as something natural, from fear, denial, imagination and fantasy to belief and transmission to others. In other words, it is anyone's Free Choice how to interpret and use this wisdom. Balanced souls will never use it for personal benefit, for the Matrix, overly ambitious ones abuse of it.

As your Elder Brothers Ayaplianos, we know that from a certain degree of evolution on, souls activate this knowledge. We are familiar with the awakening of wisdom and know that there are human beings such as scientists, investigators, explorers and inventors of whom the Internal City keeps a record. For obvious reasons, we pay attention to these activations. If the resulting actions were clearly detrimental for the planet and the population, we would find a way to block them.

There are developments that appear unfavorable for the planet – concludes the brother Interano – but over the time, result in progress and evolution and others apparently positive turn out to be high-risk operations. Humans therefore have to continue striving for responsible growth and evolution to deserve the wisdom of their creator.

48. How will erroneous psychological and psychiatric treatments affect Crystal, Indigo, Rainbow, and Diamond children today, claiming even the schools that they do not fit in the Matrix?

EL SER UNO asks that “OUR THOUGHTS BE CONSISTENT WITH WHAT WE ARE”. If parents firmly believe in freedom of the spirit, why would they not instill this belief into their children? – observes the brother Elohim – most countries already use alternative medicine and education the benefits of which might suggest the creation of a new faculty called Spiritual or Metaphysical Psychology.

> ***Spiritual or Metaphysical Psychology:*** Considers human beings in their physical, mental and spiritual expression a part of the whole. No doubt, their intimate and balanced interaction is responsible for well-being. Consequently, this therapy provides particular treatment to help patients find harmony and equilibrium to overcome the different types of disorders.
> Spiritual or Metaphysical Psychology seeks to understand the origin of suffering but also of satisfaction to identify and treat the emotions in each case. It invites to learn what this analysis can do for the soul and how it can help conquer fear and live a life of plenitude (Dictionary of Metaphysics).

It is therefore highly appropriate for the diagnosis and treatment of diverse child disorders. A psychologist specializing in spiritual treatment will determine if a child actually needs a particular treatment. He/she procures to raise its self-confidence to help it face the social environment without compromising natural-born gifts and qualities. If there were need for medication, he/she would try to avoid conventional drugs, use alternative holistic and anthroposophical medicine.

In addition, parents may opt for schools that emphasize the development of intuition – says the sister Interana – these schools have a clear humanistic orientation; they understand education as looking for the development of individual freedom incorporating artistic expression to favor the studies of other subjects. Music and painting are not only particular subjects but also have a relationship with mathematics, languages and social science. Furthermore, children from different grades attend classes and workshops for carpentry, cooking, weaving, gardening etc.

To our regret, parents look for the "best schools" with the highest possible standards of education for reasons of personal satisfaction (Ego) and social status and fail to concentrate on schools with the capacity to help these very sensible children develop their gifts and abilities. Parents thus cause them to feel insecure and frustrated instead of helping them develop the conditions to face an ever more competitive society. This shows that in your reality "Quantity", that is, numerous conventional factors are still more important than the "Quality" of responsible and solid teachings.

Reptilians' controlling force works using technology and the planetary knowledge on the left hemisphere of the brain – observes the brother Elohim – when you see your small children play with an electronic toy, you are in front of that control but do not seem to notice it. You believe that this is going to further their intelligence. In fact, their brains become very active but principally work with the left hemisphere responsible for becoming winners in life by restlessly striving for wealth.

Parents of the New Age will therefore have to ponder on the type of school they entrust their children – advises the brother Interano – a wrong decision may result in great suffering during this process of adjustment and the soul lose those outstanding qualities from past lives. We hope that this orientation will make you understand the importance of being close to those special children and truly help them start walking in this reality.

49. What occurs when members of spiritual circles headed by a channel who affirms receiving the teachings of the "Masters" mention other messages, which the channel dismisses or even forbids?

Slavery has many faces – replies the brother Interano – but many of you will have to go through this experience to understand the significance of FREEDOM. The path to freedom is one of maturity and spiritual growth and rarely spares you suffering because you have to change your routine or often remain distant from persons and environments you cherish. It means to become masters of your lives and needs brave and determined souls.

Not all are ready to walk alone and face the deep of their innermost self. They prefer to rely on "others" believing them to have the answers of the cosmos and the universe for being mediums or channels and therefore readily available solutions to their problems. This way of seeing and understanding things denotes inability to comprehend how the universe functions but, above all, fear of growing apart from families and friends.

If a channel or medium is unable to act on the teachings of the "Masters", – says the sister Interana – he/she fails to represent the correct expression of an advanced spirit. In addition, there is serious doubt about the entities with which they establish communication. True "Masters or Elevated Spirits of LIGHT and LOVE" would never show a negative attitude toward a different knowledge transmitted by brothers of the universe. Therefore, the EGO of the medium or channel who probably make a living on this might fear to lose potential followers.

Circles, institutions, sects and other credos that are not serious about the spiritual knowledge they transmit, have always existed because those who prefer not to see, hear and speak up guarantee their survival. There is proof of it everywhere with methods looking very much alike using concepts such as CREATING NEEDS TO SELL SOLUTIONS. This spiritual market works by instilling fear, insecurity and psychological dependence, a vampire that absorbs their energy and drains their pockets. The moment they understand the nature of these practices, they will banish them from their lives and walk by themselves.

To start growing and turn a collective into an individual soul, nevertheless, takes determination, courage, strength, perseverance, knowledge and understanding – observes the brother Interano – it is not an easy thing to achieve because the dependence on collective work, apparent support from others and their decisions have grown a habit very difficult to overcome.

As we leave behind what no longer helps us elevate, the universe acts to fill the vacuum – concludes the brother Elohim – you will come across people who have started an equal journey. Therefore, keep going and never desist. Feel the spirit grow in your heart and soul. Looking back someday, it all will seem a dream to you. Forgive those who hurt you and thank the universe for having made you advance always and shown you the Path of Return.

50. What is the situation of children who suffer from ADHD?

We consider ADHD (Attention Deficit Hyperactivity Disorder) a lower degree of Autism – replies the brother Interano – while you often confuse it with the Asperger Syndrome. However, both are similar disorders with almost the same treatment. Regarding the situation of the energy, it means that the thought-energy or soul inadequately incarnates during conception. The reason is that the soul does not want to incarnate in this reality but for the advance of its energy has to accept it.

The main symptom of ADHD is the dissociation of the material and astral reality, that is, the mental reality of these children creates a fluent connection between the Internal City (The Beyond) and their material world. Pregnancy and birth in most cases are difficult because these souls fight birth from the beginning. They generally incarnate unwantedly or after the mother has suffered an abortion – continues the sister Interana – these children need intense demonstrations of affection and contact with nature and animals. Since ADHD presents a variety of energy grades, many children need medication to complement psychological treatment.

Cases that are more benign only require professional orientation to find their “place” in this material reality, which means that the soul accepts the physical body. In general, symptoms continue during childhood and adolescence but tend to cease during adultness. The reason is that the soul after battling materiality for so long, finally decides to accept the teachings of this life.

51. Could you give us a more detailed explanation of the Baby-Spirit?

The Baby-Spirit is what many of you call the Holy Spirit represented by a white dove – observes the brother Elohim – here is for what they stand in your reality.

> ***Holy Spirit:*** Is the third person of Christian Trinity/Theo, the feminine energy (Sakti) of the supreme principle/Gnostic, the divine Wisdom (Sophia) with feminine characteristics, the creative power of God; The Holy Spirit (Jehovah) is the god of everything created, the Superior Divinity, the Eternal and Universal Spirit who fills, sustains and animates all beings and existence forever. When a person is safe, he/she not only turns a being of God and member of the divine family but also feels deep inside his/her soul to be a part of divine nature.
> The Holy Spirit wakes the conscience in believers that they are children of God and that His presence constitutes the divine nature of them. The power of the Holy Spirit is to spirituality what water is to materiality. Water purifies, refreshes, quenches and turns dry into fertile soil. It restores cleanness and is thus an appropriate symbol for the divine grace, which not only purifies the soul but also gives it beauty. While water is indispensable in the material reality, a spiritual life is impossible without the Holy Spirit. The white dove symbolizes the Holy Spirit. SYMBOL originates from the Greek SUN meaning just and BALIO, which means literally one thing lying beside another or one representing and explaining the other. In other words, a symbol is a material emblem that discovers and shows a spiritual truth. With symbols, the universal language makes understandable what words often cannot explain or express. Symbols are the language of the Holy Spirit (Esoteric Dictionary).

White Dove: According to Christian belief, it symbolizes the soul that after disincarnating adopts this form. It means spirituality, strength and sublimation, its color pureness, peace and joy. Carrying an olive leaf in its beak, the white dove has been a symbol of peace for thousands of years and has strong ties with Jewish-Christian culture. In the Old Testament, Noah sends out a white dove to find land after the flood. After some time, the dove returns to the Arch carrying an olive leaf denoting that the water level was back to normal and God finally in peace with humanity.

The four gospels talk about God's concern for this event while Jewish tradition interprets Genesis as "God's Spirit sheltering as a dove in the waters of the flood". Characterizing the dove as an innocent, gentle, pure, peaceful, patient, loyal and easy to handle creature means that the Holy Spirit treats believers using gentleness and persuasion rather than obligation or force.

Joshua Emmanuel advised believers to be "gentle as a dove" and thus in peace with God. The white dove may represent two situations relative to peace. When shown with the olive leaf, it symbolizes the desire for the preservation of peace. When freed during events, it represents the messenger that transmits the desire for peace (Dictionary of Symbols).

As you can see, the language of the universe always works with symbols – continues the brother Interano – these symbols have always been at your species' reach but for many reasons their knowledge has not been available to all human beings. The Holy Spirit or in our case, the Baby-Spirit presents the following qualities: Intelligence and Belief, Thinking Power, Sensibility and Intuition, Power to sense things, Will and Perseverance, Determination, Conscience of Moral and Ethics and the Knowledge of Good and Bad.

When speaking of the Awakening of Conscience, we do not only mean to see you turn "Good Persons". Awakening is to go deep into a Knowledge and Understanding that has been and is always there. It means to take the sensibility of the soul to a superior state of conscience and with will and perseverance have it walk the path of return. It is the conscience of Moral and Ethics to live this life in accordance with the canons of the cosmos.

We have always reminded you that for the Awakening of Conscience you need to take your soul to the frequency of LIGHT and LOVE where Light means Knowledge and Understanding and Love the driving force and the key to achieving positive results. The Holy Spirit and the Awakening of Conscience are synonym of the Conception and Gestation of the Baby-Spirit. Many already have initiated this process nurturing their Baby-Spirit to transcend this reality and reach higher energy frequencies that will take them deep into the Universal Mind. Others, however, are falling behind because they still are prisoners of fantasy for failing to study and understand the true meaning of the symbols in religion.

52. What does spiritual elevation tell us when giving birth to children whom we do not welcome, often because of mistaken family planning?

The advent of a new human being in this reality should always fill a couple with JOY and LOVE – replies the sister Interana – in fact, the birth of a child is a moment of great happiness for many people. However, in a number of cases, a tight economic situation may frequently overshadow parents' loving feelings.

Economy is important in a world where you have to satisfy material needs and desires. Nevertheless, you must be aware that the incarnating soul not only needs affection but moral orientation. Therefore, beware of overly material expectations. Strong emotional reactions are not recommendable either, as they often carry expressions of conflicts and passion that would remain recorded on the memory of all involved – concludes the brother Interano – furthermore, is of importance how, why, when and where conception and gestation occur because they are details that you will forever bear in your memory and hearts.

Try to control your emotions and use good judgement to avoid criticizing and hurting feelings, which would affect the spiritual elevation of the baby's soul. The baby should always be first because it has no part in the conflicts among the persons of its environment. It is not the baby´s fault, it is people around who generates the conflicts. Family is to support but sometimes they get confused. Human relationships are very complicated.

Parents have to plan the future with LIGHT and LOVE to prevent this incarnated soul from suffering the effects of the mother's possible emotional disorders during gestation or the consequences of an eventual rejection after birth. The souls we are sending are those you call souls of Indigo or Crystal children, but you should receive any new human being in this reality with wishes for plenitude and thoughts that will bring harmony and peace to his/her soul. Those special children, however, must find a true home and shelter from human prejudice, united in the LIGHT of LOVE with their parents.

53. What is your position regarding abortion?

Following the overall message of EL SER UNO – replies the sister Interana – how could we affirm that the act of abortion is correct or not? We will never be judges of any individual decision a human being has to make. Our task has been and always will be to show you how thought-energies function but only you can decide by using good judgement how you will make them work in each case. Only your heart and soul will reveal, consciously or unconsciously, the innermost truth about this.

You will always be free to decide. If you made the right or wrong decision, you would know sometime in this incarnation or after you disincarnate from the impact of CAUSE and EFFECT that this act will have on your soul and not from a possible religious punishment. The universe never judges. It only reveals the Cause and Effect relationship of ACTS, DEEDS and THOUGHTS of the soul. Since each soul is a universe of the micro-cosmos, it will have to ponder the INTENTION of its THOUGHTS.

In *EL SER UNO II,* – affirms the brother Interano – we say that "Matter-energy incarnates during the first three months of gestation. From the third to the sixth month, it develops the left hemisphere of the brain. From the sixth to ninth month, the right hemisphere prepares to receive the spirit". The Universe recycles the energies and everything takes the correct place. Remember the importance of why, how, when and where conception occurs because this is the origin of Cause and

Effect. Therefore, each case handles individually and you have to look for an answer not only to this but also to any other occurrence.

We will never tell you what is wrong or right on your acts and actions. We are always explaining the function of the energy thus it depends on you to understand the results of your choices. When you create a positive or a negative cause, this will always redound to you. The effect will return to you in different ways, in this life or the next one. Remember the importance of why, how, when and where of your acts. The experiences you live, the essence of your lives is a mirror of yourselves. Consequently, we cannot intervene in your ACTS, DEEDS and THOUGHTS. It is all your Free Will. *(EL SER UNO II – Planet 3.3.3 – The Guardians of Tera)*

From the knowledge that we transmit, we know that energy and souls are eternal – continues the brother Interano – this means that, considering the way energy works, it will not affect the soul nor will the soul compromise the energy since the universe will give the soul after an abortion because of a selfish or materialistic attitude a new chance. Nevertheless, this attitude might determine the formation of a karma for the soul.

There are many motives of different grades for it but only the universe will be able to determine the impact of this occurrence. On the other hand, only the incarnated soul will be conscious of the underlying Emotion and Intention for this decision. In many cases, religious orientation or particular ancestral tradition are at the bottom of this act, which a number of countries consider a criminal act.

As mentioned earlier, the divine laws work in a different way since the universe does not judge you for this decision, while your actions and thoughts will, as they obey to vibration frequency, rhythm and color emanating from thought-energy – concludes the brother Elohim – it is therefore important that you analyze this decision without any self-delusion to determine your true motives. If you arrive at the conclusion that your action, deeds and thoughts were negative, you need to recognize your fault as an act of contrition.

If the soul (person) lacks the capacity of self-analysis, it will clearly see the truth after disincarnating with the help of other, more advanced souls. Each soul is a universe with endless grades of thoughts that do not compare or equalize. Each soul is independent and needs particular handling.

54. What explains that so many gurus teach the path to "Illumination" by just using contemplation?

EL SER UNO is a knowledge based on the teaching of IDEA and THOUGHT – observes the sister Interana – it says that all existing dwells in an immense mind and that you, thinking beings, are its Thought-Children. How could you possibly use permanent contemplation if you have to work on yourselves with Knowledge, Understanding and Love? Why do you have thoughts if contemplation would be enough to guide you toward Illumination?

Thought-Energy needs proper recording for the human species throughout the universe, with the positive and elevated intention to reason, learn, advance, execute, elevate and eventually create to the image of its father, the Universal Mind – affirms the brother Interano.

Why would the One Origin create thought-children? for contemplation? If humans were just contemplating, who would realize the IDEAS of the Creator? Contemplation is a state of the soul – adds the brother Elohim – it is a state of the spirit as well when human minds and inner senses are in silence. This silence may develop during meditation when you manage to renounce the pleasures of materialistic thinking. This IS how you reach the state of contemplation without having to think about it, which does not mean that you stop thinking, as thinking is necessary to BE. During contemplation, the spirit in a special way starts guiding you but you do not see or hear anything yet because you are working with the LIGHT and LOVE of the inner senses that the spirit grants us. This means that Light and Love does not come to us through the sensation of the external senses but through the Universal Feelings of wisdom.

The intimate relation of the human mold (physical human body) with the spiritual faculties and the principle of life (the soul) may explain the knowledge that you receive through the Inner Senses – observes the sister Interana – although your intelligence and will stand out, both depend on and interact with the spirit, that is, your Superior Self.

You do not have to look for prayers, temples, to call on God or live in useless, idle contemplation. Contemplation is not laissez-faire or mysticism, it is neither quietness nor ecstasy. Quite the opposite, it is the consistent use of elevated thought-energies on your daily routine of acts and deeds – concludes the brother Elohim – it means that your thought-energies are always turned over to the infinite of LIGHT and LOVE.

Contemplation also means to calm and control ill negative emotions and organize your lives. It means to balance your inner self and do the best you can in an environment that you did not choose to live, with love and understanding. Contemplation is observation and the awareness that you are passing through a dense reality of fantasy. Means to look and see, hear and listen, and feel deep inside compassion to understand LOVE. You must realize that you ARE without the least doubt a part of this huge puzzle called the endless mechanism of ONE.

55. People write saying that reading the books *EL SER UNO* is as if they were breaking inner structures for revamping and feel very unhappy about it. Is this a natural occurrence in the soul?

The books *EL SER UNO* belongs to all, but is not for everyone – replies the brother Seramita – be aware of your state of mind and expectations the moment you start reading. Are you patient and calm? Do you try to make your mind assimilate their content to comfort your spirit? Do you make reading pauses between paragraphs to analyze the text? Do you use dictionaries of esotericism, philosophy and symbols? Do you share your reading with other persons?

Trying to read, understand and assimilate in haste the knowledge, they offer is not recommendable – comments the sister Interana – the amount of information is such that you should take your time to handle it. Otherwise, it may leave you drowsy or even with headaches. However, what seems to make this knowledge particularly uncomfortable to many readers is the fact that it very critically deals with traditional concepts in Religion, Mysticism and Esotericism that you carry from past lives and in your present life. The message of the books *EL SER UNO* is largely metaphysical with knowledge in the fields of Psychology, Philosophy and Spirituality – observes the brother Elohim – nevertheless, when speaking of spirituality, we refer to the knowledge of thought-energy, the process of the Cause and Effect relationship and its proper handling rather than to the religious definition of it. This may be the reason that the concepts of EL SER UNO, in general, do not meet many people's vision. You have to be sure of a soul's true needs to determine if it travels a more mystical and esoteric path and perhaps requires teachings that have more affinity with its inner nature.

We suggest slow reading of the books to give your emotions a chance to assimilate and, above all, understand these new concepts – says the brother Interano – since the books touch deeply rooted structures, the emotions of the soul have trouble to go along without the old beliefs of a comfortable routine transmitted for generations. When you read these books, you feel you lose the foundation of your beliefs and that means you have to re-structure your whole life.

Starting to walk by itself and rid of the burden it carries, will demand a soul's determination, effort, dedication, strength, perseverance, knowledge, understanding and much love thus leaving behind what produces lack of flexibility, routine, complacency, fantasy and satisfaction of the Ego and its external senses.

56. People write us confessing that after having read the books they have abandoned their job o ended a relationship. This worries me because the message of the books leaves no doubt about the importance of conscious social relationships. What would be your advice?

When reading the books, many persons seem to misinterpret the need for renunciation, which clearly does not refer to abandonment of activities or relations but to reflection about what the true needs are they have to satisfy and what whims of the Ego they should control or ignore – observes the sister Interana –their emotions responsible for quitting a job or deciding on a separation might have felt stimulated while reading but already existed. If people end a working or personal relationship means both relations no longer meet their expectations. They therefore should take full responsibility for this decision and not use the message as an excuse – concludes the brother Interano.

They nevertheless firmly disagree by using metaphors of understanding and idealism – comments the brother Elohim – while their minds and confuse emotions work to hide their unhappiness under supposed comprehension. Their decisions make them feel having found a new way to realize tasks entrusted to them by the universe – says the brother Interano – however, it is all fantasy to feel free of compromise or that their excuse may be a solid enough foundation for future realizations.

In other words, – replies the sister Interana – the books gave them a perfect pretext to end a situation they no longer could take and the strength to trade a limited for a more "secure" support. Innermost weakness had blocked the need for knowing, analyzing and facing important questions of their lives and made them choose the easier way. As you see, – concludes the brother Elohim – most people live their lives trying to escape the problems, they refuse to analyze although many of which they will have to confront again any moment.

57. We feel that the Agreement, described in the fifth book, between you and governments of the planet in 1947 and valid until the year 2013 needs major explanations regarding the following questions. Whom of the brothers had negotiated it? What are its exact terms? Why did you negotiate it? Did you transfer technology to the exterior and if so, what did you ask in return?

To begin with, this issue concerns the Brothers Interanos of the Material Reality of Atlantis – observes the brother Interano – we are spirits of the Antimatter Reality and free of reincarnation. Nevertheless, we lived that past reality, have therefore full knowledge of it and will explain why the Brothers Interanos settled that agreement and what it means.

As you know from the books, the Internal City of Material Atlantis has had communication with a certain number of humans in the exterior at all times via Orbs, Mediums, Channels and Telepathy. However, the Brothers Interanos of Antimatter Atlantis never stopped being close guiding you in dreams and memories on the path of return – observes the sister Interana – with great endeavor, historians have completed and corrected incomplete and distorted parts of those events based on documents that emerged over the time. They thus combined conclusions from their findings with the ancestral message of truth and the distorted reality we all know, deeds of those who have the power of control.

We are going to start our explanations from the Middle Ages as a time of extreme darkness and ostracism in the history of the human species

– continues the brother Interano – when the ill negative force had absolute control over the planet and its inhabitants. Most of today's incarnated souls lived that reality showing the consequences of psychological mistreatment.

In times of inscrutable conquests, slavery and domination, human lives had little value having the subconscious unleashed ill negative emotions that left the Tera-Cell in a profound state of ignorance – affirms the brother Interano – this is when we started directing the energy toward knowledge, which now was possible because humans despite the ignorance of their souls managed to free themselves of their dense and emotionally ill energies through intense suffering thus softening their petrified hearts and the Nimeos-Energy of their souls.

After this, we were able to communicate with human minds through mediums or telepathy – observes the brother Elohim – as a result, philosophy, literature and arts experimented a renaissance. Noble and generous, they helped incarnated and long dormant souls awake while the many souls that came from the Internal City to initiate their cycle in the exterior were receiving our teachings. For the first time, there were Ascended Masters who out of the Internal City started transmitting the cosmic knowledge of LIGHT and LOVE to those incarnated souls via mediums and channels.

From that time on, humans' energy went through a process of great purification. This explains why there is the counterpart of positive energy in a very ill negative world where millions of people, in the quiet of their lives, have realized outstanding work. "In the quiet of their lives" means that they are incarnated souls of LIGHT and LOVE who thus have contributed to the elevation of the energy and quality of the electromagnetism. At the beginning of the 21st century, we your Elder Brothers Ayaplianos of the eighth and ninth hierarchy of the Antimatter Reality – says the brother Interano – had a first official communication with several beings of the Russian Federation who had realized tests with mediums and telepathy and managed to make contact with other realities of existence.

For the first time, there was proof of an Extraterrestrial Presence, our presence, because we did not belong to the exterior of the planet. There was knowledge of the Internal City and of another civilization inside the planet. Aware of this unprecedented event, governments and religious institutions called on emergency meetings fearful of a possible extraterrestrial invasion. However, many failed to understand our intentions while others distorted the message of our communication striving to draw benefit from it. Nevertheless, the negative Reptilian force, after having dominated the planet for millions of years, and fearing to lose this immense control, used its power and influence to have governments recognize the need for the creation of large defense systems to protect them against possible aggressions from other countries thus initiating a huge arms race.

However, those were not defense systems against terrestrial aggressors – continues the sister Interana – but supposedly against an invasion on our part although our communications had always been messages of love and fraternity. Perceiving the union of many countries to defend the planet as contrary to their interests, the Negative Force started creating disunity among countries and religions giving rise to what you henceforth called the Cold War.

Cold War: A term coined by Bernard Baruch, an advisor to President Roosevelt, as a reference to the long competition between the US and the Soviet Union (URSS) and their respective allies after World War II. This conflict dominated international relations for almost half a century in the political, economic and propaganda but only in a limited way in the military front.

Reason for not turning a "Hot War" was the emergence of nuclear weapons. Before the Atom Bomb, war according to the strategist Clausewitz was the continuation of politics by other means. After Hiroshima, a direct confrontation of the two great powers would mean a catastrophe for the planet. The superpowers' growing nuclear arsenals were an impediment for a war that neither one could win. Nevertheless, both the US and URSS and their allies used massively propaganda, intimidation, subversion and drew benefits from regional wars.

The Cold War clearly started in 1947 after an accelerated deterioration of relations among former allies reaching its culmination during 1948-53. After several periods of distension and confrontation, under the leadership of Gorbachev, the URSS initiated a process that culminated with the disintegration of the URSS in 1991. The Cold War was over (Wikipedia).

Purpose of the wars humans fought in the planet's recent history was to show us the power of their armament. This is particularly true for the Hiroshima bombing, in World War II – affirms the brother Interano.

Although the Internal City never gave them reasons to doubt its peaceful mission, governments ignored its efforts as an intermediary. However, President Truman as an inspired member of masonry and with the knowledge Russian authorities had obtained via telepathy was willing to end the cold war.

Masonry also helped him acquire knowledge of the universal truth and he thus learned about our presence. Using the Russians' communication via telepathy, some governments established contact with the brothers Interanos of the Material Reality for a secret meeting to take place at what is today Area 51 in the State of Nevada. Since the brothers Interanos cannot take the atmosphere of the exterior, they sent a committee of Gray Clones who occasionally leave for the exterior, to represent them – explains the sister Interana – as we know, the Grays' spacecraft unfortunately considered an intruder suffered an attack with experimental electromagnetic armament and crashed at Roswell, New Mexico in June, 1947. All members of the committee died and their bodies since then remain in a cryogenic state inside the area 51.

Governments and religious organizations refused to disclose the Roswell incident and made the Brothers Interanos accept an agreement not to present themselves before the public – affirms the brother Elohim – non-compliance of this agreement would lead to sanctions against less developed countries, with which the brothers Interanos had worked more frequently and thus been able to raise the energy frequency of the electromagnetism.

Their intention was to form a coalition only with developed countries on the assumption that the less developed would not be in a condition to resist an invasion. They nevertheless sub-estimated the importance of those countries believing that the Brothers Interanos would not consider them because of their limited resources. How surprisingly ignorant they were because it never occurred to them that those countries' strength does not lie in material resources but in the energy of their thoughts.

In fact, the brothers Interanos did not present themselves but concentrated on teaching the beings of those countries universal knowledge. Governments and religious institutions did not care because to them this was of no importance. Thus, the brothers Interanos, without any restriction, managed to elevate thought-energies and free an immense number of souls from manipulation and slavery.

Throughout the 66 years of the treaty, the brothers Interanos of the Internal City of Material Reality, – replies the sister Interana – at discretion, fulfilled a task of teaching, elevating and preparing millions of thought-energies to incarnate in less developed countries as authentic and noble souls willing to remember, learn and work with conscience, confidence and love. Our Brothers Interanos of the Material Reality of Atlantis will give you further details on this topic – assures the brother Elohim – the dark forces in the planet would do anything to block the knowledge of our presence. We therefore want to protect those humans who with great determination fight for it to become public but ask them to be aware that this may be dangerous and even mean personal sacrifice. Trying to make those in power see and accept the truth of something that all have a right to know, unfortunately often has fatal consequences.

We look at one another in silence and I proceed to asking the following question

58. You say that we live our lives based on the recordings of the Nimeos-Energy. What are the consequences for doctors and members of the police who often live traumatizing events or those who regularly watch horror movies? How do they compare to persons whose lives apparently are so much quieter for benefitting from the energy of elevated thoughts?

There is, in fact, a big difference – observes the brother Elohim – in general, the Nimeos-Energy of people who assimilate continual energy from low frequency thoughts or work in an environment of dense cinnabar energies, tend to suffering from traumas. There are cases, in which those traumas not only are the cause for mental disorders but also for somatic (physical) diseases.

The process of recording and re-recording traumatic events on the Nimeos-Energy – continues the brother Interano – may cause people to confuse reality with this other reality resulting from psychical and physical disorders. Humans who lead this type of life risk absorbing ill negative energies because they do not comprehend how the energy actually works.

59. What can these persons do to prevent contamination from ill negative energies?

For the type of work they do they need preventive psychologic treatment to block ill negative energies but most important, they must be spiritually advanced and have a good understanding of the human soul, basic qualities of the mental defense system called OBJECTIVITY – affirms the brother Interano.

What is the attitude of people who work in urban sewer systems with a high degree of contamination? – asks the sister Interana – you will say that they need vaccination against diseases transmitted by animals and use protective masks and gloves same as professionals of hospitals and laboratory services. As the physical body, the soul faces infection, too, an infection through contaminating thoughts.

Therefore, professionals and in general persons whose activities permanently expose them to the risk of mental contamination, must seek to understand how the energy works to protect themselves. We your brothers of the Internal City have been and continue incarnating to help you raise the frequency of LIGHT and LOVE and will be with you for the next two hundred years. More and more human beings will thus carry wisdom from birth and be an example to follow in the Age of Awakening to Conscience.

60. How can we keep Nimeos-Energy from suffering traumas and diseases?

Fortunately, you can – observes the brother Interano – human beings with those critical low frequency energy activities, in addition to preventive psychologic assistance should make yoga, meditation and regular physical exercise a habit. Nevertheless, while these practices are an important defense, they have to be vigilant since the Nimeos-Energy are sensible to impacts from strong impressions that could turn out to be the cause for some disease.

The way those with political and economic power run the planet, as well as the profound impact of ambition, stress and emotions undoubtedly give rise to illnesses of the human mold (physical body) – proceeds the sister Interana – be aware that the soul is a sanctum where you may visualize the truth of this incarnation that connects with your superior self and where the ego no longer exists. This is where the spirit clears the way for the energies of the creation of the All, the Union and the ONE. This is how you receive teachings from the Brothers of the Light to continue your innermost work after incarnating. This is where you will remember the purpose of existence, the reality of this world and learn about truth and love. The soul is the door that opens to what you have been, to what you are and to what you are going to do in each new incarnation. It is where you go when you feel lost to reconnect with your divine self. However, if a continual flow of ill negative emotions affects a temple that is your soul, you eventually will be unable to the take the pressure and allow negativity to influence your life.

The temple (your soul) connects with the material body by a door called Nervous System – explains the brother Elohim – if the soul suffered severe continual mistreatment, this material door would open to allow an avalanche of compulsions to enter and settle in some part of the body starting to build an energy concentration that later turns the expression you call Disease.

Ancestral teachings carry verities that with the passing of the time only covered the needs of the spirit deviating from what they really were to do, provide health and well-being for the trilogy Body (matter), Soul (psyche) and Spirit (mind) – proceeds the brother Interano.

Oriental religions, for that matter, more clearly preserve, transmit and adjust to ancient teachings but some have problems with fanatic minorities. Religions in Western cultures, nevertheless, distorted those teachings adjusting them to their customs and needs to draw important material benefits from them.

Consequently, disunity of the trilogy gave rise to the outbreak of diseases that spread and worsened continually – says the sister Interana– religions' only concern was the "Spirit", governments and power groups heavily concentrated on "Matter" and scientists and investigators made the "Soul" their principal object of analysis. The result was that the knowledge about the unity of the three bodies (trilogy) disintegrated making humans create an increasing distance from the innermost selves of their souls that consequently separated knowledge and understanding.

Another consequence of the disintegration of knowledge energy is the creation of working systems without taking appropriate security measures – observes the brother Elohim – let´s consider again the last example: How do people take care of themselves when they clean the city drain?... They wear special clothes, breath in oxygen tanks, put on gloves and they do it to avoid being contaminated with bacteria, germs and viruses. Is that right? – I nodded and the brother continued...

We therefore wish to stress again the importance of protection of people who suffer from considerable health risks (sewers, hospitals and laboratories) against germs, bacteria and virus as well as the shelter of those who remain exposed to dense and low frequency energy in environments of contaminated thought-energy by the strong mental defense system called Objectivity – concludes the sister Interana – in fact, many of you have extraordinary spiritual strength resulting from well-protected souls and therefore are able to take on the densest and lowest grade energy without any opposition – proceeds the brother Seramita – souls that have come to accept to deal with very difficult situations trying to show as many other souls as they can the correct path to walk. They are what we call "special" souls – finishes the brother Elohim.

Nevertheless – remarks the sister Interana – many souls do not have this strength nor have they to fulfill a mission after incarnating. Others simply are not ready for certain tasks and suffer having to do contaminating work just because of Tradition or Habit. Yet the obligation to satisfy physical needs characterizes the exterior. This is why so many souls have to realize a type of work, with which they do not identify. Working conditions with permanent pressure and the lack of recognition also deeply affect them. Even though they try very hard they fail to resist and such is often their suffering that they develop a disease. Life in the exterior, however, is a learning process and every true-to-life experience a chance to grow – observes the brother Elohim – the purpose of life is to know from where you came, whom you are and where you are heading for, is to explore your inner self, grow self-esteem, love your fellow humans and be ready to forgive.

61. Are those you call "special" beings, able to descend to dark and low-grade energy, SPIRITUAL BEINGS? Are we only as spiritual beings able to conquer the planet's dense energy?

Real Spirituality is within the system, not outside of it. How will you recognize that you are spiritual beings if you do not know the negative energies you have to learn to vanquish and change to positive? How will you know if you are growing if you fail to work the dark side of your nature? How to overcome evil without practicing good? Spiritual growth means having gained confidence after emerging unscathed and stronger from critical situations. Only recurrent true-to-life experience will have your souls advance and make you true Warriors of LIGHT and LOVE.

Therefore, do not look for shortcuts in life believing that this will make learning easier. If you do, recurrent true-to-life experience will teach you that avoiding facing up is not the solution because it means retarding the return to your origin. Instead, you should realize that clearing obstacles in life is the fastest way to spiritual advance. Thank the universe for giving you the force to persist. Remember that the universe loves you but will always put this force to test because it wants you to be souls that with determination and perseverance are able of leaving the chrysalis of evolution to become magnificent butterflies whose elevation will take them to its very confines, the only way to become a part of it.

You often believe and feel that the emotional conflicts of your material life keep you from finding peace, quietness and spirituality – proceeds the brother – but should know that, despite feeling uncomfortable, worried and sad, perception and intuition of your inner senses are always working to help you find answers.

You often are not aware of this because of the emotion that comes from the soul and from the work with your External Senses. However, such Inner Senses as mind, sensibility, perception and intuition are generally alert and ready to deal with unexpected situations. Nevertheless, when you feel that they momentarily do not show the peace and harmony the soul needs, do NOT insist. Relax, take a walk, do some exercises, read a book, listen to music, meditate etc. Thus breaking the spell of negativity, raising your energy frequency and protecting your thoughts from any harmful interference. Life does not have any mystery. Life is about understanding and how to manage any situation.

The Spirit (divine inner force) never abandons you, however, you sometimes distance from it because of the denseness of the material world that keeps you busy with the satisfaction of needs that, though inevitable, should be in equilibrium. Although you seem to be on your own when facing problems, the spirit never stops producing Thoughts, Ideas and Solutions and always procures to give your Inner Sphere of Life, your true Reality of Existence, Harmony and Peace.

You may fail school subjects but will always have a new chance to pass them – reassures the sister Interana – there is an extraordinary force in every one of you to cure themselves and help others heal. Healing means to free yourselves of ill negative emotions that, so often producing loneliness, wrath, fear and pain, have separated you from this divine inner source. Know the most elevated expression and force of love within the spiritual dimensions of your soul and take it to superior grades of sacrifice to find happiness. Excel as human beings to conquer the so long desired universe.

Remember: The soul is the throne of your lives and the confidence in following the path you have chosen will reign with LIGHT and LOVE, indelibly recorded on the soul. The way you have been living until now will change to what it really shall be – affirms the brother Seramita – spiritual Psychologists will strive to have every incarnated soul find the work or specialty in accordance with its knowledge and experience. Therefore, schools nowadays already prepare pupils to raise their interest for future studies of science, technology, literature or arts.

62. How do many doctors deal with frustration and even guilt for being unable to save more lives despite their knowledge and great efforts?

We understand their suffering from the deep of our feelings – responds the sister Interana – you sometimes wish to have the magic wand to change things on the planet with the force of your desire transforming it into a world without anxiety, desolation and abandonment, in a place without hunger, disease, limitation of resources etc.

Who would not want food, clothing, housing, education etc. to be at everybody's reach? Why is this not so? You still see powerful countries trying to control other countries political and economically based on ideologies that long proved counterproductive or failed from the beginning. You as their brothers have compassion for the people of these countries who pay for the errors of those who have the power and use it to satisfy their ambition for more control and personal gain.

This is the environment, in which you suffer every time something very bad occurs. Likewise happens with doctors who, in spite of the progress of science and technology in your primary grade, plane and dimension, still lack a great deal of knowledge about the energy. Yet the universe knows when the time has come for a human being to disincarnate. We, nevertheless, know the factors responsible for it. Old age, genetics, inappropriate diet, poor health care, disease, unwanted pregnancy, accidents and violence.

A medical doctor knows that, by vocation – continues the brother Elohim – he has chosen a very demanding profession and that the Hippocratic Oath is a moral compromise to use his knowledge and experience on every single case as best as he can.

Doctors realize, though with resignation, that there is a limit to their efforts and that the universe has the last word about when, why and how a soul will have to depart. You, however, need more than ever doctors who not only see the patient but also the human being who trusts in their responsibility and competence. Much to our regret, health treatment does not escape inappropriate therapies, some with serious consequences because there is a growing number of medical doctors today who look at it as just another lucrative activity.

Why not, therefore, getting up in the morning with the following thoughts on your mind: "May the best of my intentions give a glow of happiness to others and help me also feel at ease with myself. May my labor produce satisfaction, enjoyment and contribute to making this world always a place a little better to live. May my action, deed and thought be an inspiration for others and my endeavor show dedication, truth and love. May my work be a part of the world I wish. May my life be the joy for all" ... Therefore, be always ready to work for the universe and let it guide you with LIGHT and LOVE.

63. We know that dreams are the language of the soul. Could you enlighten us about the following dream a reader sent us?

"I was having this strange dream about a magnificent tiger chasing after me. When I was starting to feel tired, a ladder leading up to a place resembling a spacecraft with bright silver-colored doors appeared before me. One of those doors opened and a man in a silver-colored dress with a red neckline stepped out saying:

–Come on up, you will be safe here – he said.

–Are you sure that the tiger is not in there? – I replied.

–Do not worry the place is safe – the man answered.

–Who are you I never met you before? – I asked.

–I am a Templar – he exclaimed – hurry up!

I took a chance and got up. He was tall with human features and the only person in the ship. When the door was about to close, the tiger tried to get into the spacecraft. Two very tall and strongly built beings with brownish skin came up then and finished off the tiger. After that, the dead tiger turned a little cat, which they grabbed and threw into a well."

Dreams, as we know, are the voice from the deep of the soul with expressions of the subconscious and the unconscious. Thus, emotions emerge in strange forms representing oneiric symbols. The perception of these forms in dreams and the sensations they transmit are clear signs of what the soul wants to tell you – explains the sister Interana.

The Tiger

The presence of the tiger in dreams is always terrifying because it represents instincts that threaten to affect your personality. On the other hand, the tiger also stands for what is fascinating, violent and grandiose, however without showing the dignity of the lion. It is a treacherous despot without compassion. Consequently, the tiger in your dreams means that you are under very serious threat from the instinctive and sensitive forces of brain zones one and two.

The tiger are the ill negative emotions that hide deep inside your soul but surface at a moment when they are stronger than your control based on reasoning, yoga and meditation. The tiger's paw hit you when you less expect it, that is, when you feel impotent for losing the control of a situation, start yelling, insulting and getting very angry – proceeds the brother Interano – you try running away from the tiger, which means that you are afraid of facing these emotions; you do not even want to think about them. However, the day will come when you no longer will be able to evade them and have to strive to win your control back.

The Spacecraft

While running away from these emotions because you fear to face them or even recognize that they exist, you find the solution: The Spacecraft. This spacecraft is the MIND where there is reasoning, logic, understanding, feelings of altruism, forgiveness etc. You take shelter there meeting with advanced extraterrestrials whom you accept as "Masters" because they are going to help you comprehend your emotions and protect you from any ill.

The Templar

He is the brave warrior who tells you to not only fight and win a battle but also the war inside your heart and soul rather than run away from this confrontation – insists the brother Elohim – you look at the door and expect the tiger of the emotions to enter, however, protection and comprehension from the mind are going to block a probable new attack.

Fear, escape and hiding in the mind-spacecraft made you think that you were facing a huge and aggressive tiger but that finally turned out to be just a cat. This means that problems, which appear almost insoluble in the beginning, have solutions and finally are the many "challenges" that life presents to test if you are ready to practice what you have studied and experienced.

This is how you should interpret dreams – suggest the sister Interana – in our reality, we analyze everything using symbols. This gives us a knack of understanding the situation of the soul. Likewise, you prepare to be Spiritual Psychologists and oneiric symbolism will play an important role in the treatment of your patients because it is the fastest way to understand the soul and the emotions.

64. Could you explain why a phenomenon known as Sleep Paralysis occurs?

> ***Sleep Paralysis:*** Sleep paralysis (SP) is a muscle condition caused by a loss of strength (atony). It is the organism's natural defense mechanism to prevent a physical reaction to dreams during sleep, which could be harmful to a person (REM phase without atony). According to the International Classification of Sleep Disorders, SP impedes voluntary physical movements from the beginning of the sleeping phase (hypnogogic phase) and during sleep until the wake-up phase (hypnopompic phase).
> During sleep, you are not conscious; however, some individuals are susceptible to episodes of SP in a state of consciousness. This may cause them to confound real sensations from the environment with hallucinations resulting from dreams. Consequently, they may feel like drowning, suffer from palpitations, have difficulties to breathe and other possible physical sensations. The fear that comes with SP characterizes what you call nightmare. In this state, individuals are incapable to move or speak but are entirely aware of what occurs around them, can hear, smell and even perceive physical contact and the environment with their eyes closed. Conscious SP can have "the very impact of reality" according to Robert Baker, psychologist at Kentucky University and often comes with strong sexual images (Wikipedia).

It is therefore important that you analyze the physical and mental condition of people who suffer from those events – observes the sister Interana – not always may we classify them as SP events but rather as an Extrasensory Experience such as an Astral Walk triggered by an individual's energy frequency, rhythm, electricity and colors at this moment. In this context, we are not talking about people's possible attitudes (good or bad). We just have to define their thought-energy as Frequency.

In fact, when having a conscious or unconscious out-of-body experience (astral walk) or another vivid Extrasensory Event, people are going to live these phenomena in strict accordance with the frequency of their thought-energies. When the soul vibrates with elevated frequency during an Extrasensory Event, it will automatically feel attracted to the third, fourth and fifth grade of the electromagnetism. Along an extrasensory event, the Astral Body frequently comes across advanced beings and marvelous places of harmony and peace, assimilating at the same time cosmic teachings of wisdom from grades, planes and dimensions beyond your limited third Primary Dimension – explains the brother Elohim – if, however, a soul found itself in the low vibration frequencies of the first and second grade electromagnetism, this experience might be one of anxiety, fear and terror.

EL SER UNO's teachings are that you should not just follow the desire for such a spiritual experience but look for it when you feel that your spirit actually needs it – says the brother Interano – our advice therefore is not to force an event that will only occur when the time is right. The fifth book says when going to bed to take a deep breath, visualize indigo color and enter it as if it were a bud. Then commend yourselves to the universe of the spirits of Knowledge, Understanding and Love of the elevated spheres of LIGHT for protection.

Surround yourselves with a seven-ring spiral of brilliant white light and have a good night sleep. You will see that, if the event occurs again, you mentally and spiritually will be ready for a wonderful journey. Having asked assistance from the universal entities of Light, they will guide and help your mind leave and re-enter the physical body harmoniously. During this journey, they will show you the beauty of a universe, of which you all are a part. An Astral Walk is a mental return to your origin to remember it.

65. The planet's inhabitants are fearful because of an announcement saying there will be THREE DAYS OF DARKNESS owing to the absence of the light of the Sun and any other artificial light. If

so, what is the meaning of it? What is going to happen on December 21st?

MESSAGE from the Elder Brothers Ayaplianos
THREE DAYS OF DARKNESS

BELOVED BROTHERS!!... Do not fear, as this is the beginning of a process of renewal in the cosmos with positive effects for all living beings. The energy of the MIND of EL SER UNO will undergo transformations for the following reasons:

- The Universal Mind is creating new ideas.
- Beginning of the Cosmic Alignment on July 7th, 2014, of four dimensions favoring the creativity and advancement of the Universal Mind.
- Explosions of the Solar Winds.
- Polarity changes of the planet's axis.
- Growth of the Earth-Cell.
- Transformations of the electromagnetism's chemistry.
- The Awakening of Human's Conscience.
- Departure of 20% of the souls for the Internal City.

No doubt, there is a scientific explanation for everything in the universe. According to EL SER UNO, the Cosmic Alignment will take 7 thousand years divided into 21 phases of 333 years each. You now live the first phase marked by the AWAKENING of CONSCIENCE.

The Awakening of a long-lost Conscience in humans' souls began with the advent of Ascended Masters who with their teachings reminded you of the Long Path of Return to the Center, the One Origin. It will take another 200 years until the awakening of a major portion of souls and their departure toward the Internal City. There are those ready now to go, many others, however, are going to need one or two more incarnations.

The Maya prophecies for December 21st, 2012, are a part of the first phase of the awakening. Summing the digitals of each the month, day and year you will have 12 12 12 or 3.3.3 corresponding to the first phase of the Cosmic Alignment, which is a clear indication of the forthcoming energy change, positive transformation of the soul and the Awakening of Conscience.

Those who have awaked and gestated their Baby-Spirit during the first 333 years will leave for the Antimatter Internal City after they disincarnate and continue the process of evolution and elevation there. Consequently, with no need for further incarnations, their souls prepare to continue the cosmic journey toward planes and dimensions of more elevated energies.

After the Awakening of Conscience, the second phase of the Cosmic Alignment will sink humans into an AGE OF DARKNESS from the year 2350 to 2700.

AGE of DARKNESS does not mean the absence of solar or any other source of Light but a period of ostracism and ignorance in the MINDS of HUMANITY, that is, an age without spiritual knowledge.

Remember the terribly ill negative energy called Reptilian Force. This harmful energy is going to annul humans' FREEDOM and is responsible for the Age of Darkness because it controls and dominates the planet's inhabitants blocking them from spiritual and cosmic knowledge. It is the Age of Kali Yuga.

- During the Age of Darkness, humans' thoughts become prisoners of the pleasures of the senses growing addictions and a terrible strain of the soul.
- Religions succumb to fanaticism, greed and power.
- Governments control Science and Technology.
- People suffer from power abuse, ambition and distorted knowledge about the planet.
- Governments prohibit the diffusion of cosmic knowledge under severe punishment.
- There will be persecution of positive and elevated individuals.

So bad will turn things, that the Reptilian energy will appear to have come straight from hell. However, after intense suffering and having themselves found on the dark side of the soul, humans will look up at the universe and understand that the spirit is the true wealth of their existence. They will rediscover and greatly enjoy the simple pleasures that nature offers them. When they finally overcome the Age of Darkness and comprehend the nature of spiritual existence, they will open their minds and elevate their thoughts to the universe.

Your sun's preparation for the Cosmic Alignment starts on July 7th, 2014 (777), when four dimensions will align approximating one another and thus produce an exchange of high frequency energy that will benefit planet Tera and its inhabitants. Henceforth, Tera will be much closer to other elevated constellations.

Planet Earth will begin to live the GOLDEN AGE, because the Solar Spirits will be able to communicate with humans to transmit cosmic teachings of high quality energy. Dwelling in the dimensions of LIGHT and LOVE, the elevated thought-energies of these spirits are going to nurture awaked individuals with the Knowledge, Understanding and Love of the universe. Therefore, future years will hold many a surprise for you. There will be unprecedented events that you should welcome with immense joy since they represent great scientific and spiritual progress.

Your Sun is the Solar System's Pineal Gland. Its energy will become Photonic Energy producing important genetic changes of all species and the Planet-Cell. Many of you will consider this a calamity. The universe, nevertheless, sees it as advancement and elevation of your thought-energies.

The polarity of human beings and the Earth-Cell is moving from the center to the poles. This means that the Ego's thought-energy of the Desire of Procreation is ascending through the Kundalini toward the brain's right hemisphere turning THOUGHT-ENERGY of CREATION.

The Earth-Cell is thus growing changing from a rebellious, spoiled and arrogant adolescent to a serious, studious and understanding young adult phase, willing to study the knowledge of the universe with maturity and responsibility.

Consequently, an electromagnetism overcharged with morbid thoughts, procreative egomaniacal emotions and predominantly electron-charged energy is filling with positive proton-charged energy, a change resulting from humans' endeavor of raising their thought-energies and thus nurturing the electromagnetism with the element LOVE from the LIGHT of QUARKS.

BELOVED BROTHERS and SISTERS, our advice therefore for all who are working on the Awakening of Conscience and initiating the journey toward the truth, is to keep calm because there is nothing that could make them go off the correct path. Do not worry thinking about nightmares that could fill you with feelings of distrust or even terror but look up to the universe with the light of hope and a calm spirit.

Do not forget that you are sons and daughters of love whom the universe will never abandon. Sing to the glory of the one origin that makes you share the unique universal event of new ideas. Have faith in the wisdom of the cosmos and peace in your souls while reflecting on the grandeur of the Universal Mind and the Energy of the Cosmos.

Do not let fear reign in your hearts because the ill negative energies use that emotion to make you prisoners of ignorance. Never allow darkness to command your souls. Look up to the universe and pray for those who fail to perceive the infinite Light of Love, truth of the cosmos, because theirs is the vision of the Earth and not of the Sun. Face this difficult process firmly. As mists begin to clear and light conquers darkness, there will be an extraordinary revival of the Human Soul.

BELOVED BROTHERS and SISTERS!! the LIGHT of the Soul and the Wisdom of the Spirit will conquer the forces of the dark and the vampires of the energy. Heal your Souls with Compassion and fill your Spirit with the Feeling of Love!

Message from the Elder Brothers Ayaplianos channeled on November 9th, 2012.

MESSAGE from the Elder Brothers Ayaplianos received on December 21st, 2012

Today, December 21st, 2012, humans and planet Tera start to live the AGE of the AWAKENING of CONSCIENCE or AGE of AQUARIUS. Nowadays, humanity still enjoys certain freedom despite the presence of an Ill-Negative Force, which watches over and manipulates the population but does not yet have total control of the planet. This gives humans the chance to wake up and form the Spirit of LIGHT and LOVE. According to EL SER UNO, it will take another 200 years to help about 20% or 1400 million souls transcend this reality, elevate and join the

Internal City. So, remember again the order of the events as follows: The Awakening of Conscience (2012), Cosmic Alignment of the four dimensions (2014), the Age of Darkness (as of 2350) and the Golden Age (as of 2700).

The Awakening of Conscience (2012)

December 21st, 2012 will mark the beginning of a general AWAKENING of CONSCIENCE of the human species in the universe and on planet Tera. Humans of Tera are going to wake from the fantasy of their material and psychical addictions starting to overcome the darkness of ignorance and perceive the true nature of their environment.

During the awakening, human beings will become humane and eventually turn spiritual Beings, a process, in which Knowledge, Understanding and Love are of utmost importance. By turning SPIRITUAL, humans BEINGS gain the condition as SUCH and not because of what they HOLD.

The 21st of December, 2012

Nothing will happen. It is just a new phase where humans' thought-energies undergo Purification, Transformation and Transmutation starting to raise the energy frequency of the soul. Nevertheless, no spacecraft will take them in their physical form to the Internal Cities where only a disincarnated soul can go.

Once your soul reaches the necessary energy frequency and disincarnates in a "natural" way, it will occupy the respective grade of the electromagnetism (Internal City). There, we and other elevated souls receive it to make it familiar with the cosmic guidelines of evolution and elevation.

Cosmic Alignment

On July 7th, 2014 (777), an extraordinary cosmic event initiates when the dimensions of Andromeda, Ciryus, the Pleiades and Alpha Centauri representing the spirit of Orion will align. This alignment will result in an outstanding advancement of the Southern Hemisphere where we all belong.

The Southern Hemisphere resembles an immense organism formed by planets, galaxies and constellations, constellations that represent members, head and torso commanded by the spirit of Orion. Andromeda stands for the legs, Ciryus for the arms, the Pleiades for the torso and Alpha Centauri for the head while Orion represents the Pineal Gland of this gigantic EL SER UNO.

The Age of Darkness

EL SER UNO says, "There´s no Three Days of Darkness". The real meaning of this is: You will live under the most severe control of the ill negative Force and be prisoners of pleasures, addictions, libertinage, frivolity, hallucinating from the reverie and fantasy.

We therefore ask you to stay calm, watch your diet, meditate and do not let fear dominate your hearts and souls. Strive for peace and harmony, let the spirit of love guide you and look up to the creator, the one origin.

The Golden Age (2700)

From the year 2700 on, humans will live THE GOLDEN AGE of LIGHT and LOVE whose principal characteristics are Knowledge, Understanding, Splendor and the Magnificence of Love. They will elevate their energy and their spirit will greatly advance on Cosmic and Universal Wisdom. Individuals who now awake will pass several learning grades guided by the Elder Brothers Ayaplianos Interanos at the Internal City.

There, they will complete the Awakening of Conscience by the end of the 7000 years of the Cosmic Alignment. However, along The Golden Age, the spirits of all human beings and the Tera-Cell will forever join the Interstellar Cosmic Confederation of planets, galaxies and constellations, a union that will include the dimensions of Andromeda, Ciryus, the Pleiades and Alpha Centauri with the spiritual guidance of Orion.

THEREFORE, PREPARE YOURSELVES WITH CONSCIENCE, FAITH, WILL, PERSEVERANCE, HUMILITY, KNOWLEDGE, UNDERSTANDING AND LOVE!!... We are waiting for you...EL SER UNO.
Message from the Elder Brothers Ayaplianos channeled on December 17th, 2012.

66. I wonder why after the Awakening of Conscience during the Age of Aquarius occurs the dark age of Kali Yuga. Why do we seem to suffer a relapse into darkness?

To understand the situation, we have to remember that according to EL SER UNO along the 7000 years of the Cosmic Alignment 20% (in the next 200 years), 40% (as of 2700) and 30% (until the end of the alignment) of souls will depart for the Internal City. An important part of the remaining 10% will initiate a new cycle of incarnations in the Yeti, the species to take the place of the human race on Earth. The rest will start cycles as elements in the Inferior (Planet Alpha Nova) and Creativity (Planet Ebiares) Dimensions.

Consequently, – replies the sister Interana – during the next 200 years the total population of about 7000 million people will decrease to about 5600 million. Perceiving the steady flow of disincarnating and transcending souls, the ill negative Reptilian force will use whatever means at its reach, including military and mind control equipment, to multiply its power of manipulation and domination.

They will try to keep as many souls as possible from transcending and thus secure mass slavery to continue. This extended power of the Reptilian force will give rise to the Age of Darkness of *Kali Yuga*.

> ***Kali Yuga:*** This stage says: “O wise man! In this hard age of Kali, men have short lives. They are fighters, lazy, disoriented, unfortunate and, above all, mentally disturbed individuals.” In the iron age, iron machines and weapons take paramount importance, receiving more respect than man’s life itself.
> Constant military engagements and the adoration of electronics and industrialization are imminent symptoms. Nevertheless, however violent they might be, they will not annihilate this world or change the destiny of creation but principally affect a blind, deaf and mute humanity that is living an inferior existence (Dictionary of Symbols).

After terrible sufferings and having known the dark side of the soul, humans will look up to the universe and understand that the spirit is the greatest treasure they have – observes the brother Elohim – when they finally leave the Age of Kali Yuga behind, the GOLDEN AGE of LIGHT and LOVE will welcome them where they awake and start valuing again the immense pleasure of simple things that nature can give.

67. The books talk about the Cosmic Alignment of four Antimatter Dimensions. They also say that there will be a personal, that is, a Mental Alignment. Could you explain what this alignment will be like?

We know that the date of July 7th, 2014 means a COSMIC ALIGNMENT in the universe and the beginning of a new Age of LIGHT and LOVE, the AWAKENING OF CONSCIENCE – replies the brother Elohim – for you, this date represents the cabalistic number 3 (adding the digits of the Year 2014 equals 7 plus the month and the day 7 gives the figure 777 whose sum is 21 and the sum of which is 3). This number is an important source of information and at the same time, represents the Mental Alignment of many of you when four each brain zones and chakras of the electromagnetism will align and be heading for the fourth grade, that is, the Internal City. This alignment that will activate the thought-energies crystals and make them act in brain zones 3-4-5 and 6, however, does not mean uniformity of thoughts but an entire new way of being, thinking and acting guided by your Awaked Conscience and knowledge of Cause and Effect.

By aligning, the four dimensions complete the orbit around their Center Sun, the One Origin. This occurs every three hundred billion years and is a universal phenomenon that marks an extremely important and transcendental phase in evolution and elevation of the UNO's energy. Thus, planets, solar systems, constellations as well as all thought-beings in the vastness of the universe initiate a new cycle of elevation and return to: The One Origin.

To be able to take its position in the cosmic alignment and overcome the disconnection from universal order, consequence of humans' profound ignorance of the essence of the spirit, the Tera-Cell must start assimilating photonic energy from the Sun. This is when incarnated souls will have a chance to recover this essence, which is the origin of their existence. Nevertheless, they first will have to Wake their Conscience, learn about the order of creativity, their nature, thoughts, deeds and actions. Only after having knowledge of the Cause and Effect relationship and forming their Spirit to reach the correct vibration frequency will they be a part of this alignment.

In other words, – continues the brother Interano – humans will have to transmute density and darkness into Photonic Energy. To do so, they must sort the subconscious and wake their unconscious. This new state of conscience comes from the soul, which thus turns a being of LIGHT and LOVE. The dimension's new order is to live through the spirit rather than through matter, to wake dormant cosmic energy and make it work following the universal order that generates never-ending vibration frequency in every grade. Only those who believe in themselves will live the revelation of universal changes and activate their inner senses. They are the souls to receive the message of the creator of the cosmic community. The universe will not pause as it continues its transcendental journey. You will reach out to it when you start listening to the spherical music that comes from your hearts and souls. The Spirit is a time-traveler that came to heal the Tera-Cell. Once it succeeds, it must return to the luminosity of its origin.

68. According to *EL SER UNO,* we must activate our Desire of Creation, that is, raise our vibration frequency to be able to join the Cosmic Alignment. Nevertheless, how will little children enter the alignment who do not know anything about this event nor what the Desire of Creation is like or, despite being indigo or crystal children have parents who deny the spiritual reality?

You all are very old souls no matter the phase of your physical evolution after incarnating, that is, if you are babies, children, adolescents, adults or seniors – starts explaining the brother Elohim – therefore, every new incarnation means correlation with and continuity of a soul's previous incarnations.

Let us again remember that the souls have to reach a certain frequency to qualify for the Internal City after their natural disincarnating during the 7 thousand years of the Cosmic Alignment with the following phases of departure: The first phase starts on July 7th, 2014 until 2214. During this stage, the souls will have 200 years to qualify, which means, they might need 2 or 3 more incarnations. If you can´t reach it, you will stay to the next depart; the second phase; in the year 2800. The third phase will be at the end of 7 thousand years of the Alignment.

Indigo or crystal children's souls incarnating during these phases will not suffer any setback because they come with wisdom gained in their process of spiritual elevation through past lives – proceeds the sister Interana – consequently, they carry the Desire of Creation, often already activated. If not, they have the present or future incarnations to accomplish this activation. They are under tutelage of the Spirits of LIGHT and LOVE in every new life or when returning to the Internal City.

You all have a chance to join the Cosmic Alignment independent of credo, ethnicity, language or country since all souls receive the call for cosmic and universal elevation. Joining the Cosmic Alignment means to align in a positive way thought-energies, brain zones, chakras and the electromagnetism of the physical, psychical and mental bodies using Knowledge, Understanding and Love. To do this, demands consistency of thinking and acting and being aware of the Cause and Effect relationship. To become part of the cosmos, you must be true bearers of LIGHT and LOVE.

69. Are there special requirements for the beginning of the Cosmic Alignment such as gathering in a particular place or preparing a ceremony at the city of Cuzco (Southern Peru)?

MESSAGE from the Elder Brothers Ayaplianos
regarding the COSMIC ALIGNMENT – Starts on July 7th, 2014

We know how important it is to you to get together and highlight special events – observes the brother Elohim – this time, however, we are going to break old habits and dispense with techniques and methods to encourage the Awakening of Conscience.

Nowadays, there is no need for people who have similar ways of thinking to group. This was necessary in other times. To transmute negative thought-energies that are all over the planet, you will now have to work on the elevation of a special thought-energy, that we will indicate, from wherever you are (your home, workplace, spa etc.).

The Age of the Awakening of Conscience will change your feeling and thinking through the emotions to a Universal Feeling – observes the brother Interano – this means that you are going to raise your thought-energies to the "Mental" level of Knowledge, Understanding and Love and be able to transform all that is negative using your "Mind", that is, your Desire of Creation, born from the Spirit and positive elevated Thought-Energies.

Though mentioned earlier, we again wish to stress the importance of the symbolic number 777, which results from the Cosmic Alignments' date of beginning (7/7/2014), when four antimatter dimensions will align within the Universal Mind, which prepares for the creation of new ideas to spread in the cosmos. Thought-Children present in those dimensions will capture these ideas and make them become realities that assure a never-ending continuity of EL SER UNO. This process, however, has nothing to do with the material alignment of systems, galaxies and constellations you may know.

The "Mental" Alignment is the alignment of ideas and thoughts disseminated in the cosmos of the Universal Mind. When using the term "mental" we refer to the Energy that is, to the Thought-Energies of Souls and Spirits on the cosmic journey of return to their creator, the One Origin. We shall complete this knowledge at the Internal City as soon as you are ready to receive it.

The following are the guidelines for July 7th, 2014 – City of Cuzco/Peru time 7.00 am/7.00 pm.

We are calling on all beings who wish to join us, your Elder Brothers Ayaplianos. The above date is not just the beginning of the Cosmic Alignment but also an opportunity for you and us to raise the frequency of zones one and two of the electromagnetism with the force of our Thought-Energies. There are innumerable souls trapped in these zones that need our help to raise their vibration and thus pass on to zone three for salvation.

During July 4th, 5th and 6th, you will have to prepare physically and psychically to give peace and harmony to your souls and hearts and purify the energy of your physical bodies by following the below indications.

1. Avoid the consumption of red meat, poultry and fish
2. Idem dairy products and eggs
3. Idem any type of edible oil
4. Consume carbohydrates, vegetables and fruit
5. Drink at least 3 cups of mineral water without gas every day
6. Avoid emotions such as worry and anger
7. Idem programs on TV and cinema containing violence
8. Idem alcohol
9. Idem spicy food
10. Do not smoke
11. Keep from experimenting drugs such as ayahuasca, marihuana etc.
12. Avoid beverages
13. Listen to soft music
14. Read a good book
15. Meditate 15 minutes every day
16. Wear bright-color clothes
17. If you are on some medication, keep on with it
18. Everybody, all ages, can participate on this event

Those who decide on participating in this cosmic event should strictly follow the above indications – observes the sister Interana – participation means to contribute to this important spiritual deed by jointly elevating your thoughts to the Universal Mind of LIGHT and LOVE from wherever you are at 7.00 am and 7.00 pm Cuzco time on July 7th, 2014. Raising your thoughts to the universe, you will traverse grades and planes of the energy reaching the electromagnetism of zones one and two of all the planet's beings as well as of the disincarnated souls dwelling there.

We, your Elder Brothers Ayaplianos along with the brothers Interanos, Elohim, Seramitas and Volunteers of the Spacecraft shall uplift your and our thoughts to the One Origin and thus succeed in transforming the ill negative thought-energy of grades one and two of the electromagnetism. Together we shall mentally raise millions of thought-energies (souls) and thus elevate the vibration frequency of these zones and of the planet at the same time. This way, we secure all conceptions as of the year 2014 to be of purified and elevated souls from the Internal City.

PRAYER TO THE UNIVERSE

I AM THE LOVE who reigns everything!!
I AM THE LIGHT who illuminates the universe!!
I AM THE AIR who extinguishes the flame of the fire!!
I AM THE WATER who waters the Earth!!
I AM THE FIRE who purifies the Light!!
I AM THE EARTH who feeds your children!!...

OH UNIVERSE!!

We are your children, your creation and your continuity. Today, we uplift our thoughts to ask for your kindness. Keep evil away from this reality. Free us of darkness and fear. Help us find the truth. Have our hearts feel sympathy. Send LIGHT and LOVE to the human species, peace and harmony to all who suffer and freedom to those who yearn for it. Have governments grow awareness and fill beliefs with truthfulness. Let us be generous with the poor and give our children the knowledge they need. Let there be wisdom in people's minds. Abundance to all beings.

OH CELESTIAL REALM!!

Help us conquer the darkness of ignorance in our souls and let the Light of Conscience guide us. Give us the strength to walk the path of Peace and Harmony on planet Earth. Help us trust one another. Help us being aware of the countless opportunities that our innermost beliefs may create. Make us share the benefit of gifts we inherited lovingly with others.

FORCES OF NATURE!!

May the elements Air, Fire, Water and Earth together with our inner strength help wake souls from their profound sleep! Help us illuminate the path of those who walk with us as well of those who do not yet.

OUR CREATOR, THE ONE ORIGIN!!

Have us use knowledge with humility and our gifts and qualities find the path of LIGHT and LOVE. Give us the wisdom to take our word to the confines of the planet to fill the souls with universal knowledge. Deepen our understanding and give us the courage, belief and joy to BE in the Heart, Soul and Cosmic Spirit for this is the way to be fair to ourselves and deserve to be in your Loving Mind.

FORCE OF EVIL!!

We command you, souls, to withdraw from the darkness and start moving toward the Light. We, beings of Light, will conquer density and turn confusion into clarity. We are transmitting all the energy we receive and our presence is going to spread it, healing wherever we go. We are the LOVE that cures and the LIGHT that clears the shadows.

OURS IS THE GREATEST FORCE!!

Together we shall fight evil and vanquish the ill negative force for we are the foundations of the universe. May LIGHT and LOVE cover planet Earth and the divine energy of the universe have flourished the beings of this reality!

WE THANK YOU, UNIVERSE!!

For showing us the Path of Return, teaching us to look into our innermost self, giving us the happiness to discover our many truths and calling us children, brothers and sisters. Your wisdom lives in our souls. THANK YOU for the peace that reigns in our hearts and for all the joy and happiness in our lives. THANK YOU for making us feel your LOVE and teaching us how to love our brothers and sisters.

MAY ALL THIS COME TRUE NOW AS IT ONCE DID IN A REMOTE PAST AND LAST FOREVER!!

- All who prepared as indicated in the beginning will have to repeat this entreaty at 7am/7pm (Cuzco-GMT) on July 7th, 2014.
- They will also have to repeat it on the seventh day of each month, until the end of 2014. At Same time: 7am/7pm (Cuzco-GMT).
- Those who could not complete their preparation until July 7th, 2014, may do so as indicated – preparing the physical and psyquical body for it – until the seventh day of any of the following months.
- If you wish to perform the entreaty together with other persons, you are free to do so but have to be sure to rely only on the strength and Desire of Creation of your positive elevated thoughts. In this case, the LIGHT and LOVE, with which you express your intention, will suffice.

Let us now continue our interview...

70. How can we know the type of work souls in our reality have to do?

There are many groups of souls and each one of them has to fulfill a particular task, in the exterior (as incarnated souls) as well as at the Internal City (as disincarnated souls) – replies the sister Interana – souls differ in their force of creation, the dynamic of an impulse at a certain moment related to a particular idea. However, when souls transcend this reality, elevate and turn spirits, theirs will be a universal task being able to adjust to infinite realities and accomplish multiple realizations. We shall comment further on this when dealing with the Electromagnetism and Magnetism.

71. The soul is vibration, resonance, rhythm and colors formed by the Thought-Nimeos of a collective and therefore does not carry our individual Karma. Is there a collective Karma?

Remember what happens in the Micro-Cosmos, occurs in the Macro-Cosmos as well, that is, the relationship of Matter, Soul and Spirit compares to that of planets, systems, galaxies and constellations of the hemisphere – observes the brother Elohim – therefore, you all carry Nimeos-Energies from the three bodies.

The Nimeos-Energies of the physical body (matter) are collective since they carry the record of everything existing and subject to evolution in this grade, plane and dimension of life. The Nimeos-Energies of the psychical body (soul) are half-collective and half-individual while those of the spiritual body are entirely individual in all human beings. The soul will always carry this portion of collective energies. To turn this portion individual, the soul has to register it forever as an idea of its own, which always must be positive; otherwise, the universe will consider it an ill thought subject to transmutation – observes the sister Interana –for instance, the mind holds many ideas formed from thousands of thought-energies. If a thought-energy turns idea, it gives rise to the formation of a soul. The moment, thought-energies join to manifest this idea, the soul turns spirit, that is, an individual idea.

Karma is always a collective Karma because of the lack of understanding. Once there is understanding, it turns Dharma and thus part of the spirit. Consequently, there are TASKS (MISSIONS) for the soul and for the spirit. The collective soul must strive to correct errors to wake up and start turning spirit, which will transcend this reality and rise within the universal scope of elevation. In other words, the spirit will cease to be only Nimeos-Energy and turn finally ideas of the Universal Mind while the collective souls hold our masculine and feminine expressions. This is why we, your Elder Brothers, say: WE ARE ALL, WE ARE ONE.

72. What about people who seem to perceive parallel realities? They write that after reading the books *EL SER UNO*, they started feeling the presence of souls or dreaming of unknown realities.

Those people have AWAKED turning a source of intermittent light that attracts disincarnated souls from the electromagnetism – observes the sister Interana – they should not be AFRAID as these souls are just asking to HELP them find their way back. You may not be aware but many of you are MEDIUMS with the ability to feel the presence of those souls. They should therefore accept the task to work with them in this reality and HELP THEM RETURN TO THEIR PLACE in the electromagnetism.

Once you accept, you should calm down with a deep breath and start looking for the knowledge it takes to act as mediums by asking the assistance of the universe and the spirits of LIGHT and LOVE – suggests the brother Interano – you thus will form a team with you working in the material reality and them from the Antimatter side.

You however should never do this alone because frequently you might have to face dense and dark souls and not be able to handle them. In general, these extrasensory phenomena occur because a soul disincarnated in a tragic way, does not realize the condition and feels lost. It keeps wandering and when perceiving the light that you represent, approaches it to ask for help.

Matrix or the Reptilian force has taught you to fear these phenomena and thus created a barrier between this and the "other" parallel reality (which eventually is the true one). Matrix has raised your doubts about them to the extent that you feel confused about the true nature of THE ENERGY. There are abundant science fiction literature and movies that present the beyond or Antimatter world as a place of frightful creature and bloodthirsty souls. Likewise, there would be monstrous extraterrestrial visitors to dominate Earth. In fact, the only real threat is the incarnated Reptilians force that will never desist to keep you from seeking the Freedom of the Soul.

Coming back to what is important; stay at the place where you felt the presence of that soul or perceived other extrasensory phenomena drawing in your imagination the seven protecting circles of bright shining light around you. Then ask the spirits of LIGHT and LOVE to help you ease the soul's pain by having it join again its grade, vibration frequency, rhythm and colors in the electromagnetism.

At the same time, keep sending your thoughts of LIGHT and LOVE to the soul and, as if in a personal conversation, make it understand that it has disincarnated and must continue the learning process of life on its own – continues the brother Elohim – this way, it will enter a state of enlightenment and peace ending its painful wandering.

Always remember that such presence of a soul means that it needs your help, a requirement of an AWAKENING of CONSCIENCE not only centered in your personal evolution and elevation but also in those of your fellow humans (incarnated and disincarnated). Working together is fulfilling the task entrusted to all of us by the universe.

This is the moment for the forces of your and the parallel reality of LIGHT and LOVE to join. Many human beings are unconscious of their condition of mediums and feel frightened during such an experience without the knowledge and understanding to handle it properly, they feel strange and different from other persons – says the sister Interana – if you all were conscious of the work ahead, you certainly would concentrate on clearing the first two grades of the electromagnetism since the dense and dark souls of these grades are failing to seek detachment from materialism. Therefore, they need your and our LIGHT to find the passage to the parallel reality.

Those who are mediums have no obligation to act as such. Theirs is an act of free will and LOVE – observes the brother Interano – this means that you have a compromise with the universe only when you decide on accepting this task, then however you are to fulfill it using whatever Knowledge, Understanding and Love you can give. The path of spirituality is not the same for all as every incarnated and disincarnated soul has its particular energy to meet this cosmic challenge, but it depends on everyone's Free Will to recognize, understand and face it.

73. There seems to be quite some confusion regarding the concept of Free Will. Could you enlighten us about it?

To a certain extent, there is Free Will in the third grade, plane and dimension. Why do we say to a certain extent? Because the universe still considers your ability to handle the relationship Free Will-Responsibility one of young Children – replies the sister Interana – this means that you cannot yet give children the freedom to make a decision by themselves on a particular issue but must teach them to discern what decision on given options would be the most appropriate and responsible one.

Few human beings have the capacity to use their Free Will with the greatest possible responsibility. Those who have this condition are beings who have formed their spirit – proceeds the brother Interano – they reincarnate to help and teach transmitting the knowledge as instructors of the Internal City. They present options and teach to you discern.

If you, however, made a decision based on available and explained options that eventually were unsatisfactory, your only other option would be to risk living individual true-to-life experiences meaning to deal with the Cause and Effect relationship. This would allow you to advance gradually on the condition for making appropriate decisions with responsibility.

We, your bothers of the Internal City, are always close and responsible for helping you walk the correct way – assures the brother Interano – we have to admit that this is no easy work and results often are far from satisfactory but pondering good moves and shortcomings, there is no reason for doubt that yours eventually will be the path of LIGHT and LOVE.

74. How can a disincarnated soul move material things in this reality? Many people write telling me about souls they seem to have felt or even seen them at their homes apparently making noises and causing material objects to fall on the floor.

This may occur for two reasons – observes the brother Interano – first, it is possible that the energy frequency of a person (incarnated soul) feeling strong emotions such as fear or anger be able to move things with the mind, something known as Telekinesis. Second, since this same frequency continues emanating from the disincarnated soul, it may be strong enough to move or even break objects, which would be also Telekinesis. There are the famous demonstrations of people who succeeded in bending metals or raising objects without touching them, apparent cases of Telekinesis.

When an incarnated soul is awake or has psychical sensibility; Mediumship, it is considered a flashing light for the antimatter reality. As a result, the souls of electromagnetism are drawn to this reflection. If this happens in your house or in any place, DON´T BE AFFRAID because these souls are asking for HELP.

If you feel and see paranormal facts, don´t be scared of them. You should also help to other souls to find the path of return. Many people are not aware that they are Mediums and have the ability to see disincarnated souls. If you are one, your work in this reality is: TO HELP THEM AND SEND THEM TO WHERE THEY BELONG.

75. People in many countries read the books *EL SER UNO*. Should those who identify with this knowledge form groups?

There is no need for it, – replies the sister Interana – as the spirit will guide the new ASTRAL conception of the energy rather than the soul. Your presence will be spiritual and no longer physical. There is no need for groups as in the old days, guided by gurus, masters, messengers of God etc. for the transmission of this knowledge today.

Therefore, the Cosmic Alignment is the unprecedented event to bring about profound changes of conscience creating a mental union with the energy from millions of human beings who are waking up. This phenomenon occurs every 28 thousand years, bringing great changes in consciousness on the planet. Elevated thoughts will take the corresponding grades in the electromagnetism and thus produce the grouping of ***incarnated and disincarnated*** souls.

What we wish to underline is that the thought-energies of people who never met have equal vibration frequencies, that is, affinity of souls – observes the brother Interano – in other words, souls with equal vibration frequency are going to join with view to Thoughts, Concepts,

Beliefs and Inner Strength, Harmony, Knowledge, Understanding and Love – concludes the brother Elohim.

76. How can we update concepts deeply rooted in our souls or dismiss them if necessary?

When EL SER UNO enters people's lives, it is as if "someone" has come to start cleaning and tidying their homes removing whatever is useless – remarks the sister Interana – this someone first takes a glance about the house. Starting with the garden to see if it is well kept or overgrown (to see if there is happiness in persons' work and life). Then the living and dining room (meaning how people appear before others). The kitchen (denoting or not balanced eating habits combining proteins, vitamins, carbohydrates, unsaturated fats and minerals). The sleeping rooms (representing good sleeping habits but also if their conscience is dormant or awake). The laundry area (not only washing linen and clothing but also working and purifying emotions using the detergent of understanding). Finally, the basement (storing a thousand things of past lives, many of which represent emotions that they still need to work and transmute).

The cleanliness and order of EL SER UNO makes your Ego feel uncomfortable because it means having to use more time and work – proceeds the brother Interano – you cling to material things and dislike other persons to become involved with your personal life. You feel aggravated by the truth, with which EL SER UNO confronts you and are trying hard not to look into the mirror at the entrance of your homes.

After some time nevertheless, you begin to realize what it is EL SER UNO is gradually changing in you – concludes the brother Elohim – the spaces of your homes appear wider. There is a touch of harmony, the way you arranged furniture of appropriate size and style in the living and dining rooms, the walls of which you painted in bright and vivid colors. Your windows are now wide open to let in sunshine. Decorative plants and flowers help add to the warmth and inner peace your homes were lacking before. For the first time, you feel happy at home.

You perceive the knowledge from this message as something special and of importance for your lives. Negative attitudes such as heavy criticism and attacks as well as a sensation of great discomfort turn less severe and feelings of a more positive attitude appear. You become attentive observers of your homes (souls). When finally looking at those changes feeling that they were worth occurring and having learned about the need for will, endeavor and perseverance, you are going to look at things with genuine LIGHT and LOVE and say from the deep of your hearts... “Thank you for helping change our tears to laughter”.

77. What is TOLERANCE?

Tolerance: From the Latin: "Tolerare" (to hold, to bear), defines the degree of acceptance in the face of an element contrary to a moral rule. Social tolerance in modern societies is criminally defended and seeks respect for the rights and interests of all people regardless of their individual circumstances, for peaceful coexistence.

At the individual level, it is the ability to accept a situation, another person or group that is considered different, but not all individuals are trained to be tolerant. It is the attitude that a person has with respect to what is different from their values. It is also the acceptance of an unfair situation against one's own interests or against the interests of others. It is also the ability to listen and accept each others.

This social behavior has occurred in all times of humanity and in all parts of the world as a way of peaceful coexistence. Values or rules are established by the society or group that has political power and social control, which establishes respect or persecution of the person or group considered different or problematic. Consequently, it is about respect for the ideas, beliefs or practices, when they are different or contrary to one's own. It is also the unfair respect of the ideas or interests of others compared to their own.

It is a different tolerance to freedom, and the most common in human societies is the oppression of a minority group by a majority, since the opposite is less frequent. The values of respect go to a lesser degree from tolerance to freedom, passing through social equality. Tolerance does not have to be neutral or a positive value in itself, it can also be a means by the group with social control to promote or maintain a privileged situation that is favorable to it. (Wikipedia)

Tolerance is the ability of people (souls) conscious of their virtues and imperfections to live in peaceful coexistence through mutual understanding and respect – observes the brother Elohim – all brothers and sisters of the Internal City accept and respect their different forms of expression, freedom of thinking and feelings. You, human beings, should learn and practice this quality. Respect the full right to live in peace and to be as they decide, without anyone imposing their opinions and lifestyles.

78. You do not have to worry that much about the absence of tolerance, that is, INTOLERANCE as souls at the Internal City occupy their respective grades by vibration frequency, rhythm and colors. We on Earth, however, live in a reality that does not rigorously distinguish these conditions...

Intolerance: By definition, intolerance is the lack of ability or free will to tolerate a person's ideas, condition or habits that differ from one's own. As a social or political principle, it is too open to individual interpretation because it allows a large number of conclusions. In this sense, intolerance turns out to be any disrespectful attitude toward opinions or characteristics different from one's own. In the context of ideas, for instance, it represents the perseverance in one's own opinion despite reasonable arguments against it. Intolerance therefore supposes a lack of flexibility by considering one's ideas and characteristics unyielding.

Consequently, intolerance may result in discrimination of persons or groups of individuals (or even in segregation or aggression) because they think and act different. Multiple manifestations of this phenomenon have in common the elevation of one's identity as a supreme value in an ethic, sexual, ideological and religious sense that justifies margination of any one different. An intolerant person considers that someone who is or thinks different does not have the same rights. Common forms of intolerance are racism, sexism and homophobia, religious and political discrimination (Wikipedia).

In fact, you face the diversity of ethnicity, idiosyncrasy, language and customs – agrees the sister Interana – this diversity, nevertheless, results from disorder and distortion in your thought-energies and often seriously hampers your efforts for fraternity and union. We do not have this problem – continues the brother Interano – because we all are working for a very long time already with a solid state of harmony, peace and fraternity. You are gradually overcoming this intolerance – proceeds the brother Elohim – born of disorder and distortion by conscious and respectful interaction backed by laws that seek to guarantee a peaceful living together. In the future, there will not be any separation, you all will be brothers/sisters and that you will feel it from the deepest part of your heart and soul.

79. How can we learn about the dynamic of the Universal Mind?

I asked to the sister Interana – she replied – the Universal Soul consists of an infinity of Nimeos-Energy arising from the Big Bang ideas of the One Origin. These Nimeos project lively holograms showing particular creativity of how to Work these Ideas. Following this dynamic, the soul will focus on everything created and thus fulfill its never-ending task.

As thought-beings who realize ideas, we are free to use basic holograms created by the One Origin to shape thousands of expressions. These basic holograms from the very center of the One Origin allowed us to create the existing, from elementary to the most sophisticated expressions. The Universal Soul expanded to today's unimaginable diversity of creation. This nevertheless makes it extremely difficult to anticipate any one soul's characteristics and possible cosmic tasks. On the other hand, – proceeds the brother Elohim – the Universal Soul's extraordinary development resulted in Nimeos-Energy of an unexpected quality, so elevated that it turned Universal Spirit, that is, an independent entity. The One Origin had thus created a thought-child to its image meaning the thought-energies of the Universal Mind.

As the architects and masters of your lives, you may choose out of many the path to walk using your Free Will. Whatever your ideas and desire to build a life, there are, negative and sometimes harmful occurrences you prefer to ignore and therefore often use errors for an excuse without accepting your responsibility for them. After everything you have read, learned and experienced now is the moment to calm down and start living in accordance with the knowledge your mind has assimilated – suggests the brother Elohim – it is time to stop and go to your inner world, to put into practice what you learned and make it reality.

Start tidying and preparing your intimate home to find peace, harmony and love. However, beware of the confusion that your soul might suffer for wanting all the knowledge and experience you gained to turn a palpable reality in no time. You now have reached the moment to use all this information in your daily routine from the quiet of your innermost self.

80. If the universe is a hologram, how can a hologram maintain the energy of the *ONE?*

"THE UNIVERSAL MIND projects the universal hologram. THE ENERGY generates vibration frequency, geometry, rhythm and colors. Both give thus life to the THOUGHT-CHILD who, living true-to-life experiences, creates the Form – replies the brother Elohim – this way, the beloved child's thought-energies carry the ideas of the ONE's DESIRE of CREATION without BEGINNING or END".

Holography: Is an advanced photography technique that involves the creation of three-dimensional images. For this, a laser beam is used that microscopically engraves a photosensitive film. This, when receiving the light from the appropriate perspective, projects a three-dimensional image. Holography was invented in 1947 by Hungarian physicist Dennis Gabor, who received the 1971 Nobel Prize in Physics for it. He received patent GB685286 for his invention.

However, it was refined years later with the development of lasers, as Gabor's holograms were very primitive due to the poor light sources used in their day. Originally, Gabor just wanted to find a way to improve the resolution and definition of electron microscope images. He called this process "holography", from the Greek "holos", "complete", since the holograms showed an object completely and not just a perspective (Wikipedia).

81. Where will all this end up then? – I asked thoughtfully...

If you continue the desperate journey in the exterior, you will not go anywhere – proceeds the brother Interano – you must prepare for the journey to the deep of your soul, the Internal City, and, if possible, reach your subconscious. During this long inner walk, you should seek to discover previous lives, know, understand and work your emotions to turn your soul into an oasis of Equanimity, Harmony and Peace. Learn to love yourselves and your fellow humans, the only way to transmute what keeps you from overcoming all this confusion...YOURSELVES.

You have to have plans for steering your lives and create appropriate conditions for their realization. To attain the Desire of Creation, you must generate the true Cause knowing that every breath you take is a gift from the universe to allow you enjoying its Effects.

82. Many people write asking if you are whom we call, Angels...Are you angels?

EL SER UNO says that the way many people perceive our presence may depend on their customs and beliefs. Consequently, when there is a contact with very religious persons, these persons may see images and figures such as Angels, Archangels, Saints or even deities of other religions – replies the sister Interana.

The appearance of the messenger is of little importance for the transmission of a message designed to enlighten you. From history, you know that concepts about extrasensory perception have evolved and adjusted to the new times. What today many still call an experience with angelical figures, others consider a communication with Entities from other Dimensions or Elevated Spirits. Entities from parallel realities already present themselves before you in their true form owing to the fact that scientific and technological advance has made this form of communication possible.

Through the advance of their energy, humane-humans have also deepened their cosmic understanding. Figures or images that appear in their dreams or via contacts and channeling are clear proof of this evolution and elevation. Teachings for the development of these abilities very much resemble children's school classes in your reality when, during their first years, children learn to understand the meaning of concepts they visualize through images – observes the brother Interano.

As time passes, children comprehend the symbolism of a variety of concepts recording it on their memory. Consequently, when reaching adultness, they no longer will work with images but with concepts. However, what so far had been Conceptual Analysis will now turn also Subjective Analysis, often triggered by dreams or extrasensory phenomena, but always using imagination. With the Awakening of Conscience for elevated realities of existence, their souls will start retrieving concepts stored in their memory about Science, Technology, Religion, Art, Mysticism, Esotericism etc., but always related to the recorded characteristics of each individual's Nimeos-Energy.

While you experience this transformation through Knowledge, Understanding and Cosmic Love, your Nimeos-Energy are going to turn Photonic Light that will take you to whatever places your thoughts have been able to go, that is, the infinity of existence without forms, images or pre-determined concepts that you recorded in the dense reality called Earth. Only with LIGHT and LOVE will you transcend this reality.

You therefore must proceed to self-knowledge and healing – concludes the brother Elohim – you have to look deep into your inner self and try to discover the roots of your problems. This process requires will, perseverance and time but may reward you with beneficial changes. These qualities along with self-knowledge and inner strength are the powerful and necessary tools for a true healing of the soul

You, who have already advanced on this journey reading, learning and practicing, will now have to take a deep breath and start living for good in accordance with what your minds have assimilated cleaning, tidying and preparing your inner habitat for a life with peace, harmony and love – proceeds the brother Seramita.

Confusion comes from the soul, because you expect perfection, no mistakes and fast changes. You already have enough information about it. It is time to calm down, in order to put into practice all what you have learned every day in the silence of your inner self. If you continue to desperately run through the exterior world, there will be no place to find – says the sister Interana – pack the baggages to undertake the inner journey of your souls, to the Internal City, and if possible, to the subconscious. On this journey, try to discover your lives, to know your positive and negative emotions by understanding and working on them. Transmute them into an oasis of peace and harmony and let them be reflected in the serenity of the mature and equanimous soul. Learn to love yourselves and others because that is the only way to transmute everything that makes you feel confused and uncomfortable. Which is nothing but the mirror of.... YOURSELVES.

If you were consistently using this strength and determination, you would rise to the challenge of the intimate inner enemy, which is any opposing force, and conquer it for good. Consequently, no obstacle in the exterior would be great enough to keep you from making further progress – affirms the brother Interano – nevertheless, what is the material world like? Do all humans live in peace and harmony and with their basic needs covered? Is there education and healthcare for everyone? Have wars stopped and avarice disappeared? Unfortunately, it seems that you still have a long way to go for the final battle. This is why you must invest and trust in yourselves. If your inner self is fine, the material world will reflect this well-being.

83. Many people still seem to need the image of an angel, a master or avatar to raise an entreaty to the universe. Do we have to have such an image on our imagination for that purpose?

No, you do not but you still depend on the context of images, forms, colors, time, distance etc. for directing this earnest request to the Universe. In a way, holding on to an image helps you keep your thoughts from becoming digressive and, at this point, might be necessary for sending a clear and firm message – observes the brother Elohim.

Nevertheless, more important than focusing on an image is the intention of your request. The day will come when you neither need images nor prayers but just to activate your Desire of Creation – proceeds the sister Interana – images, words, techniques etc. eventually are a loss of time and energy since they are far from functioning at the speed of your thoughts. You therefore must change the way you proceed and gradually adjust to the celerity of cosmic thought-energy.

84. Could stem cells from pigs, ducks, cattle and other animals affect the evolution of persons who use them?

Indeed, this would affect the matter-energy frequency of future generations – replies the brother Elohim – in these cases, health of the physical body improves allowing scientific advance persons to recover from serious disease and extend their life span. However, these stem cells tend to dominate the physical human body having it adopt the characteristics of animal matter generation after generation. We know that according to the human body's DNA, humans classify as mammals and therefore as animals. Nevertheless, there is an important difference between humans and the animal kingdom since the human soul has the ability to raise and thus purify its matter-energy.

If a soul during its process of mental progress and purifying elevation sent orders to the cells of the physical body, it would learn that these cells FAIL to understand those commands for being the evolution of their energy one of an animal and not of a human being. You also will have to consider the impact of the many elements that the material body receives from the animal, plant and mineral kingdoms consisting of natural and artificial products, hormones, drugs, medicine and others.

According to our vast experience with the Cause and Effect relationship, we have no doubt that humans in the future will greatly extend their scientific knowledge of the cosmos and the universe learning how to treat their Material and Astral Bodies and thus consciously lead longer and healthier lives – affirms the brother Interano – with the wisdom gained, they will be aware that those bodies never take separate ways. They will always have to work together for the conception and gestation of the third, the Spiritual Body. They will have full understanding of how the energy works and be able to transmute whatever agent threatens to unbalance or endanger it.

So far, you do not yet have this knowledge and wisdom, which makes you expose your organism to breathing, drinking, eating and injecting elements without the necessary precautions.

We therefore wish to advise you to favor a vegetarian diet that would open your cells' energy to a better and faster understanding of the commands from the soul. While awaking, many human beings are already conscious of their physical body and psyche – proceeds the sister Interana – these persons will have an active role in future investigations and disclosures. The fact that ever more humans are turning vegetarians is an important step forward in the awakening of conscience creating the conditions for the photons to take their place in the DNA and start changing genetic structures.

85. Is it true that to walk the path of spirituality and transcend this reality, we have to give up family life, jobs and friends and only listen to the voice of our souls?

The day you abandon this planet, you will have reached the necessary vibration frequency to do so and no longer incarnate in the grade and plane of a place called Earth – observes the brother Interano – however, we have to remind you, brothers and sisters, that seeking spirituality does not mean that you are free from the responsibilities of past lives, which may have become more noticeable in this incarnation.

If following the spiritual way just required prayers, gospels and meditation, far from obligations, problems and temptations, most people would undoubtedly succeed. This reality, however, would be more chaotic than ever, you be living lives of contemplation, fantasy and idealistic dreams, wishing to be angels who rise to a heaven of laissez-faire and comfort with little need for thinking and acting. This naturally would be dreaming, since nothing in the universe works that way.

True spirituality is something you build within this material world – proceeds the sister Interana – how would you know that you are spiritual beings without being conscious of the negative energies you must learn to control and change to positive ones? How will you know that your inner self is growing if you fail to deal with the dark side of human nature? Spiritual growth means to gain inner strength by overcoming adverse circumstances and conditions. Only through true-to-life experiences, will you advance and turn Warriors of LIGHT and LOVE.

Do not turn your back to life believing that this will save you from accepting teachings. If you do, you will have to go through the same experiences over and again until you understand. Backing off is not the solution, as this will slow your walk on the Path of Return. Instead, you should thank life for having forced you to clear all those obstacles helping you make an important advance on this spiritual journey – says the brother Elohim – wisdom is not so much about knowledge, but the development of an ability based on true-to-life experience and reflection to discern and truly comprehend your inner self by using common sense. This means deepening your understanding of the concept of reality and act while feeling the beat of the cosmos inside you.

You hold this mysterious conscience but are not aware of it until you experience it as the true essence of being and the closest dimensional passage to Universal Conscience. Once you have this comprehension of your inner self, strive to make it work in the exterior. Always remember: Human beings who commit themselves to Knowledge, Understanding and Love are authentic seekers of Universal Wisdom – concludes the brother Interano – therefore, be thankful to the universe and do not desist. Never doubt of its love for you. The more tests in life it makes you take, the greater will be this love, for it wants you to become souls that have the strength to break this chrysalis with endeavor and perseverance turning magnificent butterflies that will fly to the confines of the universe to be one with it.

86. What is it that makes us feel not to know whom we are and what our mission is? Must we look for some guru to open our chakras for us to know?

According to EL SER UNO, "your first MISSION is to be YOURSELVES as individuals after you incarnate in this reality". Second is your FAMILY and third everything that surrounds you – observes the sister Interana – therefore, keep from going after techniques and methods for opening chakras since they will open by themselves when you do start perceiving your ill negative emotions that do not let you live in peace. THIS OPENING STARTS AT HOME. You may travel the planet in search of answers but will hardly find any because you deep inside hold those answers. EL SER UNO also shows you that it is time to stop just using your external senses chasing after fantasies that others made you believe to be the truth – proceeds the brother Interano – therefore, take our advice and activate your long dormant inner senses. Start making your soul a place of order. If you feel uneasy, it is because you fail to understand that it is trying to tell you in a thousand ways that you do not really confront your needs and problems. When you start feeling great uneasiness, it is because your soul is without harmony and peace, which affects the emotions of your heart.

It is time for you to start the important cleanup of the basement, this place without light that is the subconscious because there you will find those answers and not through certain healing procedures. By removing what is useless in your lives, you will start discovering yourselves and opening windows of the soul to let in LIGHT and LOVE. You eventually will understand that there is no one but you to clean and tidy this basement.

87. Will we someday be able to comprehend the very message of the universe?

Every conscious human being on the planet asks this question. There however is little doubt that you in this third grade, plane and dimension are not yet ready to have a complete understanding of the "Universal Truth". This is only possible after you go through an extensive learning process – comments the brother Elohim – how would anyone in the third grade expect to receive university grade teachings? Being aware of the situation means to accept with humbleness that you are in this planet to rid yourselves of emotional limitations as a result of darkness and ignorance that keep you from advancing on this cosmic journey.

Who can really understand and explain the universal message? No one in a planet whose inhabitants still seem to have the limited understanding of very young, capricious, spoiled, fickle, egocentric, and extremely emotive people – concludes the sister Interana – consequently, to comprehend the secrets of the soul you need help via channels from the Antimatter world or parallel realities of the Elder Brothers and Ascended Masters.

They are the messengers who connect the Material and Antimatter realities, the teachers of earthly education to help you awake and find the path of return. You do not yet have the condition to awake by yourselves and therefore need to learn about the cosmic codes that your souls' crystals hold. Activation of these codes at a given moment will trigger a chemical reaction in the brain and thus the Desire of Creation for your inner transformation leaving your chrysalis to turn a magnificent butterfly. The books EL SER UNO have come to assist you on this demanding journey – proceeds the brother Interano – however, it is every one's decision to study them and use the knowledge of their message in practical life but also understand it as a guide on the path of return. On this cosmic journey, you will learn that the MESSAGE is more important than the MESSENGER and a soul has to be conscious of this when it comes to this reality to fulfill a cosmic mission. Light and Love are forever in your hearts but there will be a moment when you feel this Light as being something truly personal – concludes the brother Interano – while you advance on Knowledge, Understanding and Love making it a part of your lives, none of you will depend on the Light of others, as all will have this LIGHT and LOVE of their own.

88. What is a Spiritual Being like?

The concept of Spirituality is adjusting to modern life – observes the sister Interana – EL SER UNO says It is not against the Techniques and Methods. However, that it is not just the practice of these Techniques or Methods that might make people feel at ease and therefore believe to be traveling the path of spirituality. Spirituality starts with being authentic not for what you appear to be or have but what kind of a person you really are. It starts when you just say to yourself I AM.

Waking up in the morning and repeating to yourself that you must be a good person does not help. You are or you are not a good person. This goes for the way you treat your family, friends, colleagues and acquaintances. If you treat them day after day as a good person does, you no doubt ARE walking the spiritual path. Yoga, meditation, the use of mantras, chants and rituals may give you comfort but the universe wants your positive thoughts, actions and deeds. The rest are just ornaments and inventions by men and women who use only the external senses and emotions of the spiritual path.

Spirituality has come a long way in evolution and elevation being the promised ancestral paradise on Earth more distant than ever – proceeds the brother Interano – today's religions seem to have lost their way since real spirituality centers in the elevation of the human being's inner self. Instead, they have turned a shelter for categorical and outdated dogmas that coexist with an increasing accumulation of material goods.

Today's spirituality is something that has a place in the deep of your soul. You are creators because you carry the Origin of LIGHT and LOVE – affirms the brother Elohim – there is an extraordinary force in human conscience of Being and Feeling. Consequently, the elevation of spiritual energy has a concept of its own, which will eventually allow you to join the One Origin. Spiritual human beings will be the masters of their lives and no longer accept unconditional religious orientation – concludes the sister Interana – in fact, there is no more need for cassocks, prayers and incense. The authentic being of LIGHT and LOVE lives in a fast world of instant communication as a member of a society conscious of the need for respect and discipline.

This is a process of dismissing fantasies. Spiritual humans know that striving to advance does not mean to look in this reality for shutting themselves away but by reaffirming their values and building the strength to transform negative into positive. However, while trying to do this in the past by attending religious services and raising prayers to God, nowadays they are aware that to become a spiritual being in this reality, they have to it all by themselves and assume full responsibility.

We can say that humans in the past – concludes the brother Interano – who were looking up to a distant creator, are turning what we call a co-creator with the faculty of creating a reality of their own. There is no longer punishment for an alleged capital sin or the grace of salvation. Today's spiritual human beings with hard work and profound comprehension are going to enjoy the illumination of their eternal existence.

What is a Spiritual Being like? – asks the sister Interana – Spiritual Beings are persons who prepare the soil, sow using appropriate seeds and later irrigate it. They enjoy their work and never fail to have the seeds grow under the best of conditions but are aware that they cannot control all of them. This is why they must comprehend the canons of the universe. Otherwise, their work may vary a great deal affecting the seeds' quality and beauty.

This metaphor shows the Sowers as persons who must wake the correct thoughts, acts and deeds and irrigate them with determination, perseverance and responsibility but never allow egotism to interfere, which would severely affect be the process. Sowers know that they will hardly succeed and feel happy if they exceed control and manipulation of something that is to flow with harmony, peace and love. True Sowers therefore show respect for the natural development because this way they are going to activate the inherent qualities of everything the Great Cosmic Sower, the ONE ever created.

89. Could thought-energies already incarnated possibly occupy another adult individual's body?

For the universe that is impossible – replies the brother Elohim – during the regular process of incarnation, a mind's thoughts occupy just one physical body. Any intent of other thought-energies to enter the same body the universe considers an invasion of the body, soul and spirit of another human being nor can those thought-energies overshadow this being's soul or stop the gestation of the spirit in its Pineal Gland. All that thought-energies can do is to communicate via telepathy or mediums with the thought-energies of other individuals. Nevertheless, there are the special cases of cloning or disincarnated souls ceding this body to a very high spirit for the fulfillment of a transcendental mission.

One is the case of Joshua Emmanuel who was dying in the desert. The moment he expired; the Solar Spirit of Christ entered his body. This is when Joshua Emmanuel turned Christ. It also may occur with you when some individual disincarnates but almost immediately returns to his body. It is however not his soul that has come back because it already has transcended this reality but an Interano Spirit that needs an adult body for the fulfillment of an important task in the material world.

Consequently, two souls can never occupy a physical body simultaneously. However, advanced science of the planet often fails to study such a particular question in accordance with the universal canons and true knowledge of the Cause and Effect relationship. Sometimes technology can help on the progress of a civilization, although it can also complicate the existence due to the terrible and dangerous results that redound to the planet and human beings.

90. What makes the soul truly different from the spirit?

All is one since the energy permeates the two realities that never separate – observes the brother Interano – there is some confusion about what the SOUL is and what the SPIRIT. The human being is a SPIRIT dwelling in a physical BODY that has a SOUL. The manifestation of the SPIRIT is the development of the soul through elevated thoughts vibrating with superior creativity and knowledge of existence. It is the sublime spark for the awakening of the emotional soul to universal feeling.

This never-ending force of Light and Love illuminates the crucial moments of life. SOUL is life, the electric energy that moves everything in the universe. It is intelligence and emotion developing with creativity and manifesting itself the moment the Universal Mind's energy enters its Cosmic Spirit. The soul is lively emotion, the spirit feeling the existence.

In this context, there is a similar situation regarding Religion and Spirituality – continues the sister Interana – numerous religions have an equal number of deities. The creator of all that exists on the planet has many different names: God, Jehovah, Creator, Sovereign, Universal Mind, Adonai, Elohim, the Olam, Emmanuel, Yahweh (YHWH), Zeus, El Elohe Israel, El Eyon, El-Roi, El-Shaddai, Jehovah Jireh, Jehovah Mekaddesh, Jehovah-Nissi, Jehovah-Rafa, Jah, Jhwh / Yhvh, Allah, Yahweh and not counting the names that other religions and beliefs have given to that supreme Being , Creator of the Universe. They must also consider other religions such as Hinduism, Buddhism, Judaism, Catholicism, Christianity, Taoism, Islam, Confucianism, Zoroastrianism, Shintoism, African, Inca religions, etc. etc etc. And all the names that have been given to him on this planet.

The Western world calls this deity God – continues the brother Interano – which in Hebrew means I AM WHO I AM and considers it the GOD OF ALL. Religions have always separated the creator from the source, the One Origin. When calling on the creator with the force of your soul and heart, whatever the name you may choose, positive and elevated Thoughts, Actions and Deeds are that really matter.

To understand and explain the great enigmas of existence, humans created Religion, using it in a desperate intent to find the Light of Wisdom that would enlighten them about the secrets of their origin and destiny. Nevertheless, those religions turned organizations with sophisticated control systems and are what the public knows as an important part of today's far-reaching corporate power.

Religions introduced, from the beginning – proceeds the brother Elohim – the concept that only trusting in and worshipping a merciful God makes you feel profoundly spiritual. While calling on the spirit is always present in religious services, this seems to have lost significance with the passing of time and appears increasingly overshadowed by material interests of religious institutions. Seeing and feeling no longer spirituality in most religions of the planet, we conclude that Religion and Spirituality are not a match and probably never were. There are many religions in this world but just one Spirituality, the spirituality inside each one of you.

No matter your religious faith, the language you speak, the titles you hold, your ethnicity, if you are a man or a woman, rich or poor, all, the universe wants from you is true work for a better understanding of your inner self and the elevation of your soul. Three are the qualities that must never stop nurturing this soul: Cosmic and Universal Knowledge, Understanding and Love of an infinite existence.

Nowadays, defining oneself as a Religious Person should change to being a Spiritual Person – suggests the brother Interano – if you succeeded, visceral conflicts would certainly be over. Authoritarianism, Fanaticism and Violence would cease to clear a way for the true LIGHT and LOVE of SPIRITUALITY instead of separating you as brothers and sisters. Strive to remember who you are. Your souls are the sublime sparks of the universe destined to be ONE in this reality and thus part of the ALL. Together with so many other souls, we all have come here to help expand the Light of understanding on planet Earth.

Therefore, let Love be this Light of intense luminosity to guide every moment of your lives. Always keep in mind the Desires of Creation of the spirit and of the planet, your home. All of you are the cosmic children, you are souls and your only existence purpose is: BEING ALL YOU ARE...Remember where is the truth of heart and soul – says the brother Elohim – don´t forget you are not alone. Be conscious that the light for those who awake is everywhere. Never confound your Inner Self's true needs with the superficial whims of the Ego.

Remember, time is short. Therefore, make every effort when dealing with important places and their circumstances in the name of Light and Love. You are Warriors of the Light, which means that time is right to fight for the Awakening of Conscience with equanimity, a blazon of trustworthiness and integrity.

Most people define their beliefs as feeling sure about an idea, meaning or interpretation of something. Beliefs are thoughts the significance of which in a way has deep roots in the soul and the heart.

Believing in something is both a rational and emotional process. Beliefs guide our actions. Consequently, the foundation of beliefs must be positive, correct and elevated knowledge. It will keep the chaos in the exterior from invading your soul and heart helping peace and harmony take their place in your lives. Beware of uneasiness and fear, two favorite arms of the dark. Never forget that you are brothers and sisters of Light and Love, Children of the Stars and Seekers of the Truth. The spiritual path is a solitary one. Therefore, let conscience guide your lives always because all you have to walk this path are your Soul of LIGHT and your Spirit of LOVE – concludes the sister Interana.

Go on looking for answers – continues the brother Interano – seek filling the emptiness in your hearts. Aim for the eternal and feel as birds flying in the infinity of your intimate existence with dives for true-to-life experience in search of an almost immeasurable essence. Seek the brightness inside after that immense absence of LIGHT and LOVE... After those precious words, we all keep silent, and I feel going into ecstasies over the elevated vibration that they produce in me. I was interrupted by the sister Interana who continues saying... Terminology is very important. If you are not clear about that, you will be confused. Everybody say one thing while others reject the idea, thinking that they are not talking about the same concept.

91. Could you in a more practical way explain the difference between Thought-Energies, Soul and Spirit?

Let us use a metaphor. If someone put flour, eggs, butter, milk and sugar on a table, what would you think is the idea behind it? Your guess is that it looks like this person is going to make a cake. You are right since those are the ingredients for it – observes the sister Interana – these ingredients represent the Idea or Thoughts (thought-children) that emanate from the Universal Mind (idea-father).

However, to make the cake you need the formula, the Energy (mother) to work properly with the ingredients. The result then is a cake. This formula and the outcome (the cake) stand for the Soul. In other words, the soul is the basic formula for all that exists. If we now add other high-quality ingredients such as nuts, raisins, almonds, chocolate chips etc. we are producing a very special cake, that is, an advanced soul. Consequently, positive additions resulting in an elevation of the soul will turn it into Spirit.

Nevertheless, – continues the brother Interano – if those other ingredients were of very poor quality, the consequences might be counterproductive or even harmful resulting in a degraded cake of poor flavor. Therefore, do procure to handle the formula properly and use quality ingredients meaning thought-energies of advanced elevation – insists the brother Elohim – on your free will depends on whether you elevate or degrade the cake. The more knowledge, understanding and love you have, the better will be the cake and you thus develop the ability to advance from the basic to the highest quality, that is, help your soul turn spirit.

92. How can we define energy?

ENERGY consists of CRYSTALS. Thoughts are therefore THOUGHT-ENERGIES-CRYSTALS. There is a relationship between the color of the crystals and the quality of your thoughts – observes the brother Elohim – bright crystals let the LIGHT of UNDERSTANDING pass. Unfortunately, too many of the thoughts you produce are not only ill negative but pread planet-wide. They therefore are extremely OPAQUE CRYSTALS blocking the passage of LIGHT.

Thought-crystals function the way a prism does, that is, refracting and reflecting light, as in the case of the Rainbow colors. By elevating your thoughts, you help the thought-crystals turn diaphanous and fill with the brightest light. This means that you will receive universal LIGHT and LOVE because your thought-crystals are going to gain

Knowledge, deepen Understanding, raise their energy frequency and thus transcend this reality.

Everything begins with...

First step: THE DESIRE OF CREATION

Which starts the process of cellular and photonic activation – observes the brother Elohim – THE DESIRE OF CREATION motivates thought-energies to induce the cells to a regeneration and purification of their energy. Along this process of activation, human beings surround themselves with an energy shield called the GRAVITATIONAL FIELD that protects thought-energy against any possible interference from ill negative thought-energies by alerting the DEFENSIVE SYSTEM OF THE SOUL. The regenerative code continues forward through the energy of the positive thought.

Once humans perceive that the system is functioning satisfactorily, they must start working with their inner senses to control and transform ILL NEGATIVE into POSITIVE EMOTIONS, meaning into FEELINGS. This work requires all their Knowledge, Understanding and Love because, by thus nurturing the right brain hemisphere, they start preparing their Pineal Gland's cosmic womb for the CONCEPTION OF THEIR BABY-SPIRIT.

With their souls' positive work, they will be raising the frequency changing the electricity (electric power) of their lives to the vibration of their existence and eventually be ready to conceive their Baby-Spirit.

The Baby-Spirit

Advancing with determination, dedication and perseverance, they are going to raise the energy of the soul and initiate the formation of the Baby-Spirit, that is, the Energetic Being – proceeds the brother Interano – from the very beginning of gestation, the Baby-Spirit will guide the human-universe where it develops growing its umbilical cord to join the Universe. This is when it will start nurturing itself with Cosmic Knowledge, Understanding and Love. The human-universe of the physical and psychical bodies will be its shelter from where it reigns with LIGHT and LOVE over every Action, Deed and Thought of a human being.

From this moment on, humans have to strive for a harmonious advance of the process. It is not the time to think about techniques, methods or magic words since gestation occurs in a natural way by following the guidelines of creation as established for every species of the universe. Even though humans live in two realities simultaneously, they must always procure to proceed with equilibrium and equanimity. The Baby-Spirit will help them succeed and preserve the protection they enjoy from universal brotherhoods. In comparison with the stages of a physical gestation, the exterior of planet Tera is going to offer the Baby-Spirit only a third of its total gestation in the Pineal-Gland-Womb while the next third will occur at the Internal City of Atlantis (Southern Cone) and the last at the Internal City of Lemur (Northern Cone).

Second step: KNOWLEDGE

Gaining cosmic knowledge is everyone's personal experience, which, however, must not be just words that could become difficult-to-transmute dogmas – assures the sister Interana – to raise the frequency of your energy (energetic body) and start living with this knowledge, our advice is to proceed to vigorous physical and psychical exercises. However, before you do, you will have to check on possible habits regarding smoking, drinking, drugs, poor diet as well as emotional imbalance, which could seriously affect your astral body, block the energy flow of your chakras and give rise to what we know as Diseases.

You do have to make it a habit to live in accordance with what you believe and defend. You have to be genuinely spiritual to be able to walk the correct way. To begin with, – continues the sister Interana – you should clearly define what you intend to realize. Is there something you want to improve? What would it take to change a situation? You have the strength to develop the Desire of Creation in you because you have natural talents and abilities. All you must do is to learn to use them properly. Since you are responsible for your lives, begin to change things from now on. As soon as they are clear enough in your minds, proceed. To get the goal of your Desire of Creation, it is important to take over life, executing intelligent actions that allow you: The Realization.

Third Step: UNDERSTANDING

This is not about cognition of planetary knowledge but comprehension of yourselves as human beings using the inner senses – observes the brother Elohim – with this, we are talking about true awakening, however, not an awakening that only consists in recognizing the existence of things and situations but about full conscience of their true nature. Self-Knowledge is the ability you have to expand your inner senses and conscience to perceive whom you really are and what your reality of existence is in all grades, planes and dimensions. This awareness will lead to understanding, inner growth, freedom of the soul and wisdom.

Other than the knowledge about the exterior world, self-knowledge originates from your inner reality, from the truth that emerges when you are conscious of both external and internal events. Concepts or ideologies may not be enough to help you understand and handle the reality, in which you live. You need to gather as much true-to-life experience as possible to determine if there is a relationship for a true comprehension of your situation. You should consider that ignorant are not who suffer from a deficit of concepts but those who do not have sufficient self-knowledge.

93. Could you be more specific about the difference between Soul and Spirit?

We shall try the best we can since both are key concepts on the message of *EL SER UNO* – reassures the brother Interano.

Soul

Soul is synonymous with life. Therefore, all that exists in the animal, plant and mineral kingdoms has a soul that records their respective characteristics. As we know, the soul consists of Nimeos-Energy formed from crystals. Crystals with equal characteristics will join and advance on their evolution of knowledge and wisdom. Consequently, the tangible as well as the intangible in the universe has a soul that sustains the three bodies of EL SER UNO. The universal soul shapes all created preserving its correlation, continuity and Cause and Effect relationship. We therefore may say that the soul and all that exists in it carries wisdom without end.

Having said that the soul is life, then humans must have a soul that gives them life – proceeds the brother Elohim – the soul in the human being is the breath given by the creator. The universal soul has travelled millions of years and realized thousands of millions of recordings. However, other than the rest of the creation, the human soul (as a part of the universal soul) carries the THOUGHTS of the UNIVERSAL SOUL (MIND) realizing its ideas. Humans are very specials because they were created in the image and likeness. The Creator said: IF I AM THE MIND, YOU WILL MY THOUGHTS. It was then when its Thought-Children began to execute the ideas that existed in the mind of the Creator. The soul makes humans self-conscious recording all true-to-life experience, emotions, genetics, character traits, personality and establishes social relationships – says the brother Interano – it is intellect, intelligence, logic and has a psychological dimension. The (incarnated) soul is a part of the human being who perceives the material world through the five senses. The soul may become corrupt if the physical body causes it to enter the darkness of poor understanding.

Only when the soul WAKES its deep dormant CONSCIENCE activating communication with its "Inner Self" and the cosmic conscience of bright ancestral knowledge may we say that it started forming its Spirit. Therefore, incarnating in the material world again gives the soul a chance to work on compensations (good actions) for errors committed in past lives. These expressions of affection will help it recover lost ground and prepare for the return to its origin.

Spirit

When generating its Thought-Children, the Universal Mind (creator) left it to their Free Will of how to treat their souls – observes the sister Interana – they were free to degrade them with low-quality true-to-life experience or raise and make them show their divine and eternal nature. At this point, the Thought-Children were to choose which path of existence to walk. A degradation of the soul would mean to stay with the life of this reality while elevation be the path to infinite existence. This made them become aware of the immense wisdom inherited from their creator. Failing to handle this legacy in a positive way, could mean to lose the chance to reunite with whom is the source of life and existence, the Universal Mind (Soul).

From the thousands of millions of experiences they had lived, the Thought-Children understood their reality and started developing this legacy by multiplying the inheritance of their souls to turn it into Elevated Thoughts sheltered in a Sublime and Eternal Body. This way they had shaped their SPIRIT. The SPIRIT is inherent to humans – stresses the brother Elohim – and is the inherited soul that the creator turned into perfect elevated Thought-Energy. While they traveled the universe and learned about the magnificence of creation, the Thought-Children kept recording the best of the best on their souls. Their thoughts turned energy of delicate shades because their return to the Universal Mind was only possible in a body of LIGHT born of the highest thoughts, the SPIRIT. They then nurtured their creator with experiences full of KNOWLEDGE, UNDERSTANDING and LOVE demonstrating that they were their father's worthy children and just as creative as he was.

94. Does the soul, once disincarnated, remember whatever wrong it did while incarnated? If so, how does it deal with those emotions?

In every new life, the incarnated soul fulfills a cycle of its existence. During that cycle, it must strive to understand and transmute ill negative emotions (energies) into sound-positive ones and take them to the right hemisphere of the brain. There they turn feelings that will nurture the Baby-Spirit. When disincarnating, the soul takes whatever ill negative and sound positive with it – affirms the brother Interano.

In the Antimatter reality, the soul does remember its ill negative emotions but not the persons who had suffered from their consequences. In other words, HARMFUL ACTIONS OR THOUGHTS as such will forever be on a soul's memory that must work to understand and correct them there.

If someone is "Selfish" during an incarnation, he/she must control and correct this attitude particularly within the family nucleus but also outside – continues the sister Interana – on disincarnating, the soul must understand the ill negative emotion of SELFISHNESS no longer as a "personal" experience in the material reality but as one of "collective" understanding and existential learning. During a new incarnation, there is always a chance then to demonstrate if what they worked and learned during the Antimatter phase is producing the hoped for results with family members, friends and acquaintances in the exterior. Is in this moment, when the soul asks to itself: Did I learn not to hurt others? Did I learn not to be selfish? What the soul learn in the antimatter reality is not the whom but the why, where, and when of it acts, deeds and thoughts.

95. You taught us that the soul is the intermediary between the material reality and the spirit. Could you give us examples of how this process works?

Here is what we will use for a better understanding – announces the brother Interano – while in the middle of the hall, a large screen appears showing a design of the human brain. We see – he proceeds – that the brain divides into the left and right hemisphere. Knowing that the soul throughout nine grades mediates between Matter and Spirit, we have positioned it right between both, a point that defines the position of the Pineal Gland.

Remember that the thought-energies of the first five grades occupy the left hemisphere (electromagnetism) and the remaining four grades the right hemisphere (magnetism). The details of the grades are as follows:

Left hemisphere

First Grade: Materialism
Second and a part of the third Grade: Materiality
Another part of the Third Grade: Material
The remainder of the third grade along with the fourth and fifth grades have already developed a degree of Spirituality.

Right hemisphere

The thought-energies of the sixth, seventh, eighth and ninth grades continue their process of spiritual development at the Antimatter Internal City.

As you may appreciate on the design, the energy of the soul channels the thought-energies of the nine grades into the Pineal Gland. This is the moment of alchemy between MATTER and SPIRITUAL ENERGY– proceeds the sister Interana – when thought-energies find their balance and support to fusion allowing thus the conception of the Baby-Spirit. This means that the soul has left behind materiality and materialism staying only with the indispensable matter reality but also beginning to advance on the development of the spirit.

96. How does true-to-life experience, that is, knowledge nurture the soul?

On disincarnating, the soul only takes along the very meaning, not the many details, of each experience to expand its knowledge adding it to that of past lives – explains the brother Elohim.

In terms of your reality, you, for instance, may enjoy an excellent meal in some restaurant. All you later will remember is the quality of the food served but not the location of the restaurant or the name of the chef – continues the brother Interano – your physical body, on this occasion, and on so many others in your life does not care about the circumstances but the nutrients it receives. Likewise occurs with knowledge. It does not matter whether it comes from an avatar, an ascended master or through some religion. The soul only registers the meaning and teachings of a "message", not its origin, when it enters the Internal City.

97. Does this mean that the soul will have no memory of its loved ones from this grade and plane?

The feeling of Love for one another is what keeps its loved ones united – affirms the sister Interana – it will be forever on a soul's memory but also sufferings, conflicts, hate etc. Likewise, the soul will not remember how they occurred and who was responsible for them. All those images vanish. What eventually stays on, are ill negative or sound positive emotions. The images, however, may come back when the soul must control and work an emotion.

You want your souls to continue feeling the way they did while incarnated but this is not how things work – continues the brother Interano – souls attract one another by vibration frequency, rhythm and colors. These are the characteristics of the cosmic family where souls feel happy or unhappy depending on the place they occupy there. It is important for you to understand that the Internal City is the clearest reality of emotions and feelings but, above all, of thoughts in their most advanced expression based on broad knowledge and deep understanding.

Each one of you gains advanced knowledge from sources such as ascended masters, channels, religions, etc – proceeds the sister Interana – however, when eventually entering the Internal City, your souls' memory just carries the record of what they learned and experienced while incarnated. No names nor places. Then it may happen that one soul addresses another saying: While on Earth, I learned that without knowledge, I do not live, without understanding, I do not exist and without love, I am not. So did I, reacts the other soul. Nevertheless, neither would remember who had given it this message.

98. Is the course of our life after we incarnate subject to predestination or must we always deal with each adversity the best we can?

For you to understand the answer to this question, we have to consider that you continue the process of evolution and elevation in this reality, life after life, with every new incarnation. However, in none of them you start from scratch because your soul always carries thought-energies with a variety of positive and negative elements from past lives. It is what we call correlation of thought-energy – affirms the brother Interano – the transfer of this energy from one incarnation to another will mark the Cause and Effect relationship in your lives ahead.

This extraordinary variety of thought-energies in some new incarnation may confront you with events that you find hard to understand tending to leave a possible explanation or solution for them to the forces of destiny or good luck. Incarnations compare to a new day (new incarnation) after a good night sleep (previous incarnation). If some problem remained pending the day before, you could solve it the next day.

You certainly would take the necessary steps to avoid the problem to grow if you knew its cause – proceeds the brother Elohim – in fact, in general, you do not remember past lives, which could help you resolve situations of the present incarnation. Consequently, you take thought-energies of unsolved and growing problems of the present to your next lives.

- When you start living a more conscious life and asking yourselves about the causes of your suffering, listening to your soul for true answers from your Inner self...
- When you start realizing that your lives are always offering opportunities for improvement, seeking answers inside you...
- When driven by true needs, you strive to understand what occurs around you...

You will be ready to change and initiate the reprogramming of thought-energies (soul) that, life after life, produced an emotion called Suffering.

According to a universal axiom "Suffering is proof of lack of Understanding" – reminds the brother Interano – those who nowadays fail to seek greater self-knowledge do not seem to feel a major need for it because they may believe that their destiny is to have come to live in a predetermined way. If they think so, it is because they fail to understand the many options and chances this reality offers. Human beings, who do understand, will be eager to gain the knowledge to create the conditions for decent and happy lives using all their determination, ability and perseverance for their realization and will never desist from doing so.

The Master Life and The Master Time are on your side, provided you truly wish to change and have the genuine Desire of Creation that emerges from the deep of the soul and heart. You will then find all you need for this long journey, life after life.

99. The Beings of Light's knowledge of us is such that they are using dogmas, beliefs and interpretation to help us awake and evolve. Are we correct?

You certainly are. We the Elder Brothers know you to the extent that we have been able of adjusting to your beliefs, customs and idiosyncrasies to reach the deep of your souls and Wake your Conscience. The diversity of thoughts in the exterior is such that we need to use all available means of communication to lead you on the path to evolution and elevation of the energy – observes the brother Elohim – the process souls have to follow when walking the path of return is not the same for all because of differences in genetics and innermost beliefs. This is why every soul will assimilate the teachings in a particular way.

However, there is no such thing as "discrimination". On the opposite, going into the variety of beliefs, we find that all talk about the Inner self's evolution and spiritual messages based on the teachings from Great Avatars who came to live in the human form in different eras and cultures. Along their evolution, the souls' Knowledge, Understanding and Love kept expanding thus breaking the mold of many rigid beliefs passed on from generation to generation and transforming the energy of their DNA into cosmic energy with a much broader vision.

This is the process we call ELEVATION – proceeds the sister Interana – the Elder Brothers of the Internal City initiated it by starting from what you would call elementary school level with the use of images and chants for a repetitive practice of knowledge. In the next phase, they had you attend schools of metaphysical and esoteric studies. Finally, they presented their "masters" whom you called Angels, Virgins and Ascended Masters to be able to accept those teachings as authentic and valid beliefs.

As the soul investigates, grows, learns and more – concludes the brother Interano – those beliefs ingrained from parents to children disappear throughout incarnations. This is where new cosmic concepts enter in the soul by its own will, learning on its path of return and existence.

100. How will our souls connect with one another if, according to you, groups tend to vanish compromising the hoped for advancements?

When we say that "united you will be strong", we do not mean gatherings of thousands of people in a place but the joining of millions of positive thought-energies – clarifies the brother Interano – their vibration frequencies, rhythms and colors are going to uplift the ill negative electromagnetism of the first and second to the third grade producing what we call "Fusion of the Energy", using its elevated temperature from the interaction of matter and antimatter for the transformation of dense into light elements.

At present, there is a mental struggle between humans' negative and positive force – observes the brother Elohim.

The ill negative force battles to prevail by increasing the density of the first two brain zones, chakras and grades of the electromagnetism, thus trying to confine thought-energies of humans and the planet in these low grades.

Instead, the sound positive force strives to raise thought-energies to grades three, four and five of the electromagnetism.

By elevating the frequency of its energy, every single soul will multiply the force of its thought-energies, reaching that of a number of persons. We therefore say that, for you to advance on the path of return, physical gatherings are no longer necessary because the force to do so is in every one of you now.

101. What is the reason for this mental confrontation?

Positive thought-energies of an elevated soul nurture themselves from the universe, since they connect with the eternal universal energy and thus with the canons of the cosmos – comments the brother Elohim – ill negative thought-energies do not have this connection and need to nurture themselves from energies of their environment. We might say that they are vampire energies without the ability to connect with higher energy sources and therefore need to feed on the energy from souls of their grade, plane and dimension.

The dense souls' true motive is to keep other soul prisoners in this grade as a sole energy source, far from more elevated sources, which would be the only way to secure a permanent cycle of incarnations – concludes the brother Elohim – nevertheless, the sound positive Force strives to encourage as many souls as possible to transcend. This way, the negative force would gradually lose its energy source in this grade and eventually have to leave for the lower dimensions of new creations.

Comparing this concept with what happens in the Micro-Cosmos, that is, in your physical bodies, we would have the following situation: we can cure cancer by cutting off calorific food for the tumor cells and replacing it with an alkaline diet. This would be the beginning of the healing process.

102. Is Global Warming a natural phenomenon or Pollution the cause for it? Could it possibly be a Reptilian strategy of channeling negative energy to the Poles, which would be detrimental to the Interanos?

The cause for global warming of the planet is the proximity of the Cosmic Alignment when four dimensions are going to align in the Universal Mind of EL SER UNO – says the brother Elohim – in this natural process, the Sun absorbs and transfers the immense energy of the spirits that take part in the alignment. As explained earlier, your Sun is the Pineal Gland of the Solar System receiving millions of elevated thought-energies from Mercury, Venus and Earth. These planets are undergoing purification and absorbing photonic solar energy, which filtered during its passage through their moons, nurtures all living organisms on the planets. Given the vastness of this process, the Reptilians have neither the physical nor the mental capacity to harm the Interanos.

103. Why do we who have awaked continue accepting manipulation by persons, institutions and governments? I asked anxiously, waiting for the answer...

Does this mean to accept other people's limitations? How many people accept their own limitations? – inquires the brother Interano – you must look at the many faces of life from different angles to get a reasonable vison of them. Everyone lives what may be one of the toughest part of the path to spirituality: to understand their process and that of others and be willing to adjust to it. You are born to live with situations that would need more Tolerance, Flexibility and Adjustment, qualities that many of you carry as a remote experience from past lives and therefore must develop and understand. This, however, does not mean that you accept mistreatment without the slightest reaction. The Age of Aquarius tells you that tolerance is not synonymous of permissiveness, which could end up in ignominy and even injustice.

Tolerance means to respect other individuals' right to express their ideas about values, with which you do not identify. It does not mean that you will allow to be mistreated, trampled on and quietly have to accept it. This belongs to The Age of Pisces. The Age of Aquarius tells you: Being tolerant does not mean to be condescending, humiliated or permissive with infamies and injustices. Tolerance goes along with self-respect helping you raise self-esteem.

You cannot deal with situations unless you understand them first – observes the brother Elohim – to begin with, you should not consider them "Problems" but a chance to test your determination and perseverance. People dream of living a life without continual obstacles to achieve what they feel is best. The truth is that, while living in a material world, they will never escape confrontations that only appear to exist to turn their lives into a permanent test of endurance.

Many seem to misunderstand that life in this reality is not only a struggle for survival and success but also an opportunity to satisfy humans' inherent desire of progress. Not comprehending the reason for this challenge could mean that they are unable to meet it, that they will never enjoy the satisfaction of having cleared great obstacles and consequently lack the motivation and illumination to strive for true development and success in their lives.

You therefore must take on this challenge with the conviction that the spiritual knowledge is going to help you understand and face it by strengthening your souls, by speaking the truth, being patient and tolerant and believing in the force of knowledge but, above all, of love.

This is the moment for you to realize that it is unacceptable that many people in this planet still suffer the violence of political and economic abuse perceiving life as cruel and inhumane or without God. It depends on how they deal with their particular situation but have to understand that they suffer offense, mistreatment and humiliation because they fail to oppose to them – concludes the brother Elohim.

For a better understanding of the grades of the electromagnetism, we are going to study groups of souls and their characteristics – proceeds the brother Elohim – we call them STELLAR FAMILIES. These families of souls group in the incarnated as well as in the disincarnated state in their respective grade of the electromagnetism.

It is important for you to know that all these souls connect with one another in a certain way. All of them will feel and experience what happens to every single soul. You also will have to remember that the electromagnetism has nine grades and each one of them another nine grades. This means that you live at the same time in each grade, that is, you live 81 parallel lives. Of the nine grades, five are matter energy and four subtle energy.

104. I apologize for interrupting you but we seem to be on the edge of a war between the US and North Korea. Could you comment on this?

MESSAGE from the Elder Brothers Ayaplianos concerning the KOREA CASE

BROTHERS and SISTERS, you do not have to worry about a possible military confrontation. THERE WILL BE NO ACTION. It is an intent of coercion to make the US lift the heavy economic sanctions it had imposed to stop North Korea's threatening nuclear missile program.

This attitude is a palpable demonstration of the disease of distortion, the ill negative force that nurtures itself from resentment, indifference and hate. The more LIGHT and LOVE emanate from the thought-energies of the beings of this planet, the more fiercely the forces of the dark will fight to neutralize them.

Do not fear, brothers and sisters. We are asking all beings of LIGHT and LOVE not to allow apprehension to enter their souls. Instead, raise the frequency of your thoughts and cast the light of LOVE on that country to have it find the PEACE and HARMONY that all beings of the planet so deeply need. Have faith, for evil will never conquer LIGHT and LOVE. However, think no longer of YOURSELF but of OURSELVES as together, we always stand united.

The new Times demand fraternally working together because only united you will produce higher vibration frequency, well-being and elevation of all souls' thought-energy. May the universe always guide you on the Path of Truth and Eternal Existence!

Message from the Elder Brothers Ayaplianos channeled on April 4th, 2013.

Let us now continue our explanations...

We were saying – proceeds the sister Interana – that souls interconnect and what one soul feels all incarnated and disincarnated souls will perceive likewise

105. What does this mean?

If all souls interconnect, we may conclude that all of you carry thought-energies from the beginning of creation meaning as soon as you left the One Origin. In fact, souls, all souls, interconnect and all, one way or other, feel what every single one of them does – affirms the brother Interano.

Let us suppose that somebody's grandfather had been very selfish – says the sister Interana – when his soul reached the electromagnetism, its selfishness-energy is going to take its due place, that is the second or beginning of the third grade. This is where the healing process starts, which is to understand his selfishness and try to cure its negative energy. Meanwhile, in the exterior a descendant of his conceives a child who during the conception attracts the grandfather's ill negative energy of selfishness.

While growing, this grandson turns out to be as selfish as the grandfather had been. As an adult, he learns about this trait of the grandfather's character and wants to overcome the inherited selfishness. Analyzing he starts understanding it until he succeeds in initiating a process toward generosity – the sister pauses then continues –. The moment when the incarnated soul completes this transmutation, it aids both the grandfather's and its own energy. The grandfather out of the Antimatter World helped his grandson understand what selfishness is like and the grandson when transforming it aided thus the grandfather's soul.

This explains the transcendence of energy healing – says the brother Interano – which crosses the frontier between the exterior and interior that is between the Matter and Antimatter dimension. We therefore call it inter-dimensional healing. We want you to recall that you are thought-energies living in dense material bodies that is you are palpable holograms. Now, this energy interaction does not originate from the holograms but from programs of their souls' memory that compare to those of the hard disk of a computer.

106. What would be the conditions for a new incarnation of the grandfather's soul after the grandson transmuted his selfish energy?

The emotion selfishness ranges from light to very severe. In this case, the grandson may have helped transmute a certain part of it that lives in him but not all the grades of his grandfather's soul – replies the sister Interana – this means that the portion of selfishness in the remaining grades could continue with the grandfather or incarnate in other descendants who then would have to embark on an equal process of transformation. You all carry a great deal of emotion-energy, positive and negative, inherited from past generations – proceeds the brother Interano – you are a part of the collective soul and none of you will escape having a great variety of emotions. Imagine, however, you decided to work together on the transformation of Selfishness. In that case, this treacherous emotion would gradually leave to be a part of this reality. Unfortunately, the absence of a planet-wide mental integrity as well as the necessary knowledge of the process to conquer the ill negative force still are very difficult-to-clear obstacles for you.

You continue losing your time on courses of techniques and methods with limited results that fail to benefit people and the planet as a whole – concludes the brother Elohim – however, as mentioned earlier, to attain this global benefit there is no need for massive gatherings. You can do it in the quiet of your homes by activating the Desire of Creation and proceeding to a profound self-analysis of your inner self. Is that asking too much?

107. How can we succeed with disunity resulting from the extreme individualism that reigns in the planet?

This is the first time that you learn about the knowledge of our message and thus have become conscious of the need for unifying your thought-energies – observes the brother Elohim – you now start having a clearer view of true healing and the work you have to do to achieve it. Has religion ever taught you that psychoanalysis is indispensable to understand and work the problems you carry for so long and therefore must precede this healing process? Have some Ascended Masters truly shown you how to come out of the darkness, in which you live?

Taking a closer look at religions, masters and channels, you will find that they all eagerly built temples, schools and institutions using their believers' generous contributions for the promise of salvation – remarks the brother Interano – how do these actions match with the teachings of the great Avatars who never talked about temples and the need for money to build them? The universe does not care about your religion and if you regularly attend religious services. It works with a force called THOUGHT. Therefore, in silence and with equanimity in your souls, you can make this big step forward to advance on elevation and the formation of your spirit. Renounce the search in the exterior and enter the temple of your soul where your inner self will discover the truth of your existence.

However, you so far have eagerly been searching for the exterior and forgotten about the interior, about what truly matters in this universe: THE SOUL. You have given so much importance to the trimmings of the food you eat that you seem to have forgotten about its nutrients because you suffer from an uncontrollable ambition for visible material things – reminds the brother Elohim – your body does not need those trimmings, as with or without them it is the same food. Similar occurs with the soul. Whether it receives the knowledge in a magnificent church or in a simple garden, it is the knowledge that matters.

108. What is the emotion we have to work most?

It is GENEROSITY you need most – emphasizes the brother Elohim – while misery and stinginess seem to be everywhere in human life, you wonder why the world is what it is. Humans have become extremely selfish ignoring the suffering of a sick and unhappy society. How is it possible that you forgot about your fellow humans' need for help and support? We see a society dominated by money and ambition – observes the sister Interana – there is an amnesia of values that ever since had been important human qualities such as generosity that humans carry in their spirit.

Therefore, this is the moment to recover those values from the memory of your spirit. With the Awakening of Conscience, use its comprehension to engage in planet-wide actions of support as a sign of true goodwill without distinction of credos, ethnicities and languages – stresses the brother Interano – "THE UNIVERSE GIVES NOTHING, IF YOU GIVE NOTHING".

The day you show GENEROSITY with your fellow humans, the universe will be GENEROUS with you. That is the main reason why people get nothing...because of the lack of generosity from their hearts and souls. The Universe is a place of great order, where merit is the condition for what you receive.

109. Brothers and Sisters, I was wondering whether you could comment on Bipolar Disorder. Is this a physical or mental disorder?

> ***Bipolar Disorder:*** Or manic-depressive disease is a mental disorder responsible for extreme mood changes. It affects about 1% of the population. Feeling occasionally sad or half-hearted does not necessarily mean depression. It is, however, important to have a notion of its symptoms and seek professional help. The principal cause of the disorder may be a chemical imbalance in the brain. It sometimes is hereditary and may affect several members of a family. Men as well as women at any age may suffer from it. (Wikipedia)

It can be physical or mental or both at the same time – replies the sister Interana – knowing that you are on the path of evolution, we have found that often genetics interfere with chemical reactions producing a certain physical condition. Regarding inherited parental and past life Nimeos-Energy of the soul, it is possible that certain energy combinations failed. If the disorder is physical, it is subject to a medication that allows the person to live a normal life. In the case of an energy imbalance caused by ill negative emotions, which would affect the soul, the person needs psychological treatment to balance certain cerebral circuits. We consider ill negative emotions addictions of the soul.

110. Could you give us a few examples of what you consider addictions of the soul?

Addiction: From the Latin *addictio,* addiction is a strong habit that controls a person's will. It can be the dependence on a substance, activity or relation. For instance, "the actor had to seek admission to a clinic specializing in treatment of drug addicts", "I lost years of my career because of addiction" or "I worry about my son having developed an addiction for the internet".

Addictions control people's thoughts and behavior to the point that all they seek is to realize their desires. They therefore are prone to commit illicit, distance from their loved ones and risk their integrity, losing track of reality. Many addicts having grown in dysfunctional families suffer from anxiety or depression and there are cases of negligence or abuse that leave their victims with post-traumatic stress or a severe disorder of personality.

It is extremely difficult to escape some kind of addiction, when a possible genetic predisposition adds to the emotional suffering caused by these problems.

Addiction is a chronical primary disease with genetic, psychosocial and environmental factors that influence its evolution and manifestation. It frequently is progressive and fatal with alternating periodical or continual episodes of lack of control of something, its use despite adverse consequences and thought distortion, notably negation. (Wikipedia)

As we see in the definition of the dictionary, – observes the sister Interana – addiction is a primary disease that affects the character and personality of a person. Emotions that relate to a certain addiction tend to be deeply rooted in the soul resisting transmutation. Sadness, for instance – continues the brother Interano – people who tend to sadness deny themselves moments of joy because they feel bad (guilty) about it. This is why, they always return to this emotional state in what we might call a kind of self-punishment.

Another example is the addiction to feeling themselves always victims making other persons feel that they actually are victims – says the sister Interana – occasionally, they would enjoy a personal benefit from what we consider manipulation of emotions.

In general, strong and recurrent needs for something denotes dependence. It may affect a person's identity being an emotional disorder that impedes people to image a life without these needs. Very often, this addiction characterizes great emotional emptiness that people try to fill this way – concludes the sister Interana.

On the other hand, there is the addiction for a number of chemical substances and the pleasant sensations they produce in the external senses – proceeds the brother Interano – these sensations connect with your thoughts affecting the emotional state of the soul. Consequently, any interruption is going to cause discomfort and you will anxiously seek to restore the pleasures that these chemical reactions from the brain give you.

We therefore insist that only by giving up, by renouncing addiction you will be able to control and reorient your emotions – concludes de brother Interano – those that were positive would change to feelings, those negative you would have to transmute into positive. Humans, by nature, tend to follow strong habits that, once created, often turn addictions. Among the many addictions, the most difficult to conquer are alcoholism, drugs, unlimited ambition, power and extreme forms of materialism – says the sister Interana – there is, however, another form of addiction characterized by an exaggerated search for happiness, miracle diets, technology etc. and nowadays, a very fashionable one called SPIRITUALISM.

For a few days...

I was alone after this last conversation with the sister and the brothers. Their explanations had removed many doubts and I only was hoping not to have left out some of the questions that readers had sent. Enjoying a rest, I felt sure that they would let me know when to continue with this last book.

In fact, one morning they make contact telling me that we will talk about how souls live in the Internal City. It sounds fascinating to know the antimatter reality and the life our souls live there. This time, we meet in a different hall with several doors and large windows letting in a magnificent light and allowing a glance at a City with its bright buildings of delicate colors and people (souls) circulating. So far, our conversations had occurred in halls and I always wondered why the sister and the brothers never asked me to visit the city.

The beauty of the city is such that looking at it gives my soul great harmony and peace. In the distance, I make out splendid gardens of flowers and trees as well as many souls wearing light color clothing resembling uniforms. What catches my sight is that there are no animals, not even a bird in a tree. I make a mental note on this but remember at the same time that this is a virtual city that the brothers created to make us (our souls) feel at home.

The sister Interana gives me a gentle look and says, the animals are in a different place, you will see. We also receive their souls here to help them incarnate and continue their journey. I feel happy to hear this and smile. Then the brother Seramita who had only occasionally been present enters the hall. Looking at every one, he joins us and takes a seat close to me. We look at each other with a smile and he slightly bows. After the sister Interana and the other brothers have taken their seats, the brother Interano begins to speak...

After all – he looks at me and says – we want you to understand that we could not invite you to visit the Internal City because you have not yet disincarnated. Yours is a Conscious Astral Walk that allows you to be with us. The place where we are now is the Sixth Grade and the city you see is the Atlantis-Antimatter-City of Crystal.

The reality of this city already belongs to the Magnetism – continues the sister Interana – this is where souls have conceived their spirit and almost completed the sixth grade of gestation preparing for the seventh grade. This already formed baby-spirit needs only another three grades to be born into the spiritual and energetic reality of eternal existence. Completed the process of gestation, it will leave for the Internal City of Lemur to prepare for its journey to the Internal City of Venus.

At this point, we feel that is important for you to know that there is a process of division of planet Earth and planet Tera under way whose description does not appear in the previous books – observes the sister Interana – the purpose of these books was to provide the knowledge of EL SER UNO that would help you understand the process of transformation that you and the planet are undergoing. This means that the Earth-Cell will have an entirely positive parallel world called Tera, which your thought-energies of LIGHT and LOVE are building after conceiving your Baby-Spirit and in which you will live forever.

(Tera is an acronym formed from the initial letters of the planets Tenezia, Ebiar, Retryon and Ambiares of the Pleiades constellation, in charge of the mission to cure the seven planets – the Earth or Tera among them – victims of the fragments of planet Satien).

111. As I understand, Earth will have a twin. How is this possible?

Planet Earth has a brain formed from the thought-energies of all humans – replies the brother Seramita, who has remained in silence – until recently, you all had been a collective soul, one brain with millions of thoughts. This is changing as an important number of souls is leaving the center of this dense material brain forming a new center with a higher vibration frequency.

The planetary brain is dividing in the way a cell of an organism does. From an old and ill brain, a new spiritual brain is born. It might seem a twin but it actually is different because the souls it shelters have elevated and conquered materialism that were holding them prisoners in a world of fantasy – concludes the brother Elohim.

112. Is this the Internal City then, about which you so frequently speak?

Yes. The City that you see now is a virtual one that we created with our thoughts and where we received your disincarnated souls for millions of years – remarks the brother Interano – this virtual Internal City will however cease to exist because you will replace it for one created with your own thoughts. It will be the new planet of LIGHT and LOVE called Tera, where you, now beings of light are going to live in harmony and peace. Tera will be the long dreamed true planet Earth.

113. Many believe that it will be the very Earth undergoing transformation. Are we then creating a parallel planet?

Indeed, you are – confirms the sister Interana – the process of creation began after many of your souls had conceived their spirits of LIGHT and LOVE and started to develop the parallel brain of Tera some 15000 years ago. Therefore, many human beings very actively developed their baby-spirit and always offered to return and volunteer for the Awakening of Conscience.

They are philosophers, inventors and alchemists who incarnated once and again to help you find and walk the path of return – proceeds the brother Seramita – for a long time already, humans live cycles of great dreams and awakenings but now an immense number of awaked souls has almost completed the formation of the parallel planet Tera.

114. Is the electromagnetism of importance for the formation of this new Tera?

Yes, it is – affirms the brother Elohim – this new subtle and elevated Tera had started its formation from the fourth grade leaving behind grades one, two and three, habitat of souls that failed to transcend and therefore continue living in their world of denseness and confinement. This old Tera (or Earth) will suffer control and manipulation by the Reptilians still for some time until they start declining. Their ever-denser material bodies will no longer be able to procreate and they will try cloning, however with poor results. After several generations, progressive degeneration of the cells will eventually lead to their annihilation.

After they try cloning – says the sister Interana – they will experiment with robots, and none will have the expected results. That way, step by step, the Reptilian Men will disappear from the face of the earth and a new specie called Yeti will take their place. This evolutionary process will occur slowly in order to adjust the energy within the material body of EL SER UNO. During this extensive phase, the grades one, two and three of the electromagnetism will become one while the new Tera's fourth and fifth grade advance and join the sixth, seventh, eighth and ninth of the high and subtle reality of the Magnetism – concludes the brother Seramita – it is the very transcendence of humans and the new Tera whereas the old Tera (or Earth) will remain the habitat of this new human species, the Yeti.

115. Since the New Tera is the Internal City, will we then depart from here to the Internal City of Venus?

Indeed, – remarks the sister Interana – you have always entered and left this Virtual City of Atlantis. With the beginning of the Cosmic Alignment, however, you will enter the Internal City of LIGHT and LOVE, the new Tera, that your elevated thoughts have created in an immense effort of determination and work to conquer darkness. Having transformed your bodies into Photonic Light will allow you to leave this new Tera for the Internal City of Venus.

At the same time, she turns on a very large screen. The figure you see – she continues – is a Crop Circle that we marked on October 14th, 2013 at Avebury Trusloe, UK.

The design shows the circles of the old and new Tera meeting at the center of the Crop Circle – says the sister Interana – the small circle between both marks the position of the Internal City, entry of the souls. You also see a closed figure S in the center symbolizing the wheel of life, which is the process of disincarnating and incarnating until reaching the

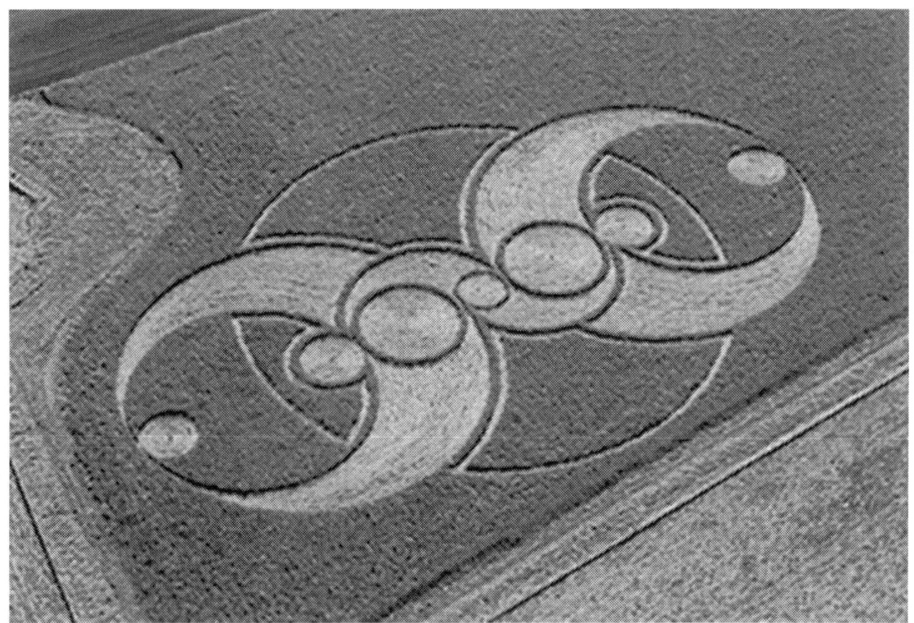

frequency to depart from it. Souls that have awaked occupy the last circle on the right side of the Internal City.

You are working to enter and free yourselves of new incarnations. Since each circle represents a frequency of vibration, your souls cannot leave the old for the new Tera unless they complete this work. As you go back and forth between the old Tera and the Internal City, the center circle keeps shrinking and the old and new Tera separate. During this extensive process, emotions make your souls become prisoners of circumstances (karmas) that you often have trouble to overcome. Therefore, only spiritual knowledge will show you the way to free yourselves from karmas that you carry from past lives.

116. Are we creating a new body for ourselves while building a New Tera?

Yes, you are – confirms the brother Seramita – by creating an elevated New Antimatter Tera, you develop the Energetic or Spiritual Body

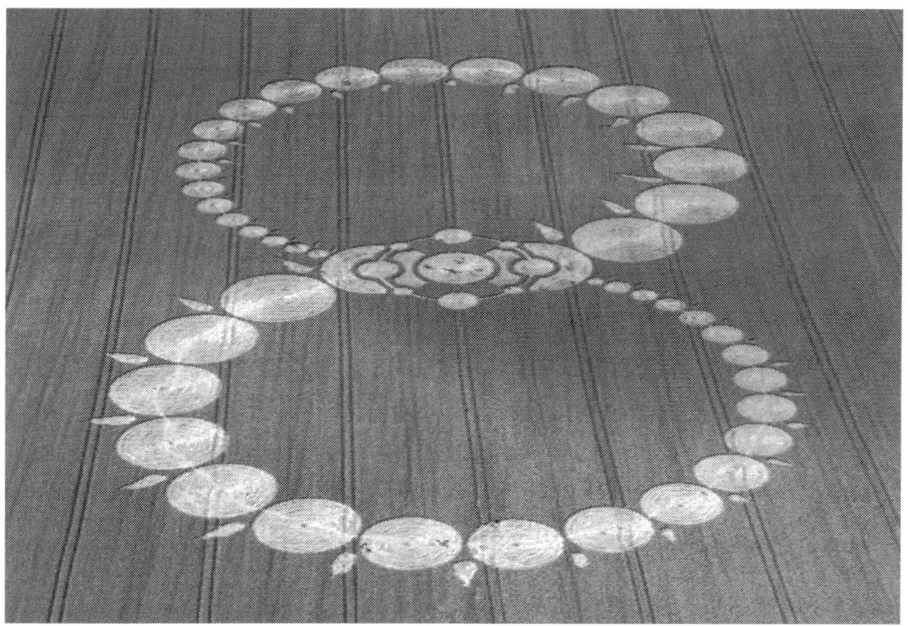

that will allow you to live this new reality whereas your dense material bodies will forever stay with the old Tera (Earth). While speaking, he proceeds to expose the following design on the screen.

The graphic you see – continues now the brother Interano – shows two overlapping circles representing the old and new Tera within the human Universe. The clear part, location of the Solar Plexus and center of the emotions, represents humans' Internal City, which they continually visit to transmute everything inappropriate for their elevation making it an Eden of peace and harmony. During this process, the two Tera circles start moving until the inferior (old) and superior (new) reality separate definitely. There, humans reach the elevation that turns their

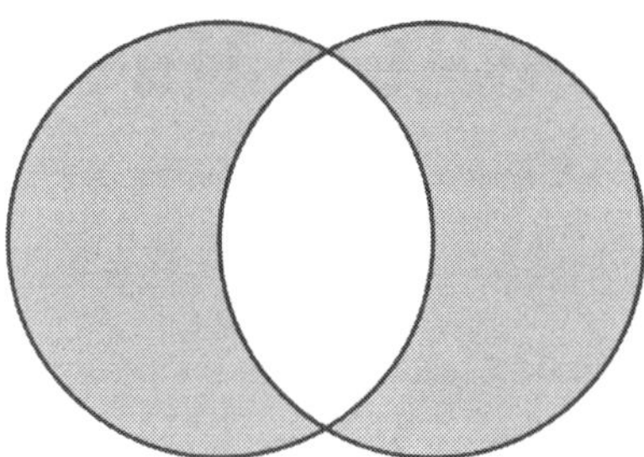

souls into spirits, ready to introduce their energetic bodies of LIGHT into the New Tera.

117. Are the Old and New Tera going to divide along the 7 Thousand Years of the Cosmic Alignment?

Yes, during this extensive period of Tera-Time, the old and new Tera will complete their separation – replies the brother Elohim – human beings who attain the New Reality, no longer need to incarnate in the dense old Tera and will be on their way to become antimatter beings of Venus, Mercury and eventually turn Solar Spirits.

118. How will we leave for Venus, Mercury and the Sun and finally go beyond?

On turning Energetic Beings (spirits), you will belong to the Antimatter reality of galaxies, constellations and universes – observes the sister Interana – we say that the Astro Sun is composed of Helium and it will be through this element where the Energetic Being will adjust and incarnate in the solar beings that inhabit it. The moment you leave the Internal City for the new Tera – continues the brother Elohim – you will be ready to enter Lemur (Northern Cone of the planet) and depart from there for Venus and Mercury. When reaching the Pineal Gland of the Sun you are bound for the Secondary Dimension. You have to do this through the Energetic Body, there is no other way. We have always said – remarks the brother Seramita – that density is only found in the Primary Dimension: Dense-Tera and other planets such as Alfa Nova and Ebiares. The rest of the universe belongs to the subtle Antimatter reality of EL SER UNO.

119. Will the Cosmic Alignment help us create and develop the New Tera?

Of course, it will – replies the brother Interano with emphasis – the Cosmic Alignment is the most important support that you and also, we, sisters and brothers Interanos will have because we, too, are going to live in that palpable Antimatter Reality, the new Tera. Our souls' vast thought-energies will join to turn spirits, Energetic Beings in this new reality of our eternal existence. Our holograms that had shown certain deficiencies before will see all the faculties of their memory restored and prepare for the departure toward the Sun favored by an increasing proximity of the dimensions during this monumental event. Profound interaction of Knowledge, Understanding and Love will make the New Tera an integral part of the Cosmic Alignment.

120. Could you explain how our souls will simultaneously live in nine planets Tera?

The nine planets Tera denote nine levels of evolution and elevation. You therefore have nine grades, chakras, energy centers, planes and dimensions and each one of them is present in you – observes the brother Interano – this might be a little difficult to understand but means that a space in the universe does not compare to a space of the primary reality where you still live. In other words, while in this reality you are separate from the cosmos, in the universal reality your physical, psychical and mental bodies connect with it. Therefore, on connecting, for example, chakra three with the third grade, plane and dimension, you mentally connect with all at the same time. When a soul disincarnates – continues the sister Interana – it passes to live the reality that matches its frequency, rhythm and colors meaning that its energy divides among the realities in accordance with the recordings on its thought-energies. This is what you call Hell, Purgatory and Heaven and the respective grades of the chakra, electromagnetism/magnetism, plane and dimension are as follows:

Hell
Grade: One, Two and part of grade Three.
Chakra: One, Two and part of grade Three.
Electromagnetism: One, Two and part of grade Three.
Plane: One, Two and part of grade Three.
Dimension: One, Two and part of grade Three.

Purgatory
Grade: Part of grade Three, grade Four and Five.
Chakra: Part of grade Three, grade Four and Five.
Electromagnetism: Part of grade Three, grade Four and Five.
Plane: Part of grade Three, grade Four and Five.
Dimension: Part of grade Three, grade Four and Five.

Heaven
Grade: Grade Six, Seven, Eight and Nine.
Chakra: Grade Six, Seven, Eight and Nine.
Magnetism: Grade Six, Seven, Eight and Nine.
Plane: Grade Six, Seven, Eight and Nine.
Dimension: Grade Six, Seven, Eight and Nine.

As you see, – remarks the brother Elohim – the universe is an orderly place, your soul cannot occupy a grade that does not match with its vibration frequency. Whatever grade it occupies, you must continue raising its energy. That´s why we ask you: What grade do you want to live: in a beautiful place or in a horror nightmare? It depends on the thought-energies of every human being. Every place we have mentioned, is a Tera-Reality, where you all live forked at the same time in those realities.

121. Do we then live in nine realities at the same time?

That is correct – affirms the brother Elohim – your densest and darkest part of the thought-energy (soul) still lives in a Tera of Hell. On conquering this reality, you are raising your thought-energies and going to live only the reality of the purgatory. Those who awake to Conscience will live different grades of that purgatory but will not yet have reached the Heaven of Tera. When finally entering the Internal City, they may say that they have found Heaven. Nowadays, all of you occupy diverse grades of the Purgatory, with many of the fifth grade preparing for the Internal City (sixth grade).

122. Does this mean that we, from now on, are a part of the Antimatter reality?

You indeed are – replies the brother Seramita – since you are now Energetic Beings, we will be able to proceed to the fusion of all our energies and thus prepare for the return to our origin. Remember that the universal body of EL SER UNO is almost entirely Antimatter. There is only a minimum density in a few grades. While the main purpose of your material bodies is to purify the dense and ill Nimeos-Energy, the passage from the third to the fourth grade already requires a subtle energetic body.

123. Speaking of which... Could you briefly explain the origin of the word "Nimeo"? I can´t find it in the dictionary.

Ni = In *Spanish,* it is used to add strength and intensity to something denied. Symbol of the chemical element of Nickle. Coordinating union with negative value. It means – says the brother Elohim – neither positive nor negative, it is neutral. ***MEO*** = Mi in *Latin*. It means – continues the brother Elohim – ***MIO***, which is, The One Origin.

Nimeo is the term the Lemurians used to define something immaterial of little importance – observes the sister Interana – much later, it turned NIMIO from the Latin NIMIUS changing its meaning erroneously to being something abundant or excessive.

Around the year 1650, it received the term MONAD from the Greek MONADOS, which means FUNDAMENTAL UNIT – proceeds the brother Seramita – we therefore could call the Nimeos "metaphysical atoms". Similar to the physical atoms in their natural state, monads are neither undividable nor self-destructible. Their disappearance would mean the annihilation of the One Origin's creativity.

The universe consists of an infinite number of Nimeos-Energy, independent and different from one another, which nevertheless united take the forms that the Geometry of the Desire of Creation asks them to adopt – adds the brother Elohim – consequently, they are elements that can be dense as your material grades and subtle as the antimatter reality where we are. They represent the universe with its innumerable realities and expressions.

124. What are Thought-Nimeos?

They are particles that carry thought-energies responsible for the correlation and continuity of thoughts – replies the sister Interana – while ideas and thoughts fill both the tangible and intangible universe, the Thought-Nimeos' task is to create the universal language of words, telepathy or symbols.

125. What will happen to those dense material bodies in the planet?

Along the seven thousand years of the Cosmic Alignment, the dense human-mold will experience a positive or negative transformation – remarks the brother Elohim – it will depend on how everyone has recorded the energy on his/her soul. This means that evolution will shape the Nimeos-Energy's characteristics. The overlapping circles of old and new Tera have not yet completed the process of separation leaving an open space (center) between them you call Limbo. Disincarnating souls remain prisoners of this center, unable to enter the subtle reality of the new Tera because they still must work on ill negative emotions and addictions continuing their battle between the old and new reality.

As we know, only about 20% of all souls will transcend the old Tera. This along with the souls and spirits that already made the transition will help complete the separation and independence of both realities. The majority of those humans who remain will gradually develop physical Reptile-like traits such as scales, oblique eyes, hairless bodies etc. thus manifesting the true nature of their energy – observes the brother Interano.

However, despite their great advance in science and technology, – says the brother Elohim – an extensive Ice Age critically reducing Tera's calorific combustion will finally force them to leave the planet and settle on planet Mars. Adapted to live in an environment of permafrost, the

Yeti will take their place turning the dominating species on the planet while in areas with higher temperatures other species will emerge. It is the recurrence of the planet's Stone Age.

126. Will animals and plants also transcend?

Many of them will be a part of the new Tera because of the proximity of the energies, despite the difference in vibration frequency and the love you have for them – observes the sister Interana – your union with the souls of the animal and plant kingdoms will occur in your minds and they therefore be able of taking along the essence of those kingdoms toward the infinite reality of LIGHT and LOVE.

The animals you cherished in the old Tera will be in your heart and spirit and thus live on with you in the new Tera. Your imagination and creativity there are such that by activating the Desire of Creation you will connect with the souls of those animals that had always been close.

This, of course, allows you to join the disincarnated souls of any human being you ever truly loved – proceeds the brother Seramita – otherwise, a union in the new Tera would not be possible since every spirit will take the way marked by the vibration frequency of its energy.

127. Eliminating animals such as rats, cockroaches, scorpions, spiders etc. when they threaten our health, will create a karma?

While you continue generating ill negative thoughts, you will continually add to the animal kingdom's lower grade energies – replies the sister Interana – the energy expressed through the thoughts and words will take place and shape according to the intentions: ugliness or beauty. Since preservation of the species in the universe is first, those animals need an appropriate habitat and severe control. Many new species in the future will appear as well as others will disappear. It depends on the evolution and elevation developed of the electromagnetism energy. Everything in the universe transforms. Nothing is static. As the Human-Being raise their thoughts, these species will disappear from the face of the earth, and other harmless ones will emerge.

Therefore, instead of decimating them, you should make serious effort to limit their proliferation. Elimination of animals that are essentially inoffensive will result again in negative and violent energies creating the conditions for the appearance of aggressive ones. Adverse outcomes such as the birth of cruel and poisonous creatures is an expression of your hearts. There is always a reason for the universe. If you leave a wide-open space, someone else will come to occupy it – says the brother Interano – for example, if you kill a whale that is a harmless animal, the cruel act created from negative-thoughts will cause horrible, bloodthirsty and brutal animals to emerge elsewhere as the same created thought.

The many forms, by which life expresses itself in the planet, first existed in your thoughts. Rats' threat of infection, disease and even death – says the brother Elohim – symbolizes dense and low quality thought-energies. It is important to study the symbolism of everything around you. The knowledge we transmit therefore aims at making you understand not only the diverse lifeforms on the planet but also what they may represent in your dreams.

128. Will we have physical bodies in the New Tera?

They will not be the way your bodies are now – remarks the brother Elohim – they are energy, vibrate with the magnetism and allow you to live in the element helium. They will resemble those of the Interanos and make you invisible for your fellow humans in the old Tera. Having equal vibration frequency, you will be able to live with them and incarnate in their bodies, as they will in yours. It is the energetic fusion of evolution and elevation between Ayaplianos-Humans and Interanos exchanging at the same time Knowledge, Understanding and Love. The fusion also includes the brothers Elohim. Together, we will proceed to the spacecraft of the brothers Volunteers at the Northern Cone and from there depart for the Internal City of Venus, Mercury and the Sun and finally go beyond leaving the PRIMARY for a different dimension of existence, the SECONDARY DIMENSION.

129. If those distorted and ill-Reptilian souls must leave the old Tera for Mars what will happen to souls that have serious addictions but good characters?

They will always have a chance to transcend the old Tera during the seven thousand years of the Cosmic Alignment – replies the brother Interano – if they failed to overcome their vice or to reach the necessary frequency, they would incarnate in the Yeti to help this species evolve. However, this will probably not occur because they generally manage to correct these anomalies during successive incarnations.

Those who gain the New Tera are going to aid their brothers the way we do with you through channeling, apparitions and dreams – adds the sister Interana – in the New Tera, you will learn how to transmit the teachings of our message in a proper manner.

You are preparing for this work of LIGHT and LOVE while the spirits who have transcended are striving to save as many souls as possible. Many feel that time is already short but do whatever necessary to contribute to the Awakening of their still dormant brothers and sisters.

After we remained in silence for a while, the sister Interana speaks:

"May LIGHT and LOVE always guide you on the true path of return. May the force of the cosmos be with you in this journey and goodwill, endeavor and perseverance the shield for your souls' battle against the darkness of ignorance in this Earth. May Knowledge, Understanding and Love enlighten your evolution and make you feel the vibration of whom gave you infinite existence!!"...

CHAPTER II

ACCELERATING THE HEALING PROCESS

It has been about two months now that we had our last communication. I am back to my daily routine but wondering when they would make contact again. This happened when I least expected it. One morning, the sister and brother Interanos and the brothers Elohim and Seramita established communication asking me to meet with them, as before, to continue our conversations.

Our meeting started dealing with...

Reprogramming the healing process

There is need to accelerate the two-hundred-year process since the use of techniques and methods to avoid errors kept you from seeking the origin of the problem and thus slowed the process – explains the sister Interana – the purpose of this book is to help you do things faster and establish an exact vibration frequency for the energy.

How will you gain time? – asks the brother Elohim – by ignoring prayers, mantras, magic words, rites and chants every time you prepare for a healing service. Wouldn´t be better if you go straight to the cure process? To the Cause and Effect relationship? Try to analyze the patient's problem(s) by asking support from the universe. Our task will then be to assist you and the patient, conscious of the procedure from our reality. This way, you will avoid feeding the ego and will prevent patients' inclination for considering you having superior abilities.

True healers – continues the brother Seramita – will start their work by showing patients how to treat their souls to prevent recurrence of a problem (illness) in this life or its possible appearance in future incarnations. They will use the power of reasoning to have patients understand that the origin of suffering lies in their subconscious. Consequently, healers and patients will have to embark on a journey into the patients' inner self to try finding the source of the suffering and a possible solution for it.

130. How can we connect with the patient's subconscious?

The Subconscious

The subconscious is an archive with many keys holding information that you do not know or, if you do, fail to understand – remarks the brother Elohim – it is also a place of multiple emotions. To enter it, requires maturity, common sense, responsibility and a solid knowledge of how human emotions work.

Much of this information is of vital importance and needs to become a part of your conscience – proceeds the sister Interana – other, accumulated during many incarnations is no longer useful but it also takes knowledge to transform it into recyclable energy. Furthermore, there is a memory of great suffering and illness whose access requires precaution to avoid contamination.

On carefully entering patients' subconscious and drawing forgotten experiences, healers will make them relive and bring those events to the present – continues the sister Interana – thus, healers will make contact with entities (energies) that beg for healing. In general, symptoms from the material body will guide them in this task.

Healers make frequent contact with the subconscious using designs, images, colors or the interpretation of dreams whose symbolism is the language of the soul – explains the brother Interano – another way of communication with the patient is through telepathy (distant healing) or the patient with him/herself . the Inner Self will communicate what is correct to do.

Meditation and profound reflection are important tools to access the subconscious – advises the sister Interana – in this case, healers and patients develop a combination of analysis and self-analysis. Nevertheless, on trying to discover the origin of problems by using what you call "gift", healers cannot do without the assistance from doctors of the antimatter reality who will help those read thought-energies and emotions – continues the brother Interano – in this context, the use of the infallible inner senses is almost common practice with healers and doctors representing an ideal combination for this type of energetic work.

The above exercises may be of help to both the Healer and the Patient to reach the subconscious – emphasizes the sister Interana – which is the key to the knowledge of the soul and holds the memory of all the lives with multiple experiences that the soul has lived. You also live the many realities of the nine Teras in the subconscious. There is, however, a difference between the reality in the exterior and the true reality of the soul, the source of your oneiric experiences. We, therefore, must emphasize that your memory holds a Rational Consciousness regarding the exterior and the Emblematic Conscience of your inner Self.

Rational Consciousness

Knowledge and Understanding of everything you studied in the planet are the foundation of Rational Consciousness, which we call the Collective Consciousness – remarks the sister Interana – it is self-understanding and the comprehension of everything around you as perceived with the five senses, an objective reality not considered within your subjective reality. "Seeing is to believe", would define this consciousness, which human beings developed by establishing certain parameters and ways of living and existing and call "Evolution".

Rational consciousness guides the lives of most human beings because it best adjusts to the reality, in which incarnated souls live – proceeds the brother Elohim – while humans conceive their reality from both an individual and collective perspective, the universe of the Ego holds thoughts that center on self-esteem but actually more on egotism. This will make those thoughts become fragmented and inconsistent trapping people in a life of loneliness, isolation and an often-uncontrollable sensation of failure. The problem with rational consciousness is that people fail to activate their Subjective Reality and Imagination holding on to stereotypes instead of analyzing and understanding concepts with an open mind.

Emblematic Conscience

Going deep into the Conscience about Symbolism is hard work for both healers and patients – observes the brother Interano – a good rest and relaxation are indispensable for connecting with the Subconscious, a reality that never stops functioning and holds ill negative thoughts that are responsible for draining patients' energy until often leaving them physically and energetically exhausted.

Analyzing thought-energies and determining their chakra of origin is the best way to connect with the Subconscious – explains the sister Interana –knowing their state and grade will allow healers to broaden the analysis and help avoid precipitated or false conclusions that could affect the healing process. Healers have to make a thorough analysis of the Objective Reality of the patients who must consider themselves observers and not actors of their existential problem during the procedure.

Thoughts, actions and deeds originate emotions that healers must analyze with impartiality. Once concluded, patients will have to remove inappropriate and introduce useful concepts. To do so, they have to be very alert, calm and aware keeping useless thoughts from getting in the way – continues the brother Elohim.

At this point, patients must make a profound reflection about the way they have been living their lives and how they choose to continue. This means to check on and probably change their diet. They must avoid what may produce a feeling of emptiness in their lives and learn to deal with the Cause and Effect relationship more consciously. They should be aware of the impact thoughts and words have on moral and ethics and therefore use their external senses the best they can.

131. What should be the next step after both healer and patient perceive an ill negative emotion?

When this occurs, you should remember that emotions always connect with a brain zone, chakra and grade of equal vibration frequency – replies the brother Seramita – in general, this kind of emotion connects with the brain zones, chakras and the grades of the electromagnetism no. 1 and 2. Once they detect this ill negative emotion, the healer or the patient – in case of self-healing – will have to place their right hand on the solar plexus and in their imagination make its emotion-energy leave.

Sustaining it with their right hand, they then proceed to transmute this emotion, again in their imagination, into a sphere of white brilliant light and introduce it in the left hemisphere of their brains, that is zone 3 where this now transformed positive emotion will join the corresponding grade – explains the sister Interana – however, this emotion-energy will not entirely be sound and therefore remain in quarantine since it may suffer a relapse. This is when the healing process actually starts.

Both healer and patient will have to embark on a work of psychological analysis to understand the underlying problem of the emotion meaning, above all, whether it has its origin in this life or rather in past incarnations. This true alchemy from the joint efforts of healer and patient will eventually produce the long-expected result.

Introducing the transmuted and now positive emotion into the left-brain hemisphere practically neutralizes former negative energy as a cause for some physical or mental disease. It is, however, imperative for the patient to preserve the positive emotion's health by being always conscious of its origin and thinking and acting accordingly – emphasizes the brother Interano.

If the joint procedure healer-patient were incomplete, the following serious error could occur. Should healer and patient after the removal of the ill negative emotion from the subconscious fail in the treatment as indicated this emotion-energy may start wandering and invade other persons or even return to the healer and patient for a new cycle of contamination.

ELEMENTAL DIMENSION

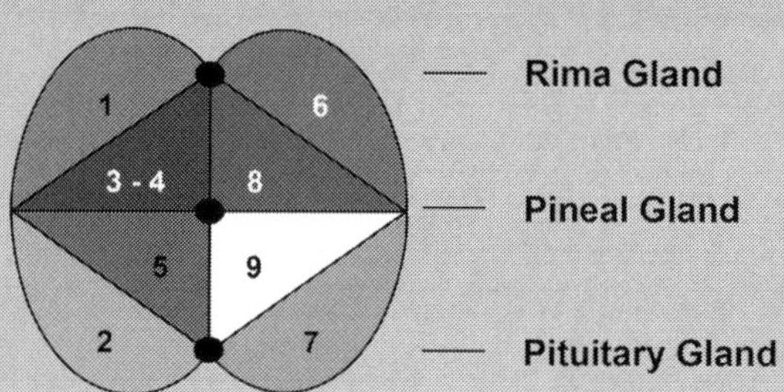

SECONDARY DIMENSION

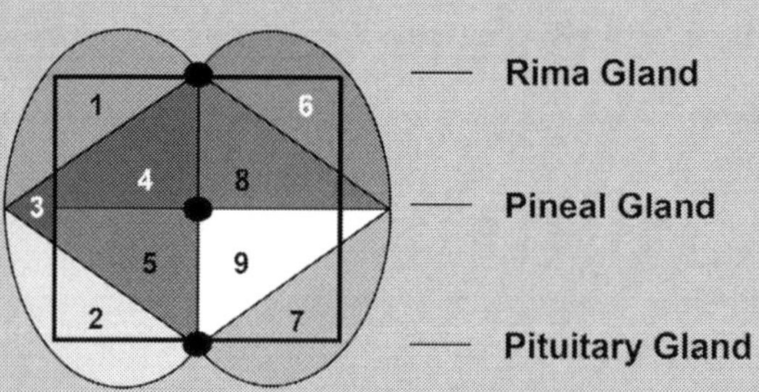

REGULAR DIMENSION

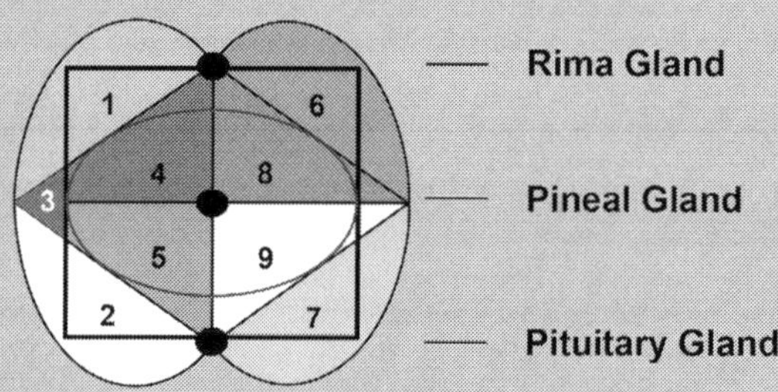

FIGURE A

Nevertheless, until now, you are only halfway toward the cure of the disease. Although you have given proof of Knowledge and Love by showing determination for analysis and action, you still must deepen your UNDERSTANDING to complete the process – concludes the brother Elohim.

Understanding means to have an intimate knowledge of your soul – proceeds the brother Seramita – this becomes evident when you look at the relationship between understanding and the external senses. Human beings develop understanding through those senses and the greater their sensitivity the deeper will be the understanding of their inner self and the world around them.

Your natural ability of external perception has its limitation and allows only a certain internal penetration but with endeavor, you will manage to activate your inner senses. To reach, however, the profound subjective nature of your soul, you have to use this special gift only humans have called the ABILITY TO UNDERSTAND.

132. Must there be appropriate physical and mental nourishment during healing?

Chakras are centers of energy invisible to most people and may vary owing to changes of thoughts and feelings – replies the brother Interano – ill negative thought-energies but also an unbalanced diet may affect your inner equilibrium while inappropriate energetic stimuli could activate certain chakras more than they would others.

Meat or spices in excess on your diet, for example, may have a strong impact on the inferior chakras leading to an increased absorption of calorific combustion. This could result in heavy stomach trouble, some form of sexual perversion and violence. Therefore, a balanced alkaline diet is indispensable. It provides alciatic (alkaline) combustion that, entering and leaving the chakras o brain zones, favors harmony and peace of heart and soul.

133. Will semiprecious stones (crystals) work with healing?

With the passing of time, this practice has suffered distortion since your ancestors already used crystals and colors turning a technique as many others. However, when talking about crystals for healing, we refer to thought-crystals as an energy responsible for this process of transmutation – concludes the brother Elohim – consequently, once you have learned to handle healing as looking for the origin of a patient's suffering there will be no need for stones (crystals), magnets or mantras to proceed. When will you learn to summarize and specify the healings and go straight to the cause? As we said, you don´t need to use stones, magnets and anything of that.

You are the masters of your minds using imagination and the Desire of Creation to heal yourselves and help your brothers do likewise. Therefore, try freeing yourselves of obsolete methods, rites, chants and magic words that many of you still seem to need for achieving the hoped-for results. Those are placebos and addictions of the soul – continues the sister Interana – we no longer lose time and energy on this using a conscious and loving desire to transform ill negative into sound positive energy. The soul must also learn through the knowledge and understanding that it cannot feed those diseases and make them emerge again.

134. When we pray calling on the Angels and Archangels of our religion, we wonder whether they actually listen to our prayers.

Humans use to work with their five external senses. Suggesting now to seek the origin of a problem without using them, might be asking too much, above all, from people who still need Figures, Images and Symbols to keep them from feeling that their prayers may just vanish in the vastness of the universe – comments the brother Interano.

This means that they still very much rely on their Rational Consciousness, which is sight, hearing and taste, smell and touch – remarks the sister Interana – they cannot do without those senses because these hold the roots of beliefs and emotions of their Egos and are a very hard to overcome psychological condition. This is because it takes time to build an Emblematic and Subjective Conscience. The essence of their souls already holds everything that exists in the exterior but not being aware of this Knowledge makes them believe that it is the exterior, which provides the positive results. In fact, the one positive outcome, so far, has been the development of the Desire of Creation and the Intention of their Thought-Energy – concludes the sister Interana.

However, once they perceive that they no longer depend on answers to their prayers – proceeds the brother Interano – their souls are going to feel agile, light and, above all, FREE from a burden they carried during many incarnations.

135. A reader writes me that she feels the presence of an entity at night fondling her and even touching her intimate parts. How is this possible?

Yes, this may occur. We call it Energy Transposition from one soul to another – explains the brother Interano – we will try to explain it the best as we can. Let´s check the meaning of this word:

> ***Transposition:*** Disappear behind a distant object. Transpose a corner. The action of transposing something. The act or process of changing something from one position to another. Transposed a novel to the cinema. In music, transposition refers to the process or operation of moving a collection of notes (pitches or pitch classes) up or down in pitch by a constant interval. Displacement of an organ to the opposite side. Surgical operation that consists of transferring a graft without completely separating it from its place of origin, until it has been attached to its new location. (Dictionary)

During several incarnations, the souls transpose each other, – continues the brother Interano – owing to a very strong relationship that they had in past lives. Consequently, the energy and emotions of two souls may join until forming one single Energetic Being or Spirit. In some cases of intense passion or serious conflicts.

These types of souls, join their lives and stick together for several incarnations. As a result, they will have to work hard (at least one of them) to separate and detach themselves of those emotions such as passions, conflicts, murders, rapes, complicity, and more – concludes the sister Interana.

136. Could you give us details about Energy Transposition of the souls?

Going back to the case of the woman who felt an intimate contact with some entity – replies the brother Elohim – we would say that the entity is her husband. Both had been mediums in past lives, during which they called on dense cinnabar energies that unfortunately turned out to be harmful to a number of persons. After he disincarnated, she continued calling on him.

Owing to this lasting and very intimate relationship, they share the transposition of energy of their souls having thus created one single vibration frequency. Therefore, whoever remains incarnated is going to seek to maintain contact with the disincarnated. If this woman fails to restore and raise her frequency or correct bad karmas from past incarnations, the entity (energy of her husband) will continue molesting her because according to him she still owes him "favors".

Souls that suffer from the Transposition of Energy must be aware of it to be able to transcend their energy and consciously block the transposition from the other soul's energy. Therefore, only she, by raising her frequency and using her ability as a medium to serve human beings, can manage to disconnect from the other soul – concludes the sister Interana.

137. How can we recognize that our soul suffers from the Transposition of Energy?

Here are the symptoms – responds the brother Interano.

- You clearly perceive the presence of a negative entity and register emotions such as uneasiness, fear, aggressiveness etc.
- Disincarnated entities transmit negative behavior, unhealthy desires and habits that may affect an individual's personality.
- The entity turns an energy vampire drawing vital energy from a person who starts feeling tired or ill. The entity may also enter an individual's subconscious triggering physical, emotional and mental disorders.

- Individuals who absorb this energy but are not aware of their relationship with disincarnated personalities may turn cases of Schizophrenia, a disease that characterizes the presence of two or more personalities in the mind of a person. Generally, the strongest among them will have the control over this person.

Unbalanced emotions may be an indicator that an entity is proceeding with the Transposition of Energy causing an individual to show continual signs of negativity and thus unconsciously level his/her frequency with that of a disincarnated entity.

On the other hand, some people frequently blame an entity or entities for all kind of ills and even existential problems. If these people were emotionally or mentally weak, they might invite in such an entity – remarks the brother Elohim –now, if they leave their emotions to chance or worse, lose complete control of them, they run the serious risk of having to face such a situation.

Nowadays, many people want to be Mediums or Channels to make contact with entities of other dimensions or ask "Guides, Ascended Masters etc." for assistance – comments the sister Interana – those are risky practices because if they lack the knowledge for it or the guidance from the spirits of LIGHT and LOVE, they are about to turn candidates for mental abduction by dense and low frequency entities. Therefore, to become aware of those forces requires the Awakening of Conscience, which means sound Knowledge and Understanding of the Cause and Effect relationship. Otherwise, misinformation and an initiative out of simple curiosity could have dramatic consequences.

Just wanting to do this for a good reason is not enough – proceeds the brother Elohim – a person should never "invite" the soul of a loved one to join him/her and ask favors from that soul. This attitude will benefit none of them. On the opposite, asking "help" from a disincarnated soul will make it cling to the person's soul and thus turn a lost soul, one that neither knows its place in this nor in the Antimatter reality.

The Desire of Creation of both souls triggers the Transposition of Energy. However, an incarnated soul should never invade the space of a disincarnated soul by invoking it but respect its new reality. You may think that calling on these souls, is an act of love – continues the brother

Interano – but it is not because it means to slow or even impede its spiritual advance. Nevertheless, there is a way to help such an entity (soul) find the LIGHT to guide it.

You should ask help from healers who deeply believe in LIGHT and LOVE, and consequently have the support from the Antimatter world, when treating patients – says the sister Interana – they form working groups for an adequate treatment of disincarnated souls.

Perceiving that a person suffers from Transposition of Energy, true healers procure to guide the errant disincarnated soul with much love on finding its way (LIGHT) in the antimatter reality and thus free the person (patient) of this energy – concludes the brother Interano.

Healers or mediums have to be sure that the entity (soul) is on the right way and complete the work with the help of their Spiritual Guides. On the other hand, they will instruct patients to follow certain guidelines to keep them from repeating errors. They will show them how to raise their vibration frequency, practice psychological self-healing, control ill negative emotions, strengthen their self-esteem, think and act positively.

138. What happens if people fail to ask for help allowing an entity or entities to stay with them in this life or in those ahead?

In these cases, we are talking about souls with emotional addictions that join life after life owing to unsolved conflicts. – replies the brother Elohim – such is the accumulation of those conflicts that their thought-energies firmly join producing malign psychical energy. This is when physical and mental diseases start and proliferate.

The universe bans the Transposition of Energy because it hampers the transmutation of ill emotions and compromises the formation of the Spirit – concludes the brother Elohim.

139. You say that Souls are collective while the Spirit is individual. Would this collectiveness of souls not be a Transposition of Energy?

When speaking of the Transposition of Energy, we always refer to ill negative energies – replies the brother Elohim – sound positive energies will never give rise to an agglomeration of energy or its invasion of souls while Transposition is negative and ends up in control and domination of one soul over another.

When two souls come together with love and respect, they will never transgress their energetic boundaries but rather exchange knowledge.

140. What is the work in this reality of those who are Mediums?

Life after life, mediums keep on developing their faculty of communication with disincarnated souls – observes the brother Interano – but the soul of e v e r y human being actually has this faculty, which consists in the soul's clairvoyance of the subtle expressions that characterize the Antimatter reality. Therefore, humans who are aware of this faculty, develop and use it are Mediums.

This condition does not hold any privilege for those who have made it common practice although many think it does – continues the sister Interana – to decide to act as a medium essentially means helping disincarnated souls, out of altruism, work and elevate their energy but also use the condition for guidance on important personal matters.

Using it for personal satisfaction (Ego), instead, weakens mediums' spiritual faculties and exposes them to dealing with disincarnated souls of low vibration. Consequently, respect, responsibility and, above all, LIGHT and LOVE should guide them on why and how they proceed. Remember that communication with the Antimatter World will always depend on an elevated energy frequency of mediums' souls. Furthermore, they must never stop studying the human psyche (soul) and act with true dedication in fulfillment of the canons of the universe – concludes the brother Elohim.

The Perceptions about the world are not very pleasant – says the brother Interano – have you ever wondered why and what is Mediumship for? Human beings of extraordinary sensibility, mediums feel affected by the emotions and sufferings from past and present lives they perceive, may times trapped between the two realities (matter and antimatter). This task is for strong spirits who have made helping others on the path of return a life-long compromise – observes the sister Interana – apparently, it's very modern to feel the antimatter world, but the reality is different. Mediums are connected with the pain and suffering of the planet. With the passing of time and practice, mediums learn how to control those energies, whether harmful or encouraging, by keeping a certain distance.

Authentic mediums succeed in harmonizing their energies with what they perceive and live through knowledge and a great sense of responsibility.

141. There are certain devices using the process of Bio-magnetism, which is healing with the help of magnets. Do they work?

> ***Bio-magnetism:*** It is a therapy that employs medium intensity magnets for pH control and stabilization by eliminating virus, bacteria or parasites thus improving the energy supply for the organism and acting on emotions. Findings are that specific combinations of microorganisms produce most diseases in humans including those, for which it sometimes is impossible to detect a microbial etiology such as diabetes, cancer, arthritis, fibromyalgia, sclerosis, lupus, Alzheimer disease, glaucoma, stress, tunnel of car piano, lumbago, osteoporosis, influenza, epilepsies, sinusitis, conjunctivitis, meningitis, liver cirrhosis, hepatitis and others. Affirmations are that bio-magnetic treatment gives fast and notable results that other therapies usually fail to produce (Wikipedia).

According to Ayapliano-science, this therapy eliminates only a portion of virus, bacteria and other elements that affect human emotions. It produces relief but fails to purify the human body for good and therefore has **No** healing power – explains the brother Seramita – the reason is that those magnets generate static fields that do not conduct energy – adds the sister Interana – without this energy flow, the magnets do not have the force to adjust PH values nor can they eliminate ill energies drawing them from inside the cells' nuclei where those energies produce diseases and anomalies.

We want you to realize that it is not the magnetism of any device but the electromagnetism of the healer or patient and their firm belief in the cure that will transmute ill negative energy – insists the brother Interano

– nevertheless, it is only the beginning of a new therapy. Broadening your knowledge about energy and magnetism, you will be apt to heal with it in the future. So far, for you this science is still of a limited reach as it only allows to detect anomalies but not to treat and cure them.

If nevertheless for some reason, it worked out it would not be for long and with the risk that the ill energy migrates to other parts of the body. We therefore advise against this therapy for now and rather suggest the laying on of hands and the use of the combined electromagnetism of healer and patient as well as the brothers' magnetism from the antimatter reality – advises the brother Elohim –remember that the healer must always work with assistance from the spiritual doctors.

142. There is a therapy from Hawaii using self-forgiveness, self-acceptance and self-esteem for healing oneself and others from situations of the past and present and in the future. Is this a correct therapy?

We have used this type of treatment for a long time with good results – remarks the brother Interano – this therapy seeks to solve problems deeply rooted in the thoughts teaching that the very thoughts can cure them but showing that also the memory of past lives carries emotions that may trigger disease if not properly understood.

Resembling what we are trying to help you understand, this therapy connects the patient with his/her inner self emphasizing self-forgiveness for healing and transmutation of ill negative emotions to restore the relation he/she lost with the spirit, creation and origin, which is the Universal Mind – continues the brother Elohim – it thus will make the soul perceive its divine essence and with love reach mental emotions or the subconscious to release those transformed negative emotions into an environment filled with the energy of forgiveness and love – concludes the brother Elohim.

It is good work since both healer and patient get to the bottom of the problem, which may be of the incarnated soul or of souls whose energies the incarnated soul carries – remarks the sister Interana – however, while this therapy centers in the divine essence inside you, it fails to allow the incarnated soul to record the work and nurture the Energetic Being in gestation.

Leaving everything to the divine essence is not appropriate because the healing process has not concluded yet – proceeds the brother Elohim – the soul feels that its register of emotions has remained an empty page. It is therefore a mistake to believe that this technique with just one or even several performances will complete the cure. It is true that love will fill the patient's soul but is not enough to transmute ill emotions entirely.

What we say is that the therapy does transmute thought-energies or negative emotions but those not transformed (not understood) are going to occupy the left hemisphere of the brain and stay there – explains the brother Elohim – the patient trusts in having reached a total cure, but not knowing how to maintain emotions balanced may have to repeat the entire healing process.

We therefore want you to remember that the patient must have complete understanding of the healing process and ascertain if he/she really worked, understood and transmuted the thought-emotion-energies – continues the brother Elohim – the healer on his/her part must again explain their origin, when they turned ill negative and during which life this occurred to help the patient avoid new errors.

Let us go back to what we explained in the beginning – suggests the brother Interano – only the patient, that is every one of you, can complete this healing process. You may need help on the way because you still do not have the knowledge to do it all by yourselves or just believe you cannot do it. This is when you call on healers and most will be of help. Nevertheless, the conclusion of any healing process is to make you understand the truth about your emotions. Words such as I am so sorry, please forgive me, I love you are therefore just the beginning of true healing – observes the sister Interana – the problem is that you (the patient) instead of working and understanding ill negative emotions make them pass from your Subconscious to your Unconscious. This means not conscious of them, that you will always carry them with you.

Nonetheless, when disincarnating the soul will be unable of taking the energy of those emotions to a reality of higher frequency since, hidden in the Unconscious, it could not understand and less work it. We therefore insist – remarks the brother Interano – that using techniques you often keep shifting ill negative emotion-energies back and forth without ever understanding, working and transmuting them. Similar occurs with the use of medical drugs, treatment of physical diseases, social and family relations, work etc.

With great affection, we recognize your efforts by using so far methods and procedures that do produce results. You, however, must be aware that they often suffer from distortion, fancy ideas of magic and miracles, mystery and egotism creating an atmosphere that affects the advance of a soul's energy. Control and certain manipulation of the healing process may have slowed your pace in life because of a healer's ego and economic interests or your ignorance of the very process – concludes the brother Seramita.

Knowing the profound truth of Cause and Effect, – says the brother Elohim – we insist that there is no better cure than healer and patient proceeding together, acting the healer with altruism to show the patient the way of the cure and the patient comprehending that healing needs all his/her determination and perseverance to occur.

"When this happens, JOYFULNESS in the heart will fill the mind with the Light of the day and lasting serenity since the transformation from negative to positive means SERENITY. There is FREEDOM when you live with the rhythm of nature and creativity, HAPPINESS because of an elevated enjoyment at every instant, SUCCESS for maintaining a balanced and objective behavior and finally WISDOM for being able to judge what is essential and what is not".

143. We have also a technique that helps us detect possible family conflicts transmitted from one generation to another that might determine present psychological disorders. It is not a genetic but rather cultural inheritance a person carries that, beyond individual teachings, has its origin in the particular family life of that person's parents, grandparents or distant relations. Would you consider this technique useful?

This type of technique correlates incarnated and disincarnated family members – replies the brother Elohim – as it allows incarnated members to establish an intimate contact with those who left them an inheritance of unworked and non-understood matters you call Karmas. The idea of this form of healing is to use a joint family nucleus for treating those trapped emotions to comprehend the Cause and Effect relationship. This technique works on stablished patterns of human emotions where members of the family should understand the structure – continues the sister Interana – these patterns are schematics and are based on human natures such as the daily routines, family, work and social relations of problems of the present.

It sometimes gives positive results but the passage of ill negative energy from one person to another can be detrimental owing to its power of contamination for an emotionally weak brain – says the brother Interano – we therefore advise against group healing as a general practice. Group healing as a form of psychological treatment also tends to stir other emotions with the risk of additional alterations.

As mentioned earlier – continues the sister Interana – these techniques can resolve the emotions of people in a group. However, those such as anger, bitterness, sadness, etc, that hide and contaminate other people come to light. By this we mean, – says the brother Interano – we are dealing here with low frequency energy that can severely affect persons who are prone to develop those emotions and even trigger collective hysteria.

These techniques of that kind are not entirely wrong because they always reveal the origin of some of the problems. Nevertheless, group treatment is not an appropriate manner to understand and work them – sustains the brother Interano – since it deals with emotions many of which do not concern some of the patients present because they already worked and transmuted them in past lives.

Whenever possible treatment should therefore be individual considering every patient's particular needs as the only way to determine the origin of the emotion and an appropriate therapy for it – concludes the sister Interana.

144. Can we use the frequency of musical sound waves for healing?

It is possible – replies the brother Elohim – if the vibration of the thought-energies' sound has the proper frequency. This obviously is not about the sound from musical instruments but a kind of music that energetic sound waves of the soul produce. Their resonance from the physical, mental and spiritual body is extremely important for your physical, and mental health – observes the brother Interano – this is why we emphasize so much the importance of your raising the vibration frequency, a frequency synonymous of Harmony, Peace, Light and Love. As conscious beings, you are capable of healing the energy through elevated sounds of your thought-energies but since you still move back and forth between the left and right brain hemisphere, you are keeping a low sound voltage instead of adjusting it to the resonance of the universal sound vibration frequency.

The natural vibration frequencies result from the friction of the crystals that form vast universal energies. These frequencies are joining light, time, space, matter, gravity and magnetism with your DNA code and conscience. The energies' sound frequency can modulate the vibration frequency of thought-energies thus producing the cure and improving the quality of life – continues the sister Interana – the condition for the process to work is the fact that the atoms of human cells react with the vibrational waves, which then spread throughout the electromagnetism.

Your failing to be in accord with the frequency of the universe is the main cause for the lack of harmony of your inner self while an adequate frequency of your inner music (sound) will be the key to reaching higher grades of energy flow. Positive emotions tend to flourish producing joyfulness and peace – concludes the brother Elohim – without this harmonious energetic flow, your inner music will express negative emotions and give rise to physical and mental disorders. Elevated inner music, instead, will help you be in symphony with the sphere of LIGHT and LOVE, habitat of the spirits of the universe and the beings of conscience and wisdom.

145. Is it true that we can heal using Chromo therapy?

Chromo therapy: The use of colors in healing has its origin in ancient Egypt. This treatment, today called chromo therapy, is a complementary treatment some physicians use to improve patients' health. Some professionals who specialize in alternative medicine employ

> colors to balance physical, emotional, mental or spiritual energies. According to them, colors influence sensations, thoughts and feelings... Using light with different colors on the human body, chromo therapy favors relaxation, strength, unblocking and projects a particular image or personality. Colors trigger reactions in the brain and conscience stimulating in most cases unconscious responses from the nervous system. Affirmations go that colors influence people's behavior and mood and that there is a relationship between people's character and their favorite color (Wikipedia).

Both Frequency and Color use similar concepts – replies the brother Interano – while the energy must vibrate at an elevated frequency and its crystals be in symphony with the frequency of the universe, the colors of the soul's energy have to be bright and diaphanous. However, bear always in mind that it is not the Technique of Chromo Therapy that cures you from physical or mental disorders but the inner colors that shine with your Thoughts, Actions and Deeds – observes the brother Elohim – we therefore wonder why you keep employing this deep inner knowledge to create techniques for miraculous treatments when the very knowledge of your soul offers you a "natural" cure.

Nor will colored stones on your bodies or the sight and mental visualization of colors cure your energy. Colors represent the significant emission of the body or soul's energy at a certain vibration frequency of sounds. True healing occurs when you raise this frequency to produce bright and diaphanous colors. Which way do you create those colors? On elevating your Thoughts, Actions and Deeds, energy crystals automatically start producing the proper frequency that will join the cosmic frequency – observes the sister Interana – likewise occurs with the colors of the crystals and the energy that forms the soul.

Do you know the origin of the words Christian Philosophy? – asks the sister Interana – Christian originates from CRYSTAL while Philosophy (in Greek FILO SOFIA) means LOVE FOR THE WISDOM, which makes Christian Philosophy the LOVE FOR THE WISDOM OF THE ENERGY CRYSTALS. The ancient knew this meaning but modern times distorted it causing confusion that keeps you from channeling the true meaning of this wording.

146. If techniques fail to reach the deep of the soul, what would you say is of true help for healing?

In fact, many techniques and teachings are far from reaching the soul – agrees the brother Elohim – because they just worry about the beauty of the house with paintings and flowers in the dining room etc. but omit to deal with the somber basement that hides things you have been accumulating in many lives. Perhaps those techniques let you enter this part of the house closed for so long and full of old dusty furniture, but leave you with no idea what to do with them?

You cannot live hiding ugly secrets by keeping up appearances – proceeds the sister Interana – such as sensations you are unable to face and the memory of sufferings, buried deep in a soul that is desperately looking for help. It is the basement of your lives, where the soul hides from the light of reality.

However, once you humbly admit that this basement exists – continues the brother Interano – you will have taken an important step to deal with it. Nowadays, multimedia communication allows you to learn about the many problems that you carry there. Not taking advantage of it could mean that you are unaware of this source of information or just unwilling to proceed because your concern for material needs is such that you seem not to find the time to deal with your inner self.

For this to occur, it takes discipline, order, determination, culture etc. In general, the beings of this planet have little interest for self-knowledge and rather seek the pleasure of the senses that an intense social life can provide. We therefore are trying to have you realize that the Awakening of Conscience means to be truly conscious of yourselves and the world around you – concludes the brother Elohim – this mental cleanup starts at home. If you are ready for it, you will succeed by using meditation and reflection, studying and analyzing your thoughts, actions and deeds.

Scrutinizing your emotions, you will understand and consequently be able to work and transform them, thus avoiding prejudice or errors of judgement. This means to recognize and correct mistakes that may affect others. Educating yourselves by making good reading a habit is therefore of great importance. This will help you deal better with certain rigid standards or distortions of education in society. On the path you travel, of great help, above, all will be your ability to learn from other persons by just listening.

If you feel you cannot do it alone, try looking for help from your family, friends, centers of studies or professionals for psychological and spiritual orientation. It is true that even the spiritual way for inner healing has a cost but there is abundant information available at a minimum charge if you only decide to activate your Desire of Creation. Always remember: If there is a will, there is a way.

147. How do you actually define Karma?

Karma in Sanskrit means: Source. It is the correlation of Causes and Effects that makes the Universe a place of Order – remarks the brother Interano – it is the growing cumulus of thoughts and emotions life after life with ill negative emotions proliferating and creating confuse situations. These situations mold the existence of every individual who passes a great deal of conflicts on to others, which results in immense collective ignorance and suffering. Therefore, being the Universal Order the reality of everything created – proceeds the sister Interana – in any of its thoughts, actions and deeds, the mind must procure to maintain this order. This concept has to permeate all states of conscience of the soul. Without that Order or Equilibrium, thought-energies tend to look for a solution in some other way to restore them.

Since the Desire of Creation or Procreation will always manifest its origin, those thought-energies are going to adjust to this expression. Consequently, a Karma emerges when thought-energies are unaware of the Cause and Effect relationship of that expression creating an energetic vortex that will block their freedom of expression.

Once people know and talk about the origin of their Karma, they will begin to control that vortex and the moment they really understand all its implications, there will be silence and that expression, in a positive way, have become a part of them.

148. Is it true that we should not neglect our daily routine while looking for the spiritual awakening? How do we manage to complete that transmutation toward the conception of our Baby-Spirit?

Could a woman abandon her daily routine keeping a distance from her loved ones only because she is expecting a baby? – observes the brother Interano – on the contrary, she will have to do the best she can within this particular true-to-life experience she is living. Thought-energy should never hide and always remain connected by interacting with other thought-energies. This and a great deal of information will help you continue the journey of return, on which every one of you must continue with a particular rhythm and understanding – proceeds the sister Interana – no prayers, rites and chants will take you to a different reality of existence. Only the objective of your thoughts, actions and deeds will allow the energy of your soul to reach the frequency that a subtle and higher reality will attract

149. Do we need solitude, silence and introspection for the transmutation of our emotions and elevation of our conscience to advance on the path of return?

A soul often needs a moment of silence for a better understanding of the reality it lives – agrees the brother Elohim – you call it Meditation. However, silence does not refer to stop communicating and expressing your feelings; – continues the brother Interano – it is rather transforming wrong expressions into Elevated Feelings that would result in a beings' thoughts, actions and deeds. True silence is the Innermost Wisdom from which a feeling without words emerges.

Therefore, while the books EL SER UNO needed to use words to transmit this message for you, the moment you finish reading all those words will have turned feelings of comprehension and plenitude – concludes the sister Interana – when Knowledge and Understanding become feelings, you no longer need words to express them. This is when your soul embraces silence, without the need for convincing itself and others of anything. Your soul just IS and will express itself through its attitude and example.

150. Is it true that to raise the energy of our soul and transcend this reality, we have to renounce sexual life?

Not at all – responds the brother Interano – sexuality as money, food and other material needs is energy that you have to handle properly. There is nothing wrong with sex unless you fail to live it without wisdom by distorting its functions and emotions. Sexuality is an essential part of the human-form of planet Tera to guarantee the preservation of the species and the solution we found for the incarnation of the divided and dissipated thought-energy. Sexual activity is pleasure of the senses. Now, if your senses were suffering from some form of distortion or degeneration, so would your sexual activity. Since sexual energy is fundamental in human life and associates intimately with the emotions, the solution is not to block it (no sexual life) but that every human being manages to cure and enjoy it with LIGHT and LOVE.

151. Is there a relation between the energy we all carry when incarnating and the signs of the zodiac that represent the four elements (earth, air, fire and water) with fire and earth absorbing the cinnabar energy, but air and water rejecting it?

We know that the planet's axis is making an upside down movement meaning the inversion of its magnetic poles. How will this affect astrological charts – ponders the brother Elohim – you all probably are asking yourselves that question. However, changes are imminent as the Cosmic Alignment is going to create a completely new panorama for the planet and its inhabitants. Consequently, the setting up and interpretation of astrological charts will have to be in the same way. An individual's zodiacal sign will change. For instance, those born under the sign of Libra will be Aries. This means that the present charts are no longer valid – proceeds the brother Interano – since the year, day and hour of birth are of no importance. You all will belong to one single sign: Aquarius – the brother pauses then goes on – souls are unifying. What until now had been predominant in the soul of each one of you, now you have to see and understand in a general way. Your souls are turning spirits and as universal bodies, spirits are not a part of the planet but belong to the universe and therefore do not allow the set-up of astrological charts based on the constellation between the planet and the zodiacal signs.

Aquarius: Symbolizes friendship, thirst for spirituality, fraternity, universal love; collective striving, trade-unions, revolutions, altruism, humanism; progress, technology, electronics, cybernetics, alternative medicine; vibration, rhythm, inventions; freedom, democracy, solidarity and union of peoples. Element: Air, Season: Winter; Character sociable, altruistic but also unpredictable and obstinate.

Aquarians have a strong and attractive personality. There are two types of Aquarians: one characterizes sensible and patient, the other exuberant individuals capable of hiding their true personality under a frivolous air. Both types know how to convince and make people see the truth but are ready to change their opinion if there were solid evidence for it. They have an ability to capture two or more aspects of an argument, which makes them one of the most tolerant and unprejudiced signs of the zodiac. They are open to accept the truth and ready to learn from others. Aquarians are humane, sincere, sophisticated idealists. They are perseverant and know how to make their point in a moderate and good-humored way. Intelligent and logical, many are psychic and have great imagination. However, sometimes they feel they need a distance from their environment for thinking and meditating. They never follow crowds but despite their open minds and the desire to help humanity, they do not seem to make friends nor open up their hearts (souls) easily.

Normally shy and calm, they also can be determined and even eccentric but are profound thinkers and always eager to lend a helping hand. Of great intellect, persons born under this sign are extraordinarily independent with logic following their intuition. The two personalities look at each other without prejudice, which makes it easy for them to solve problems. While perfectly adjusting to their environment, to restore their energy they need to be far from the crowd. “Imagination” characterizes Aquarians. They are capable of seeing a world of options even when it seems that there is none. Their element is Air, which makes them use their minds to find a solution in any situation. If there were no mental stimulus, they would miss the motivation to strive for a better result. Uranus governs Aquarius. Though a planet of aggressive nature, it makes Aquarians develop visionary qualities helping them anticipate events some five or ten days away. It also allows them to adopt quick changes, which makes Aquarius the sign of thoughtful, progressive and humane human beings who enjoy group or team spirit.

Aquarius is the guardian of the water that cures people, animals and plants and stands for the continuity of life. This is why Aquarians are so eager to feel that they are a part of the life cycle and will do anything for its preservation. Their delicate parts are wrists and the circulatory system. For good health care, frequent check-ups by a doctor are therefore the best thing to look for. The worst thing for them to feel is limitation. Their desire for freedom and equal rights for all will always make them seek to act and speak freely. On the other hand, they have a reputation of discreetness and seem to lack empathy. This, however, is to prevent a relationship from getting to close at the beginning. With the passing of time, they learn to trust other persons and show their feelings (Dictionary of Symbols).

Let us go back to what we said about the transformation of your souls into spirits. Similar occurs with the elements – observes the sister Interana – because until now you lived with the four elements Earth, Water, Fire and Air. The Age of Aquarius will add Ether and Helium. You no longer can predict the elements present at your birth since awaked parents will give their children the six elements with the conception. This is why there are special crystal and indigo children. All those AWAKED souls that incarnated some 60 years ago as well as those that are going to incarnate during the first 200 years of the Cosmic Alignment will belong to the universe. They are free and the planet will have to consider them souls that no longer fit in an astrological chart or correspond to some sign of the zodiac because this was when the souls answered to the laws of the planet and the Karma after incarnating.

152. Does this mean that reading the cards, divination, premonition etc. does not work anymore?

In fact, no AWAKED human being nor those who incarnate during the 7000 years of the Cosmic Alignment will need any of it because they no longer subject to the planetary canons after having conceived their spirit. Nevertheless, souls that fail to transcend denseness will be unable to elevate during the Alignment and do have to continue the cycle of incarnating and disincarnating. This means that their energy will adjust to the very vibration frequency of the planet, their inheritance and lineage that comes with procreation but owing to cosmic changes their astrological charts will certainly have to consider the new planetary and cosmic parameters.

153. Comments are that there will be two suns. How is this possible?

As so often, you are trying to explain symbolism using only physical evidence. The appearance of two suns refers to the Star Sun and the Inner Sun of your Pineal Gland – observes the brother Elohim – the relationship of both represents the union of Cosmic and Human energy. However, you should use your knowledge of the Pineal Gland, your psyche's big mystery and according to scientists the source of Melatonin, rather than only the symbolism of astrology to understand their "interaction". The impact of solar radiation is important because it is responsible for altering the production of Melatonin, a chemical element that functions as a neurotransmitter to balance the biorhythm of your sleep – concludes the sister Interana.

Defined the functions of the physical Pineal Gland, let us have a look at the activity of the Inner Sun of the soul's Pineal Gland – suggests the brother Elohim – to begin with, it perceives the invisible inner LIGHT in the form of a magnetic field in your thoughts' Nimeos-Energy. This inner LIGHT is what you call the Third Eye or Rima Gland, situated between your eyes. The Third Eye is the soul's holographical vision allowing a perception with the inner senses. It is the dimensional gate, through which the human brain perceives the realities of other dimensions. Your Spirit reigns in the Pineal Gland where it reincarnates over and again until completing the formation of the Energetic Being – proceeds the sister Interana – electromagnetic energy is going to help open that cosmic gate whose photonic LIGHT from the inner Sun will provide humans with this special energy raising their thoughts and greatly illuminating their cognitive abilities. The teachings of important personalities in human history always highlighted that illumination through the Third Eye (Rima Gland), which through the inner senses captures the profound changes of human conscience.

154. Trying to live according to your teachings with harmony and peace, little emotional devils, when less expected, make us feel as if what we are doing is in vain, causing sadness and dejection. How do we keep our equanimity to overcome those doubts?

You may have forgotten that you are Probability, the X Factor – reminds the brother Elohim – you must pay close attention to this factor, on which you still have to work. Let us have a look at the way it functions.

Some 150 years ago, humans still lived very much their lives in accordance with the external senses. Brain zones one and two dominated prevailing instinct and sensation. They lacked the capacity to decode scientifically the psychological behavior of the thought-energies because their brains did not know how to shape them appropriately failing to understand, correlate or handle the inner language of emotions and dreams.

After great thinkers and investigators of the human mind started discovering their nature, important and long-hidden mysteries in the psyche surfaced. Humans began to study themselves becoming aware that they were more than just physical bodies but another different reality that connected with others to make them truly understand themselves and the world around them.

As they went along, their cognitive capacity activated the Time Clock (sand hour). You may wonder what this means – says the sister Interana – it is your Biological Clock within the X Factor represented by the figure eight, symbol of The Infinite.

The Time Clock has been with you since the creation of the human-form. We installed it considering that humans would have a biological

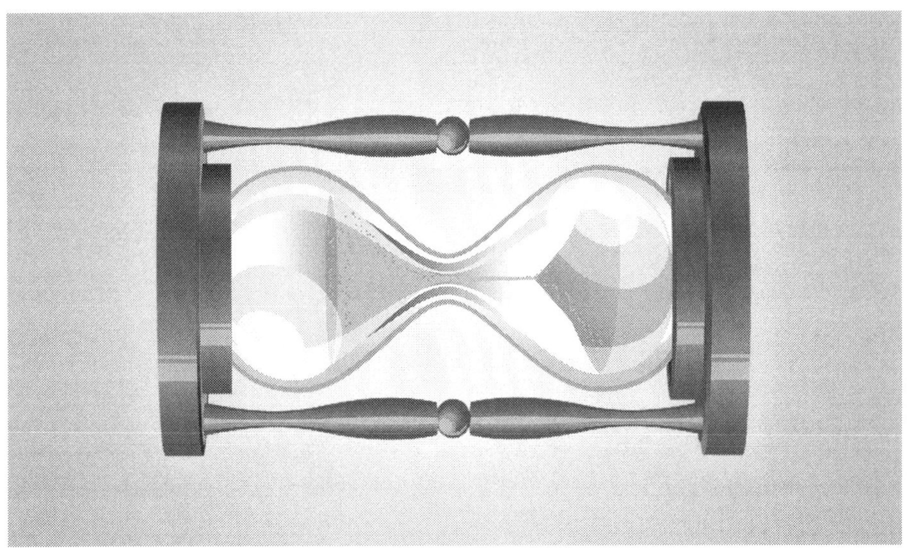

development to be able to continue their evolution. For a long time, it functioned horizontally on purpose because it would time allow to transcend the left and go to right brain hemisphere. This process favored the evolution but was very slow. Anyway, while the brain kept advancing, the Time Clock was marking humans' evolution.

As of July 7th, 2014, the Time Clock will be in vertical position in the cosmos, the planet and in human beings to mark the first three hours meaning the first three hundred years of the Cosmic Alignment of humans and the planet with the Energy of the Universal Mind. This is when humans and planet Tera are going to define their thought-energies.

Souls that fail to control and transmute ill negative thoughts will be denser and denser turning dark, petrified and remaining prisoners of materiality. Those healing and transmuting their thought-energies are going to leave denseness behind and prepare for the Internal City to continue the learning process, elevation of their energy and the three final months of gestation of their Baby-Spirit.

155. How does the Time Clock work?

The Time Clock or Infinite eight, as you know it from earlier explanations denotes the passage of thought-energy from the left to the right hemisphere of the brain – observes the brother Elohim – for thousands of years, its exclusive function was to provide the brain, habitat of the soul, with a maximum of thought-energy for the evolution of the human-form.

The Time Clock always functioned in a horizontal position occupying the center of the Solar Plexus and passing through the chest and arms of a person. The narrowest point where this passing energy crosses the Solar Plexus we named the X Factor. In this position, it greatly helped humans' evolution by nurturing one brain side the other. In most individuals, it still works this way and many will never change it because they do not know how or firmly hold on to lives of materiality.

You therefore will meet with very intelligent and professional people, particularly in science and technology, denoting advanced evolution but only an incipient elevation. On the other hand, those who predominantly seek to satisfy a desire for material goods, fail to control ambition or correct distortions, certainly have little or no elevation – proceeds the sister Interana.

In the horizontal position, the Time Clock's ill negative thought-energies and emotions are wandering from one side to the other. It therefore is unable of turning them into a vertical position to work and transmute them so that the superior reality of its universe might return those negative energies to the left-brain side and once worked, take them to the right side for nurturing the Baby-Spirit.

Human beings who have experienced the Awakening of Conscience, care for their spiritual progress and, satisfying their souls' need, seek to follow the advance of the energy that the spirit demands. This means that they are about to move the Time Clock into the correct vertical position. From there, they will be able to transmute low quality energy and

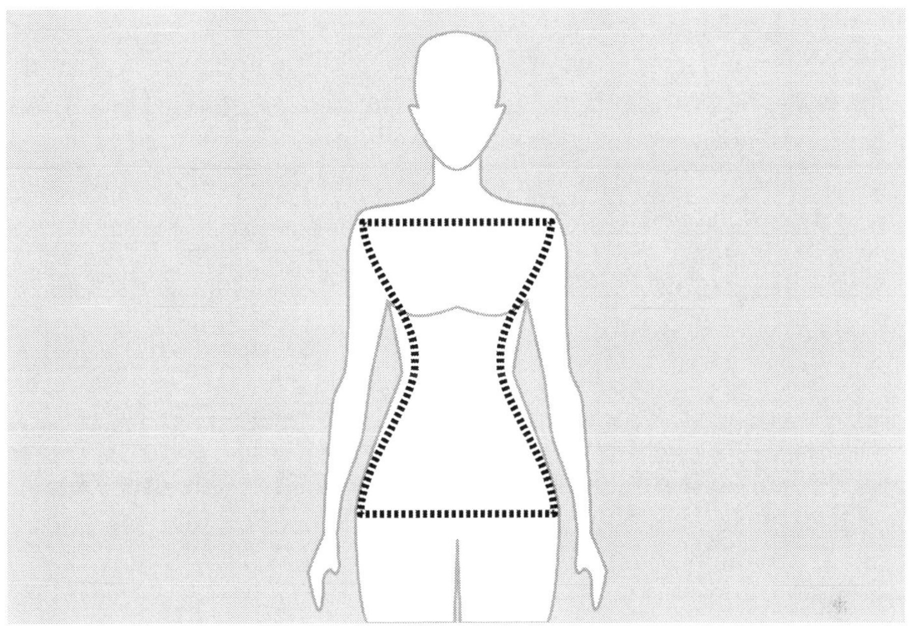

take it to the left side of the brain. Transformed by this inner work into sound thought-energies, these will go to the right side or Pineal Gland where the Baby-Spirit receives them to grow.

Once humans' Time Clock works in the vertical position, countdown of their spiritual elevation begins when they will be able to join one of the three departures souls will make during the Cosmic Alignment starting July 7th, 2014 – observes the sister Interana – with the Time Clock in that position, human' food turns nourishment, which is how they will raise the chakras and kundalini of their thought-energies.

Nevertheless, to turn the hands of the Time Clock, they had to fill the domes of the Pineal, Pituitary and Rima Glands with information from the brain. Consequently, their souls had been able to expand knowledge, understanding and love – affirms the brother Elohim – the clock reached its maximum expression when, moved by its weight, turned from the horizontal into the vertical position and dense thoughts descended to its lower part, the location of the first chakra.

This lower part of the Time Clock is replete with ill negative emotions and dense thoughts that occupy the inferior chakras waiting for you to take them to the left side of the brain to understand transmute and cure them. Nevertheless, before they rise to traverse the Solar Plexus, center of emotions, the sorting out of those that are ill and useless must already start in the first Energy Center through the infinite figure eight, now in the vertical position. Imagine a collecting device following the pointed line on the above figure picking them up over and again and taking them to the left hemisphere of the brain – remarks the brother Interano – this device will descend from the right side of the brain, cross the X Factor and finally reach the chakras below the navel. Reaching chakra one, it proceeds to chakra two, three and four. Ascending further, it crosses again the X Factor picking up those emotions that had remained in the deep of the soul. However, the device will reach the higher chakras beyond the X Factor only after having recycled other ill negative energies of the Solar Plexus. When finally occupying the left side of the brain, it will discharge all those emotions it noticed on its way. Should the brain fail to understand this recurrent process, it will feel confused, sad and discouraged.

Misunderstanding the process, the brain will be accumulating the defective thought-energy it cannot recycle and cause this energy to descend through the nervous system contaminating everything in its way. This is how multiple disease spreads in organs and systems of the physical body and deteriorates matter energy to the point of being unable to execute orders from the brain. If humans understood and worked those emotions of the Solar Plexus, they would be able to transmute them into feelings to occupy the right hemisphere of the brain and nurture the Baby-Spirit helping it reach safe and sound its fifth month of gestation. By raising the transformed emotions, the lower part of the Time Clock will remain empty allowing the soul to distance from materiality, start transcending this reality and prepare for the Internal City of LIGHT and LOVE.

We sent you a great deal of information through the Crop Circles explaining this knowledge and will go on doing so – remarks the brother Interano – the below figure supposedly appeared on June 25th, 2013 at Silbury Hill, Nr. Avebury, Wiltshire/England. Although allowing a number of interpretations, it well could represent a large Sand Hour that shows a cross – standing for humanity – on the side where the sand (time) seems to be running out – observes the sister Interana...

156. What shall we do when this happens?

You certainly remember our arrival as depicted in the first book – says the brother Elohim – when entering this reality, the first thing we saw was an agonizing antimatter crystal with an imperceptible beat, unable to move.

Therefore, we created a parallel and ethereal replicate. Nevertheless, this replicate turned a shadow of itself and became dense and opaque because its elements lacked the brightness of the original crystal. It was just a bizarre twin.

On cleaning the original crystal, we found that the disease from Satien had become a part of the opaque crystal without light. Thus, we did save the original anti-matter crystal but should also have transmuted its shadow since the Universal Mind is light without shadows. Our task has since been to eliminate the shadow, under which the disease spread neutralizing understanding but where we decided to incarnate in the human-form to explore the darkness. This was the only way to vanquish the dreadful influence of Satien's energy.

After creating the shadow (replicate), we realized that we found ourselves in a bizarre environment where our deepest thoughts had become reality. Observing them, we were able to know our true nature from deep inside our minds.

You are not what you think you are. You are a part of our souls but at the same time the shadows of non-understanding, not understood thought-energies and the subconscious deep inside our souls.

From the Anti-matter reality where we are, our unworked and not comprehended thoughts separate and occupy the shadows we created. In fact, we all are Soul Mates when, understanding what occurs, join to become ONE. You therefore have to return to your origin, to our spirits of LIGHT and LOVE. The Internal City hopes to receive you soon for the celebration of a reunion restoring thus our alliance of the past.

157. What would be the proper system and material for Hydroponics? We understand that the use of plastic devices is inappropriate owing to the presence of cinnabar energy (oil contaminants). Is it convenient to install a pump to keep water with nutrients circulating? What would be the quality of water to use? Should we operate an in-door system receiving sunlight through large windows or rather decide on an open-air operation?

In fact, operation of Hydroponics should NOT use plastic or metal apparatus. We suggest the use of glass or wooden devices as well as a water pump for circulation – replies the sister Interana.

You should use running Mineral Water without additives from rivers, lakes or similar natural sources. For this type of plant growing, the devices should receive indirect solar radiation to prevent water from heating.

158. What actions should we take regarding current armed conflicts employing chemical weapons? Would giving the Nimeos of those arms the order to transmute their malign into sound or

innocuous energy work? Could a single person succeed in producing this change or would it take hundreds of individuals?

In fact, it would take hundreds of thousands – replies the brother Interano – the forces of darkness, BELOVED BROTHERS and SISTERS, keep using the energy of fear of military power based on massive arms production and trade, involving huge economic interests, to terrify the planet. Despite important nuclear arms treaties, "but not all that glitters is gold", there are ancient ambitions for power and enormous karmas that the ill negative emotions of incarnated souls carry from past lives.

We say that "standing united", positive thoughts, firm decisions and actions made it possible to block escalation toward a planet-wide war – concludes the brother Elohim – in spite of powerful interests, the forces of darkness failed to resist the strength of thousands of millions of human beings asking the universe for PEACE on Earth.

This proves that thoughts can move mountains. The souls and hearts with LIGHT and LOVE of a vast number of persons generated the extraordinary power to prevent humanity from suffering another devastating disaster.

159. What is the meaning of the image on the front cover of the books EL SER UNO?

This image represents the nine dimensions where all that exists lives and develops – replies the brother Elohim – you call it the Flower of Life, which is the Pineal Gland of EL SER UNO, source of the One Origin's ideas, where our thought-energies enter and leave in an infinite cycle fulfilling the desire of the creator's extraordinary ideas of LIGHT and LOVE.

Each part of the image stands for a grade, plane and dimension appearing in this form in the Macro and Micro Cosmos and owing their existence to the creativity of the Flower of Life – continues the sister Interana – we have projected this image in a plain way for easier understanding, but you should consider that it actually presents itself in 3D – 4D – 5D – 6D – 7D – 8D and 9D, the comprehension of which your current technology, however, does not yet allow.

Let us now use imagination – suggests the brother Interano – since the image you appreciate is never a static one. Always moving, it continuously adjusts to the conception and gestation of a new idea from the Pineal Gland of EL SER UNO. With the conception of the idea, all dimensions join up to form a flower that points to the center.

When this occurs, the dimensions or petals of the Flower of Life open up giving rise to the Big Bang and launching this new idea to the confines of the universe. After the dimensions have assimilated the idea, its gestation and execution will begin. This process resembles pollination in the plant kingdom.

We say that this is what happens in the Pineal Glands of all human beings because everything repeats in the universe. The thoughts that align in your brains and souls are aiming at a different reality of life and existence. By elevating your thought-energy, you are creating a new parallel antimatter Earth that will shelter souls that with determination and perseverance have transformed their dense into subtle energy.

Depending on the type of idea – proceeds the brother Elohim – the petals adjust and combine its requirements, which makes, for example, number one join number six or number four number two.

Since the One Origin never stops creating by opening and closing the Flower with extraordinary celerity, only the Sublime, Divine, Ethereal and Perfect Dimensions that surround it are going to understand the idea's vibration frequency, rhythm and colors expressing it with the celerity of their creativity.

The other dimensions will have to wait for these superior dimensions to transmit the meaning of that idea. Once it reaches your Primary Dimension, the Secondary Dimension will be responsible for helping you comprehend its exact meaning – ends by saying the sister Interana.

With the beginning of the Cosmic Alignment on July 7th, 2014, the human brain zones will adjust to the vertical figure eight and align with the thoughts of the universe – proceeds the sister Interana – thus, souls and spirits will become a part of the new universal idea of LIGHT and LOVE. However, for this to occur, they must open their minds to share personal, planetary and cosmic transformations. Inflexible minds will fail to adjust to these new ideas of the cosmos remaining trapped in obsolete concepts and beliefs.

This is what happens in your Pineal Gland – emphasizes the brother Interano – the Flower of Life nurtures itself with new thoughts, which makes its petals vibrate in higher frequencies resulting in new ideas with advanced Knowledge, Understanding and Love. This nourishment from more developed realities becomes stronger with the beginning of the Cosmic Alignment.

160. A CROP CIRCLE located at Hod Hill – North Hanford Dorset/UK discovered June 1st, 2014 symbolizes EL SER UNO and the announcement of the beginning of the Cosmic Alignment by the Elder Brothers Ayaplianos. In this sixth and last book, the Brothers explain the perfect lines and their meaning of this most interesting crop circle saying that we are going to receive more signs from them, the planet and the cosmos.

Meaning of this crop circle

This Crop Circle was found on June 1st, 2014 in England. It is the symbol of EL SER UNO. This Crop Circle shows the nine dimensions of the universe that represent the Pineal Gland of EL SER UNO and therefore the One Origin or what you call the Flower of Life – comments the brother Interano – the nine dimensions move at an incredible speed in the form of a flower whose petals flutter and rotate in a constant up and down movement. This movement makes the petals capture the creation of the One Origin's new Cosmic Ideas.

You of the Primary Dimension have not yet developed the condition to read the symbolism of these movements and ideas emanating from the Pineal Gland of EL SER UNO, which the superior dimensions handle perfectly. They perceive, analyze, understand and transmit them in a way to the Regular, Secondary, Primary, Inferior and Creativity Dimensions that allows these to assimilate and execute them in accordance with their particular conditions of comprehension.

The larger circular figure of the Crop Circle represents the Pineal Gland of EL SER UNO, the smaller one planet Earth, connected through an umbilical cord with the One Origin but not integrated into EL SER UNO – continues explaining the sister Interana – most incarnated and

disincarnated souls of planet Earth still are building their Energetic Being (spirit) and therefore following the process of Conception and Gestation meaning the AWAKENING of CONSCIENCE.

Once concluded this process, they will become a part of and participate in the important thoughts and ideas of EL SER UNO. With their integration, they will be EL SER UNO. After all souls of planet Earth formed their spirit, the umbilical cord will break. However, before the New Antimatter-Tera-Cell or New Tera can join the dimensions of LIGHT and LOVE, it will have to pass through every one of them until finally enter the Pineal Gland of EL SER UNO and thus the Creativity of the Universal Mind as a true Living-Antimatter Cell.

161. Many of us understand what you explain in the books but what happens to those who do not or never met with this knowledge.

When talking of the unification of EL SER UNO, – observes he brother Elohim – we cannot expect all human beings to have the necessary knowledge nor does elevation depend on the books – the brother makes a pause and proceeds – what is important is that you raise the energy frequency of your beliefs and of how you lead your lives. Neither reading or not reading the bible and the books EL SER UNO nor following closely the teachings of Ascended Masters, will help with the elevation of a soul's frequency. It all depends on your essential inner values, worked-on emotions transmuted into universal feelings and true conscience of not falling victims to illusion and fantasy.

The intenseness and continuity of every one's inner work will mark the difference among the souls. However, neither religious faith, spiritual guidance nor the size of your library will make you vibrate in accordance with the Vibration of the Universe if you do not to listen to the voice of your soul to understand the importance of Compassion and Love – concludes the sister Interano.

162. Which way will we become ONE?

To become ONE in the universe does not mean to live, talk, dress and behave as OTHERS do – advises the brother Elohim – but rather to show that you share the universal vibration frequency, rhythm and colors with other human beings no matter their ethnicity, language, beliefs and customs.

Whatever prayers, techniques, methods, chants, meditation and mental exercise you may use, most important for reaching the necessary frequency are ACTIONS, DEEDS and the true positive INTENTION of the soul. Becoming eventually, ONE means to embrace Knowledge, Understanding and Love of the COSMIC CANON of the ONE.

"El SER UNO is a phase in the journey of the soul, a fountain of cosmic water to quench the thirst of the Spirit. It is a place for travelers to stay and live for some time to gain true-to-life experience through

Knowledge, Understanding and Love. Duly provided, they set out again looking for other phases and sources to show their Hearts and Souls the path toward LIGHT and UNIVERSAL LOVE. Cosmic travelers will come across thousands of sources in their infinite existence. It is the souls' journey of return to the place from which they came, the ONE ORIGIN"... EL SER UNO

163. A week ago, a plane of the Malaysia Airlines crashed. Since rescue operations were unable to determine the area of the accident, rumors on the internet go that the Intergalactic Federation of the Internal City hijacked the plane. Is there any truth in this?

MESSAGE from the Elder Brothers Ayaplianos regarding THE LOSS OF THE MALAYSIAN AIRLINER

"You should not seek the Awakening of Conscience through speculations, inventions and fantasies in the form of a competition where Egos strive to prevail. The soul's truth does not consist in trusting the information or not but how every one of you feels about it. Do you really believe that we your Elder Brothers Ayaplianos of the Internal City of Atlantis would hijack an airplane with 239 passengers in a demonstration of power before the governments of the planet? How could we who live and work with LIGHT and LOVE inflict on those passengers and their families sufferings of fear and pain?...

Brothers, pay attention and feel the voice of your hearts and souls. Beware of the power of negative thoughts. They are as harmful as a virus affecting your innermost beliefs and work of LIGHT and LOVE. The truth never remains hidden; it sometimes takes time but eventually becomes known. Raise your thought-energies with Peace and Harmony in memory of the passengers who disincarnated and for all the families who accept with resignation but deep affection the loss of their loved ones (end of the message from the Elder Brothers Ayaplianos of the Internal City of Atlantis)". (03/21/2014)

May this message help you understand the need for inner work with discipline and humility – says the sister Interana – and that EL SER UNO has not come to argue over premonition or divination. EL SER UNO is a knowledge of LIGHT and LOVE to help you use intuition by working with your soul in silence. It is each individual's Free Will to decide on living the turbulence of a river that is the exterior or the tranquil waters of the inner world. Life presents thousands of challenges forcing you to sort them out and decide on how to deal with them.

Not prophecies, omens or prediction will help with your spiritual elevation but an arduous and conscious endeavor day in, day out, to fill your souls with the Universal Wisdom of Knowledge, Understanding and Love.

Message received through channeling in March 2014.

CHAPTER III

A BROTHER OF THE SEAS

Looking at each one of them, I thank them for having answered so readily all my questions. Since you seem not to have any further question – proceeds the sister Interana – we wish to continue our conversation to give you another important information: the Knowledge of a species unknown to you that until now is just a part of human mythology. This species does exist having undergone a process of evolution similar to yours but, for some time already, is on its path of return.

There is a moment of silence. Then the brother Elohim addresses me saying: We have discussed an important number of issues in the previous books, answered many questions but spared this information for the sixth and last book. The reason is that we first had to transmit all you know now to prepare you for this final knowledge – proceeds the sister Interana – it is time for you now to know about the existence of other brothers and sisters of the species whom you never saw or met but whose presence many of you never doubted.

Old books call them children of the gods while legends describe them as having special powers, but no one actually knows anything about them nor about the deep of their habitat, the seas – continues the brother Interano – where innumerable species remain undiscovered. It will surprise you to learn about their real characteristics because in ancient times people considered them sinister marine monsters with huge eyes and sharp teeth producing terrifying guttural sounds. There might be some truth in those visions, but they evolved and developed their true Ayapliano nature. We therefore can say that they are ready to continue evolution and elevation and eventually return to their origin.

May we introduce to you – says the brother Elohim – the BROTHER AYAPLIANO SIREN-LEMURIANO that you know as Sirens (females) and Tritons (males). We call them LEMURIANOS and are going to tell you everything about them so they may join and try helping you prepare for the return to your origin, The Pleiades.

This is how their story begins…

It all starts at Lemuria – proceeds the brother Seramita – where the brothers and sisters Ayapliano-Siren-Lemurianos built their physical reality.

AYAPLIANOS-SIREN-LEMURIANOS

Millions of years back in Tera time, we came to this reality in the form of LIGHT (and stayed for a long time in our Bubble-Sphere-Spacecraft as related in the books) – reminds the brother Seramita – proceeding to in-depth studies of the environment, a very dense and dark reality entirely unknown to us, before we decided on leaving the spacecraft.

We were replicate energies of ourselves traveling at the speed of thought lacking physical bodies but were able to descend protected by the Bubble-Sphere that had adjusted to the denseness, gravity and all that existed and still exists on the planet. Our mission was to cure the Tera-Cell and return to our origin.

At that time, – continues the brother Interano – the planet's surface did not have continents consisting of one solid land mass called Pangea surrounded by the large Panthalassa Ocean and presenting extremely low and high temperatures at the same time. With the passing of time, Pangea divided into Laurasia comprising North America, Europe, Asia and Gondwana formed by South America, Africa, the Antarctica, India

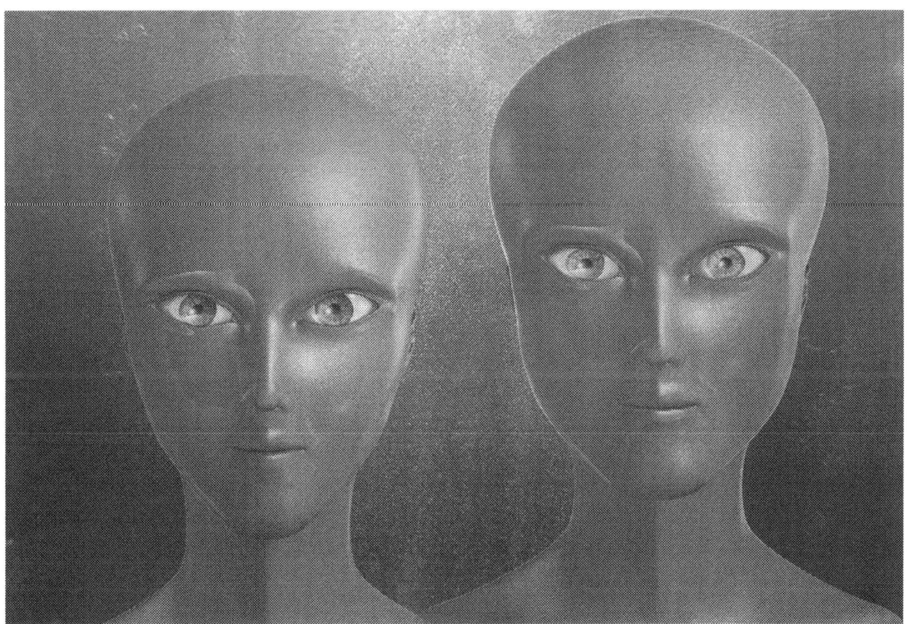

and Austral Asia. As related in *EL SER UNO I – The Arcana of Thoth,* we had to stay for three hundred million years Tera time in the Bubble-Sphere-Spacecraft where we developed the dense physical bodies in which we had to incarnate to become a part of our Ayapliano species settlement in Tera.

Our task had been to imagine the human-form using our Desires of Creation and produce a dense human-thought-hologram to be able to incarnate in our own thoughts and visit the surface. To do so, we first created a dense cone crystal duplicate and gave it the Breath of Life, thus forming an Astral Body that would shelter us and other energy across the planet, which had no other way to go.

In this dense reality, it took our Desires of Creation such a long time to manifest themselves that they failed to execute their thoughts in the imagined forms, which gave rise to strange variations. The number of expressions of our minds was such that we created innumerable dense-forms with the passing of time, the animal and plant kingdoms, among them. However, we continued imagining thus coming closer and closer to the dense expression of the human-form that would allow us to leave the Bubble-Spheres to explore this strange new reality.

On replicating an ethereal crystal clone from a material crystal clone, – says the sister Interana – we were building the Northern-Cone-Internal City of Lemur that ever since shelters us. At this Internal-Antimatter City, we imagined every single life form on the planet you call Earth. While doing so, we also were able to build a material version of Lemur in the exterior naming it the Material City of Lemuria to receive us when the time would come.

Our priority continued to be the creation of a Human-Form that would preserve all our characteristics within this dense reality. However, while imagining this human form without succeeding to realize our true Desire of Creation, we were creating bizarre forms of creatures that started developing on the surface or in the watered-down quartz crystals generated by the Interstellar Cosmic Federation.

When we came to the planet, part of the animal and plant kingdoms already existed since the cosmic dust in the universe, similar to plant pollen and via a steady energy flow takes life to one planet after another. However, everything was in a very primary phase and fluctuating elements joined in a most surprising way.

We must emphasize again that despite living in an ethereal-crystal-cone, we had great difficulties in realizing our Desire of Creation because the imagined perfect human-form, once introduced into in the matter-crystal-cone, presented distortion showing unexpected characteristics. The subtle turned grotesque denoting once again the negative impact of the Satien fragment having contaminated the planet matter as well as the plant and a part of the animal kingdoms. Thus, the life forms we created under the influence of reptilian energy resulted in creatures of reptilian aspect that expanded until reaching full growth. On perceiving the extremely harmful and dangerous contamination of the exterior, we started creating life in the watered-down quartz that had turned oceans, rivers and lakes – observes the brother Elohim – we realized that life in liquefied quartz did not suffer from distortion as it did on the surface and therefore risked to create human life there. On the other hand, we noted that some under water species in the course of evolution emerged to continue their development in the exterior.

Consequently, we predominantly used our Desire of Creation to create human life in the water. The first forms did not quite meet that desire but gradually advanced. We, however, remained in general unsatisfied with their development because they only could subsist by extracting oxygen from the watered-down quartz and not from the atmosphere of the surface as we had hoped.

At that time, we created the Ayapliano-Siren-Lemurianos. Our idea had been that they should start developing under water and after reaching a certain advance, emerge to continue their evolution in the exterior. After an extensive period of experiments and adjustments, a part of this human-form eventually managed to leave the deep waters and adapt to the conditions of the planet's surface.

The need to live in the exterior made the individuals of this human form develop more and more in accordance with our Desires of Creation. They started evolving by adapting their eyes, skin and inner organs to the sunlight and, at the same time, shared the process of evolution with another creature of their new habitat, the monkey, with whom they fraternally and harmoniously coexisted. Before we decided on developing the human-form, we had created dolphins, whales and several other marine creatures to help us advance toward the human-form. However, despite having some human characteristics, these did not evolve in that direction and therefore never could leave their watered-down crystal habitat, the oceans and rivers.

After the human-form had emerged from the water, we knew that our Desire of Creation had finally come true, and it all now depended on its further advance. From now on, our task was to help with its development by instilling our DNA in it and thus mark the correct course of evolution. Humans in the exterior of Tera evolved during millions of years and we have been, are and will always be responsible for following up on this evolution introducing corrections, whenever they might be necessary. Meanwhile, other life forms we created in the exterior advanced in their evolution. One of them was the Monkey, a human-like creature building ties between the two species in fraternal coexistence.

Despite obvious differences, the human-form did identify with its brother, the Monkey. There was a time when they were very much alike regarding the way they behaved and assumed their respective identities. While at the same time the human-form in the exterior developed creativity, the other human-form in the watered quartz grew characteristics of evolution of its own. Nevertheless, Ayaplianos-Siren-Lemurianos and Ayaplianos-Humans are brothers of the same origin and both very close to reach the highest expression of evolution and elevation.

164. How did you manage to create the human-form with your thoughts?

We are children of the Universal Mind; therefore, our thought-energies have this ability – replies the brother Seramita – it created us to its image making our creativity match with that of the One Origin.

165. May we Thought-Children achieve whatever we wish by just using thought and the Desire of Creation?

Yes, you may – replies the sister Interana – but all depends on the Desire of Creation, as it will occur with the vibration frequency of your desire. Whatever your Desires of Creation or Procreation, they will materialize when time is right. The vibration frequency of those desires will determine when but never impede it to occur. The more elevated the thought-energy and closer it is to the One Origin, the better and faster will be the creation. We call this STATES OF CONSCIENCE.

> ***States of Conscience:*** The state of conscience is one in which all Superior Neurocognitive functions are active allowing the perception of both individual and environmental psychical knowledge. In medicine, the states of conscience are subject to studies of psychiatry, psychology, physiology and neuroscience in close collaboration with physics to explain the function of synaptic connections in the brain. These studies have focused on altered states of conscience from a physiological perspective. Consequently, to explain the type of alteration, they use the dynamic of neurotransmitters and over or under stimulated brain zones.
>
> When studying the mental manifestations of saints or mystics such as visions, ecstasies etc., scientists classify them as pathologies due to neurochemical alterations of the brain. The state of conscience presents a number of phenotypes of which good examples are sleep

and wakefulness. Modifies states of conscience may show induced or artificially altered phases of wakefulness.
Drugs or discussions, autosuggestion, hypnosis, meditation but also exhaustion, insomnia, fasting, dehydration, intoxication, manias and schizophrenia may cause those altered phases. It is, however, important to differentiate mental states from states of conscience. While mental states are subjective that is only the individual registers them, the different states of conscience are objective meaning that a third party may perceive them (Dictionary).

There are neither false nor true realities but just the perception or not of them, meaning different STATES OF CONSCIENCE – observes the brother Interano – the all where we are we call the UNIVERSAL MIND...Where will we be in that mind? Where we will find answers. Therefore, whatever our reality, we always must be aware of that reality.

166. If you are elevated spirits, why did you have such difficulties to make the human-form?

At our habitat, the Ethereal-Cone or Internal-Antimatter City we never had any problem to create the human-form in our thoughts – replies the brother Elohim – but when introducing the imagined form into the dense Matter-Cone, this material human-form suffered serious deformation. Similar may occur when you, after creating a thought-desire in your imagination, fail to turn it into a material reality. Our true difficulty was that the energy of the Matter-Cone forming this perfectly imagined human-form turned out to be distorted and ill.

167. What about that part of the plant and animal kingdoms created by the Cosmic Confederation?

In fact, both the Confederation and we are responsible for the creation of prototypes imagined at the Ethereal-Cone and later introduced in the Matter-Cone for learning about the process of transformation of our Desires of Creation – replies the brother Seramita.

168. How did you divide the Matter-Cone to form the Ethereal-Cone?

We make an energy duplicate – replies the brother Elohim – imagine the formation of cones by rotating triangles with their basis in the center and points in a superior and inferior position, which, overlapping, will form the six-pointed Star. What we have to do then is to close the triangles of these cones as if they were wings of a butterfly. When covering each other they form a wormhole, through which our thoughts are going to pass from one reality to another.

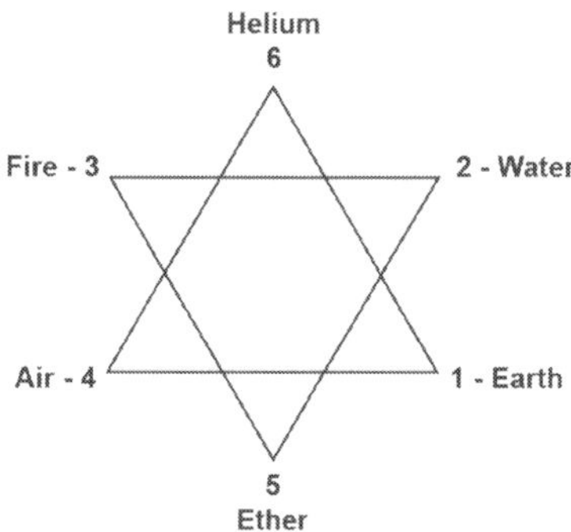

169. Did you this way pass the ethereal human-form from one reality to another?

This is what we did by introducing the imagined human-form in the watered-down quartz crystals of the dense Matter-Cone, since in this subaqueous environment the material human-form presented less deformation than in the exterior – explains the sister Interana – we sincerely regret the severe deformations that occurred in the beginning with the appearance of terrifying creatures, many of which have survived in the deep of the seas and in the exterior. However, the human-form's structure gradually gained stability. Today we dominate this dense energy and use it wherever we feel convenient.

170. Did those human-forms you created under water emerge and mix with us in the exterior?

We continue creating human-forms that host our minds allowing us to follow up on whatever concerns the evolution and elevation of the planet and you – says the brother Interano – those human-forms that move among you are palpable holograms that we created for particular tasks of observation and study of the exterior. Once we consider them to have completed their work, we withdraw them.

171. Would this not be a kind of espionage?

We only do this to study and analyze the advance of the energy at all levels – replies the brother Elohim – our state of conscience would never allow us to think and act for any other reason.

172. Do governments know about this?

Yes, they do but fail to comprehend our good intentions and do not want us to intervene in the advance of evolution and elevation. With no belief in the spiritual way, power, ambition, distrust, invested interests, control and manipulation reign in the exterior.

173. Do ghosts or souls make this transition as well?

No, – replies the brother Interano – they do not go from one reality to another because they live in the electromagnetism of the same dense reality, the matter-cone. When referring to the transition, we are talking about the passage from magnetism to electromagnetism that is from the energy grades nine, eight, seven and six to the grades five, four and three.

174. What are the brothers and sisters Ayaplianos-Siren-Lemurianos like? – I asked surprised by those explantions.

We already gave you a short description of their principal characteristics – observes the brother Interano – but as mentioned earlier, had to conduct innumerous experiments to improve the imagined and created human-form, all of which stored in the Akashic Register as well as in your and our memory. In fact, you all originate from the Internal-Antimatter City of Lemur and later became a part of the Matter City of Lemuria in the watered-down quartz crystals, the seas. A number of them left for the exterior and, initiating the process of evolution with our help, abandoned their aqueous conditions turning what they are today: Ayaplianos-Humans.

Most brothers and sisters Ayaplianos-Siren-Lemurianos remained in their aqueous habitat for having entirely adjusted to this life form and reality preserving the human-form, however, with a few exceptions.

175. How did those forms develop their characteristics?

Energy is quite flexible and adjusts to its environment – remarks the brother Seramita – therefore, the image of the dolphins inspired the Ayaplianos-Siren-Lemurianos and made them develop almost identical characteristics, something that also occurred with you when adopting the monkeys' form of development making both appear very much alike. Nevertheless, a brain and the soul of the Ayapliano species marked the difference in evolution between the Siren-Lemurianos and the dolphins as well as between you and the monkey.

The Ayaplianos-Siren-Lemurianos

These brothers and sisters are very able representatives of the human-species – proceeds the brother Elohim – they have considerably advanced on investigation and turned expert oceanographers with vast knowledge of the marine life. Although physically almost identical to you, their respiratory system allows them to draw oxygen for breathing from the water.

When taking in water, their lungs separate oxygen from hydrogen. This allows them to remain submerged for hours and often for days. Formerly, they never left the deep waters. Nowadays, they manage to surface, breathe in the exterior and even can take sunlight for a few hours.

176. Does this mean that the Ayaplianos-Siren-Lemurianos still exist?

Yes, but their natural habitat are tepid waters of the oceans as deep as 500 meters – observes the brother Interano –they can see in an environment of low luminosity, have sensitive nerve cells on their skin that allow them to anticipate any possible hazard and always move in groups. They live and work in communities with active social relations.

Male and female individuals enjoy equal living and working conditions. They have great cerebral capacity, are intuitive, perceptive and sensible and communicate through telepathy. With their vast knowledge of the marine animal and plant kingdoms, they are the masters of the seas. As vegans, they respect the life of all other creatures being their diet plankton and algae. Free of emotions but with feelings and an extraordinary evenness of mind, they strictly live in accordance with the canons of the universe. They are pure souls of heart.

Their bodies are the same as yours inside – continues the brother Elohim – but other important characteristics of their skin, beside the deep blue color due to chlorophyll and their diet, are great elasticity with an epidermis without sweat glands about 10-20 times thicker than that of other mammals and an adipose panicle holding fats that guarantee a steady thermal isolation and body temperatures of 35-36 degrees C.

In the course of evolution, their formerly joined legs have separated showing broad feet with five toes that resemble flippers. Strong muscles allow their powerful up and down movement and displacements at a considerable speed. Their webbed five fingers, joined by an elastic and flexible membrane hands, give them great agility while swimming and diving.

An average two meters tall (men and women) and of great physical strength, they are capable of covering long distances under water, an ability that reminds us of their close relationship with the dolphins – observes the brother Interano – they can swim at fifty miles per hour. They have vivid communication with these and the whales using sounds over long distances under water while among their fellow Lemurianos.

The Ayaplianos-Siren are very intelligents and their brain mass work at 90% capacity. They are intuitive and telepath thus they are capable of communicating through telepathy over thousands of kilometers. We could say that they are the king of the oceans and all the creatures of the sea knows about it. Their daily diet is made of seaweed and plankton and live in big communities. They live in large quartz caverns at the North Pole, with both underwater and surface structures spending about 70 % of their lives at the submerged part and the rest in the exterior. Outside, they sleep for short periods to recover energy.

Sexual relations, conception and gestation (9 month) are no different from humans' – remarks the brother Interano – but as a rule, the female Lemuriano gives birth to her child under water. She feeds the baby with breast milk. She, however, takes it to the surface not long after birth to make it familiar with the conditions of the exterior. The Lemurianos society is a just and balanced one formed from family nuclei with solid relations in both environments.

177. These surprising revelations – I remark smiling – appear to confirm the nine realities of the Ayapliano species on planet Tera. Is there any other?

No, there is no other – replies the brother Elohim smiling back – the nine realities are as follows:

1. Ayaplianos-Volunteers of the Spacecraft
2. Ayaplianos-Siren-Lemurianos

3. Ayaplianos-Seramitas
4. Ayaplianos-Elohim
5. Ayaplianos-Interanos
6. Ayaplianos-Humans
7. Grays
8. Reptilian Grays
9. Nefilins

They coexist on planet Tera as parallel and ethereal or physical realities but all are brothers (and some also sisters) of the species that came to this planet some 600 million years ago. The first four brothers mentioned live in the parallels and ethereal realities: sixth, seventh, eight and nineth grade of the magnetism. The other five brothers, they live in dense realities of the electromagnetism and they have physical bodies as you all.

178. Is it then true that the Siren-Lemurianos are our brothers and sisters?

Yes, they are – assures the brother Interano – however, before we could think of creating any dense human-form from our imagination to face the inhospitable environment of the planet, we as beings of light of highly subtle human forms, had to change the slow and dense crystal core of the planet to a fast and diaphanous one. We therefore founded the first Antimatter City of Crystal naming it LEMUR. We then started developing a human-form that would allow us to live in the dense reality of Tera. As mentioned earlier, we had to go through a long process until succeeding in creating a human-form that would preserve the elements it needed to grow. However, for this to occur we had to introduce the human-form from our imagination into the watered-down quartz matrix. Although we could not prevent distortion, we found that this was the only way of transiting between light and darkness.

Darkness: Is the absence of visible light and something not too difficult to produce. Absolute darkness from a scientific viewpoint does exist because light does not only have a visible but also an invisible electromagnetic spectrum. Any part of the universe has a certain amount of radiation although imperceptible to the human eye. This means that in theory total darkness only exists in the proximity of a Dark Hole. Human emotional response to the absence of light has inspired metaphors in symbolism and arts. Earlier in history, it appears sometimes as a substance in its own right in some fantasy literature. In this context, people call darkness also shadow (Esoteric Dictionary).

In the end, our light projected a shadow – proceeds the brother Interano – a shadow that was reaching the denseness we had expected. You are our shadow and we are the light in this shadow. We therefore always say that you are we and we are you. This was the moment when we beings of light started adopting the dense human-form of the planet, perceiving ourselves as if we were looking into a mirror. We were Light and Darkness at the same time. It was as if we had produced a photographic picture from a negative. One imitated the movement of the other. We thus had reproduced ourselves in a reality we did not know and had to investigate. However, this way the dense human-form started defining and projecting itself in the watered-down quartz, which was of great help owing to the divergence of the colors that turned denser filling spaces properly and starting to form the filaments of organs and systems. Summarizing, the planetary human-form originated from the imagination of our Desire of Creation, the watered-down quartz, the colors and the electromagnetism. We call this form of creation, Photographic Chemistry.

Photographic Chemistry

To initiate this process, we turned chemical and electrostatic energy into an appropriate form using light – explains the brother Elohim – the change in the photo-sensible crystals drew certain substances from the quartz transforming their structure, something that only occurs in the presence of light – proceeds the sister Interana – the chemical crystals of our imagination are light. When exposing them to the darkness, they produced chemical reactions such as oxidation and reduction resulting in what we compare to the process of photography. Some other chemical and physical changes occurred, after we managed to produce an impression of the image.

A good deal of your creation occurred through Photosynthesis, the process that guarantees the preservation of the plant kingdom in the planet using their chlorophyll to transform inorganic into organic matter and solar into chemical energy – continues the brother Interano – heterotrophic organisms such as animals and a number of plants depend on these energy conversions for their sustenance. In addition, on transforming carbon dioxide and sunlight into carbohydrates, photosynthetic organisms produce important amounts of oxygen. The Brothers-Siren-Lemurianos and you, nevertheless, originate from components of the water and quartz elements.

Water: Consists of molecules formed from hydrogen and oxygen (H_20). Hydrogen (H) is a reactive gaseous, colorless, and odorless element with the atomic number 1. Oxygen (O) with similar characteristics is slightly magnetic and the most common element on the planet. Water is the main component of organic matter by representing 50-90% of the mass of all organisms. Protoplasm, the living material of the cell, contains fats, carbohydrates, proteins and salts in solution. Water is a carrier of those substances decomposing and combining them chemically. The blood of animals and sap of plants hold large quantities of water for an adequate distribution of nutrients as well as the elimination of waste material. It furthermore is essential to the metabolic decomposition of proteins and carbohydrates. This process called hydrolysis occurs regularly in living cells (Dictionary).

Quartz: Is a silica compound (SiO_2) and an oxide in accordance with the Strunz classification. Despite its high silica content, it may contain traces of lithium, sodium, potassium or titanium. It is not susceptible to exfoliation. With a number 7 hardness on the Mohs scale, it may produce scratches on common steel. There are two quartz type structures. Alpha-Quartz and Beta.6-Quartz, the first called low quartz has a trigonal structure and resists temperatures up to 573 degrees C. The latter classified as high quartz results from the low quartz above that temperature forming a hexagonal structure. At temperatures above 867 degrees C, it gradually turns tridymite, another silica type mineral. Quartz develops pyroelectric and piezoelectric properties under tension or pressure (Dictionary).

To create the form from our imagination until completing the formation of the Siren-Lemurianos and Ayaplianos-Humans obviously took us hundreds of millions of years – observes the brother Elohim – this included the definition of what elements were necessary to give life to these physical bodies and from there on guarantee their adequate growth and development. We therefore created both Siren-Lemurianos and Ayaplianos-Humans at the very same time (in unison) in the watered-down quartz whose nutrients we found were turning these forms organisms.

Almost 300 million years passed until we succeeded in completing this immense task, because we needed beings who would bear our very characteristics to host and give us the conditions for fulfilling our mission: The Cure of the Tera-Cell. Once completed, we would return to our origin, the realities of Alpha Centauri and The Pleiades. While in the watered-down quartz, the human-form developed magnificently – continues explaining the brother Elohim – from a certain moment on, evolution would have to go on beyond this habitat to face the challenges of the exterior.

We therefore divided the human-form into two groups. One would stay at the original habitat, the seas, the other continue the process of evolution on the surface of the planet. We went on experimenting with both groups creating mammals close to the human-form - among many other species - such as the monkey, which nevertheless did not develop the energy and intelligence as expected.

Similar occurred with the mammals of the seas that developed traits close to those of the Siren-Lemurianos but without reaching the conditions, they would need to host us. Therefore, both humans of the exterior and the seas, brothers of the same species, gradually adjusted to the characteristics of their respective habitats – proceeds the brother Interano.

179. Are the Siren-Lemurianos aware of our presence?

They, indeed, are but fearing to be hunted down and become objects of studies they avoid making contact – observes the sister Interana – they communicate with us and know the Internal City of Atlantida, which they access by traveling from their submarine homes through subterranean rivers.

180. Do they have any source of light living in caverns?

Small crustaceous in some caverns as well as plants emit photonic light. They have channeled this natural light using its energy for their sustenance.

181. Do they have any electric power source?

They use the natural energy of the marine currents since artificial electric power is not a part of their reality. Lemurianos lead a very natural life with no need for metallic materials or machinery nor for any of the apparatus that you consider inevitable in your lives. Their habitat consists of materials that the seas offer them. Their reality is quite different from yours and so are their needs.

182. Has the energy of the Siren-Lemurianos suffered the distortion ours has in the exterior?

No, they never had this problem – emphasizes the brother Interano – they preserved the pureness of their energy because they never stayed long enough in the exterior to risk distortion by taking in ill negative energy or eating harmful diets. Nevertheless, what helped them maintain their crystals pure was the watered-down quartz.

183. Is the Energy of their Spirit then pure?

Yes, – continues the brother Interano – because the brothers Ayaplianos whom they hosted preserve their original energy. However, evolution in this reality has enriched their Energetic Being with a knowledge they did not have in their planet of origin, the wisdom (of the seas) that they are going to take with them when finally departing as will all the brothers who live in this reality of Matter and Antimatter.

184. Are they going to form their Energetic Being (spirit) the way we will?

They already formed their Energetic Being because they never suffered distortion.

185. Did you create particular human-forms to gain an overall knowledge of the Tera-Cell?

We indeed fulfilled what our brothers of the superior dimensions had asked us to do before leaving for the Tera-Cell – confirms the sister Interana – since nothing occurs by accident in the universe, your living in a dense and contaminated reality and suffering distortion was within their plans – says the brother Elohim – consequently, we created all the human-forms and material-suits to be an explorer and a researcher for those unknown realities, to find out about the disease that was attacking the Tera-Cell and assigned them the following Tera areas for investigation:

- The Center to the Ayaplianos-Nefilins
- The Exterior to the Ayaplianos-Humans
- The Interior to the Ayaplianos-Interanos
- The five Grades of the Electromagnetism to the Ayaplianos-Elohim
- The four Grades of the Magnetism to the Ayaplianos-Seramitas
- The Oceans to the Ayaplianos-Siren-Lemurianos
- The Poles to the Ayaplianos-Volunteers of the Spacecraft

This is how we realize in-depth studies of the ill cell – observes the sister Interana – the vast information of each Ayapliano Grade is the wisdom that we together will take to the Interstellar Cosmic Confederation. Thus, WE ARE ALL, WE ARE ONE. To fulfil this immense mission, we had to separate but we will all join again. The physical human-form is of great importance to us for being the shelter we need for our investigations. However, knowing that we cannot take this dense form with us, we have to create the most favorable conditions for our energetic body to initiate the long path of return to our origin.

We all always had full conscience of the place we hold and why and that those human-forms are finite. You, however, still seem to believe them to be your one and only reality and therefore fear the moment of disincarnating. Your fear is such that we, so far, failed to help you understand that belonging to the even reality you live a life of fantasy in this odd reality, which you have created and therefore must work and understand to transcend.

186. Are the Ayaplianos-Siren-Lemurianos aware of your teachings that these books transmit?

Their awakening of conscience is complete since they never suffered distortion nor were oblivious of their even (antimatter) reality – affirms the brother Elohim – we created the Brothers Siren-Lemurianos to help us learn about the benefits of the watered-down quartz that we all would enjoy. We created everything on this planet, which in all truth, means that its environment was and still is a non-existing (odd) reality in this antimatter universe from where we all originate.

187. From the books, we know what our return will be like. How the Brothers-Siren-Lemurianos are going to return to their true reality?

Just as your souls must elevate, the Brothers Siren-Lemurianos will have to undergo their particular process of forming the spirit for the return but with the help from the Brothers Volunteers of the Spacecraft, the Brothers of Light, they will succeed. In reality, both of you will benefit from this extensive learning process providing and receiving knowledge to keep advancing – observes the sister Interana – although the Brothers Siren-Lemurianos spent most of their lives in the quartz-water habitat, their evolution compares to yours. Exclusively created to live in spacious under water caverns of the planet, they gradually adjusted to breathing oxygen in the exterior since after some time volunteers decided on incarnating as humans seeking to complete their evolution and elevation. Despite having to face an adverse environment, they found a way to face this process conveniently.

To give their souls the chance to adjust to this new habitat, they decided on consecutive incarnations in children who suffered from different grades of autism. This allowed them to know their way around in the exterior and learn how to use the human language for communication without creating curiosity among humans about their origin. Their souls nevertheless preserving the deep love for the ocean, in dreams sometimes live and breathe in their old habitat remembering past times and lives.

188. Are all autists incarnated Ayaplianos-Siren-Lemurianos?

No, – replies the brother Elohim – only a small number of them incarnated some 180000 years ago during the foundation of the City of Atlantis.

189. Did we incarnate in their reality as they did in the exterior of the planet?

The reality of the brothers Siren-Lemuriano took a different way of evolution, both developed characteristics of their own. One of the canons of the universe reads that, while elevated thought-energies (souls and spirits) may descend to the lower grades, low vibration souls cannot rise to the higher grades – explains the brother Elohim – this means that they as Spirits of Light may descend and incarnate in a human baby born with an elevated soul.

The Brothers-Siren-Lemurianos not only can incarnate in the exterior but also join the brothers Interanos, Elohim and Seramitas at the Internal City. They are the only to rise and descend owing to the great pureness of their energy, which shows a blue tone after disincarnating. Spiritually, many of you know and communicate with them that is, with the City of Lemur.

190. Must those incarnated Brothers Ayaplianos-Siren-Lemurianos forever live in the exterior or may they return to their original habitat, the Quartz-Water?

Some return but most continue in the exterior as professional oceanographers and investigators transmitting their vast knowledge of the seas – replies the brother Interano – their wisdom made an important contribution to the evolution of the planet and its inhabitants. After numerous incarnations, they finally are Ayaplianos-Humans.

191. Why do the souls of the Brothers Siren-Lemurianos show a blue color tone?

In reality, it is the projection of form and color of their last incarnation – observes the sister Interana – their souls are not actually blue but the thought-energy recorded their reality that way. On disincarnating, the Siren-Lemurianos proceed to the Internal City of Lemur while you enter the Internal City of Atlantis however, in both cases, this antimatter reality energy has the same characteristics but may differ in elevation, vibration frequency, rhythm and colors – adds the brother Elohim.

192. Have they formed different ethnicities from the four races that came to the planet the way we did in the exterior?

Yes, they have – replies the brother Interano – along the process of procreation and evolution, groups and communities developed particular characteristics owing to the composition and temperature of the water as well as variations in diet. As a result, many of them made fast and positive advances while others suffered a slow-down in their evolution and elevation.

193. Which are those Ethnicities that descend from the Ayaplianos-Siren-Lemurianos?

As well as you who distinguish developed from developing countries (societies) based on advances in education, health care, security, economy etc. the brothers Siren-Lemurianos come from a large process of physical, psychical and mental development, which included extensive migration – explains the sister Interana – nowadays, most live at the North Pole while other smaller communities established habitats underneath the Australian continent and at the South Pole.

We can say that the two material cities at the poles greatly benefitted from the influence of the Internal Cities of Lemur and Atlantis whereas the city underneath the Australian continent has had a slower development. The element helium, pureness of the quartz-water and the plankton and algae diet have greatly accelerated the Siren-Lemurianos' evolution. However, a part of their society is still behind owing to warm climates, low-quality water and a crustacean diet – remarks the brother Interano – there are no overwhelming differences, but they are big enough to consider this part of their society as belonging to a lower evolutionary grade.

As you had a similar situation in the exterior – continues the brother Interano – when starting your evolution from the four original ethnicities such as, Yeti, Gorilla, Chimpanzee, Kuturo Monkey, and Malasya Monkey. The brothers Siren-Lemurianos also divide into four grades of evolution differing in physical appearance as well as social, scientific and technological advances:

- Siren-Lemurianos
- Siren-Assos
- Siren-Frigus
- Siren-Atlantidos

SIREN-ASSOS and SIREN-FRIGUS

They are the brothers whom we first created in our Antimatter lab – observes the brother Interano – owing to certain factors, the fell behind in evolution to the point that their physical bodies deteriorated and turned terrifying creatures. We nevertheless preserved their energy sending it to incarnate in you, with a chance for them to continue their development.

They are the legendary sirens who attracted ships with their singing feeding on dolphins, whales and even humans – continues the brother Elohim – facing them several times, the brothers Siren-Lemurianos tried to change and help them develop but failed for having suffered the energy of those brothers from extreme distortion. We Interanos of the Internal City accepted the task to help them evolve, however, no longer in their usual habitat but in the exterior. To make it work, took us the past 180000 years because they had to incarnate at a very low grade to develop gradually cognitive abilities and other human faculties.

None of those brothers incarnated again under the sea and only about 300 remained incarnated in the exterior – says the sister Interana – although presenting physical and psychical disorders at the beginning, they succeeded in adjusting to their new habitat and we could say that their descendants today are entirely human. Ancestral memory of their past lives in the seas sometimes comes back as flashes in their dreams. However, once their energy (soul) is ready for it, they will remember those remote experiences in detail.

SIREN-LEMURIANOS and SIREN-ATLANTIDOS

These brothers – says the brother Interano – made magnificent progress in evolution never losing the essence of their origin and feelings. As brothers of the same species, they developed in parallel with you. Their natural habitat was and still is the watered-down quartz of the ocean, while yours is the atmosphere of the surface. You have been successful in developing the technology to explore the deep of their habitat. They nevertheless succeeded in rising from the water, separating their legs and breathing the helium-purified oxygen of their crystal city giving them protection against diseases and a life span beyond yours.

The brothers Siren-Atlantidos have tall and strong physical bodies, slender arms and legs, blue skin, large eyes as well as small noses and ears. Their broad five-toe feet resembling fins, but entirely apt for walking, and skin-webbed hands make them very fast swimmers.

Having a sharp sense of direction and great subtlety, they communicate telepathically. Their clairvoyance allows them to anticipate action against any upcoming danger. They live submerged or in their crystal city but cannot surface because the contaminated oxygen of the planet's atmosphere in the exterior would suffocate them. Therefore, no one has ever met them in person but those who have raised the energy of their souls may perceive them in their dreams or visions. When disincarnated, they might see them as spirits who sometimes incarnate and present themselves as Ascended Masters in the exterior.

After we had come to this reality, we stayed for 300 million years in our spacecraft knowing what would happen to us if we left. Making, however, good use of this extensive timeframe, we managed to create dense material bodies that would host and allow us to explore the exterior of the planet. While most of these bodies adjusted to the conditions of the quartz-water, a good number of them gained the surface and adapting to its particular environment developed into what humans are today.

Both the Brothers Siren-Lemurianos and Siren-Atlantidos live in large cavern-cities at the North and South Pole, respectively. The Siren-Lemurianos have Material, Psychical and Spiritual bodies and in their disincarnated state share the Internal City with us. They never present themselves in their physical form, but many had incarnated before to study and learn about the conditions of evolution in the exterior. This last happened some 180000 years ago. After that, the immense contamination of thought-energies across the planet's electromagnetism made further investigations inviable.

Therefore, all those who incarnate in the exterior have to complete the same process that is, once disincarnated enter the Internal City of Atlantis and proceeded from there to their true habitat, the Internal City of Lemur in the Magnetism of the planet.

194. Have we also incarnated in them?

No. For you to incarnate in them, you first would have to heal the dense and ill negative part of your energy – observes the sister Interana – which means that before your soul can join the Internal City to incarnate in more sophisticated bodies as those of the brothers Siren-Atlantidos, it must undergo the purification of its energy. This is why you first must enter the Antimatter Internal City and prepare your energy for this process.

195. Thank you, brothers, for all the enlightenment. With your permission, I would like to change the subject to ask your comment on the following. There are rumors that an eclipse to occur on April 15th, 2014 will show a red moon. Should we prepare for a particular meaning or even danger regarding this event?

It is not the first time to happen and will happen again – comments the sister Interana – at all times, the moon has presented a reddish or even blue color but humans continue holding on to superstition and prophecies announcing imminent disasters to scare and confine them to lasting nightmares.

You rather should use knowledge and discernment to understand planetary and cosmic events and therefore need a broader scientific knowledge of the planet's history. The books EL SER UNO put it this way: YOU USE RELIGION FOR EVERTHING YOU DO NOT UNDERSTAND and CALL SCIENCE WHAT YOU DO UNDERSTAND. Let us see how science explains the details of this eclipse.

The moon's reddish color appears when it approaches the horizon but not at full moon. This reddish to yellowish color tone results from the dispersion of blue, green and violet light in the atmosphere. To reach us when the moon is nearing the horizon, its light has to travel more than three times the distance within the atmosphere than it does at full moon. The moon may show the yellowish color tone at any time of the year but sometimes the phenomenon even occurs with the moon in a perpendicular position to the horizon owing to atmospheric pollutants such as smoke or dust that affect the color we finally perceive.

Lunar eclipses occur when the earth comes between the sun and the moon blocking the sunlight from reaching the satellite. When fully eclipsed, the moon takes on the reddish tinge that you tend to associate with prophecies and disasters...Do not let those impressions interfere with your emotional balance and the work with your inner self and have PEACE, HARMONY and LOVE in your hearts.

CHAPTER IV

LEMUR
CITY OF LIGHT AND LOVE

Let us tell you the story of Lemur – continues the brother Elohim our conversation – after his words, the place where we are suffers a complete change. It is no longer the large hall of our previous talks. We are now in an environment I actually find difficult to describe. From what I can see, it is a place without windows and doors but with a brilliant white LIGHT filling every part of it. All I can see are the brothers. I do not know if I sit or are on my feet, in fact, I am unable to feel if I have a body at all. However, I notice that I continue with a clear and lucid conscience. There is deep peace making me feel that everything flows in a subtle, quiet and loving way.

The brothers put me in a circle they have formed. A sphere of white LIGHT emerges from its center. In a split second, I understand that I am in the presence of one of the brothers Ayaplianos Volunteers of the Spacecraft and that the place is the Antimatter City of Lemur. I only regret that except the brothers and the light there seems to be nothing more around me. I feel the brother of LIGHT close to me saying – the forms within the light are very different from the matter-forms in the exterior, the only way to perceive them is with your imagination.

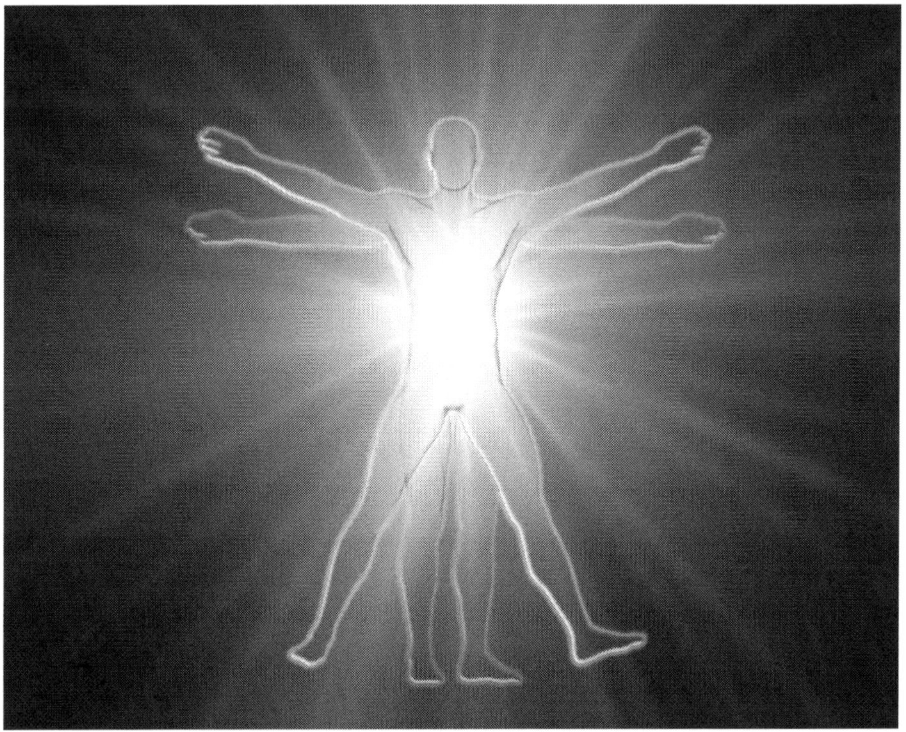

The LIGHT – continues the brother – is the sum of all that exists. Within the light, the Desire of Creation makes you perceive your existence. Whatever you imagine and desire becomes real. However, you must understand that we do not have material needs. Our only desire is to satisfy the needs of our Energetic Being. You are experiencing an antimatter reality – he proceeds – where nothing physical can emerge; what we do is create elevated thoughts-feelings, which joining form ideas that may adopt a diversity of forms in accordance with the intensity of those ideas. We all are LIGHT but coming to this dense and dark reality, we had to adjust this Light to the Darkness, which resulted in the vast number of processes as transmitted in these books.

The LIGHT is internal however, the forms are expressions that physical needs forced us to project but again, behind the forms are we all, brothers of LIGHT and LOVE – observes the brother Seramita – this Antimatter reality is the place from where we all will return to our origin. To succeed, we have to recover the essence of the LIGHT – the brother pauses then continues – from everything the six books describe we know that we all came as spirits (holograms) from the Secondary Antimatter Reality of Alpha Centauri and The Pleiades volunteering to cure the seven cells of EL SER UNO's universal body, stricken with the cancer of Ambition and Distortion.

What is your origin? Who are you? Where are you heading? Broadly speaking, we have commented these questions providing information that your minds will record and use in your next lives. All you know now and will learn in the future about EL SER UNO will become a part of your thought-energies and you will be able to activate it whenever necessary – concludes the brother Seramita and proceeds the brother of the LIGHT – we Elder Brothers Ayaplianos of the Light together with the brothers Seramitas, Elohim, Interanos and Lemurianos will be explaining in the present book how we built the Internal Cities and created all that exists in this planet although as Volunteers of the Spacecraft never descended to its surface.

This city, a Bubble-Sphere located at the North Pole Antimatter Cone has been our habitat for 600 million years Tera time and preserves the reality of our origin providing all we need for our sustenance as beings of Light with no physical bodies. From there, we have been able to access, protect and correct the planet cells that had suffered distortion of varying intensity.

196. Why do I only see *BRILLIANT WHITE LIGHT*?

The Pineal Gland of the Sun reflects this White Light deflecting other colors by refraction owing to the presence of magnetism – observes the brother of the Light – in this process, magnetic waves turn extremely amplified laser light. Consisting of fast-traveling photons, the white light's energy passes through the Nimeos-Crystals causing the refraction of colors. Nevertheless, neither you nor we are real nor anything you see now but rather a projection of the LIGHT owing to the effects from the magnetism of the Internal City of Lemur – continues the brother Interano – this tells us that white light is formed when colors overlap, deflecting refraction, that is, going through the crystals and as each crystal is different from each other, they cause the bifurcation of light creating different colors. We can also adapt this explanation to the composition of our figures, of our presence, which have been made by magnetic waves and by the amount of crystals, through which white light passes creating the prism effect, in this way it has formed the figures. of all of us including yours.

197. Are we then holograms?

Yes, – replies the brother Seramita – but instead of being the projection from a display device, we are the projection of our mind through the prism of the Pineal Gland. When a positive and elevated Thought or Desire of Creation forms in our brain, they rotate at a certain speed producing a reflection from the crystals of the Gland. The Pineal Gland then releases this Desire to take on the intended form at a given moment.

198. Are we a reflection of the Pineal Gland?

We are indeed – replies the brother Interano – our Pineal Glands hold the divine inner force of every Nimeos-Energy particle of our energetic body, which projects the hologram of the bodies we see now. You call it the Ethereal Body that also appears in your dreams. Many times, this Ethereal Body splits taking with it your thoughts but has no form.

199. Do we find ourselves in some Pineal Gland if we are within that White-Light at Lemur?

Yes. We are in the Pineal Gland of the Tera-Cell – replies the brother of the Light – remember that there is no material universe. Future interstellar travel will give you proof of it. The only palpable matter-energy are the Solar System and other systems of the Primary Dimension's third grades and planes. The Primary Dimension is of varying density, which means that you will only be able to deal with densities similar to yours. There is a Bubble-Sphere that shelters your Solar System nurtured by the Sun. Everything beyond it is of subtle, ethereal, gaseous and impalpable nature.

200. If Lemur is the Antimatter City, is Lemuria then the Matter or Material City?

The history of both cities begins – observes the brother Seramita – after we came to a planet whose crystals rotated with great difficulty and, very distant from its source, was no longer able of attracting the energy it needed to regenerate its elements – he pauses and continues – We will not repeat the history, but we start telling you that your Human-Forms were made by us. You were created by the reflection of LIGHT, which was projecting its own shadow. As a result, this shadow took the form in a given moment. We could compare it with a negative photo. In fact, with this explanation, we can say that you are the negative part of us.

201. Are you, brothers of the Light, Lemurianos?

No. We are the Volunteers of the Spacecraft – replies the brother of the Light – as described earlier, Lemurianos are your brothers Ayaplianos Siren Lemurianos conceived and created in unison with you after we had founded the City of Light called Lemur at the Antimatter North Pole, which is the Bubble-Sphere-Spacecraft that brought us to this planet. This immense spacecraft is our habitat, from where we watch over every single manifestation of life. Together with our brothers Seramitas, Elohim, Interanos, Lemurianos and Humans we have studied the kind of cure planet Earth needs to transcend and form another Tera, a reality of LIGHT that will take us all back to our origin.

202. Who are Lemurianos?

300 million of years ago, we founded the City of Lemur. You all who descended from the first Human-Forms we conceived at the City of Lemur are Lemurianos. This internal city continues until today at the Antimatter North Pole near large Quartz deposits. Parts of these deposits that we had watered-down turned oceans, rivers and lakes in the exterior but a large portion of this "quartz-water" remains inside the planet – explains the brother of the Light.

The quartz-water of the exterior became our labs where we experimented with the first Androgen-Human-Forms. This Human-Form was tall, strong complexion, androgen and hosted the Energetic Being of some of the brothers Volunteers and whose incipient development and growing physical needs we accompanied from the city of Lemur. The Human-Form started projecting images according to its needs but different from the Energetic Being. Slowly, the material needs of the Human-Form, which we created, were expressed.

Such was the development of the Human-Form in the quartz-water that we built a submarine city of great proportions for a permanent habitat naming it Lemuria. This city offered entire satisfaction of the needs that material beings have in compliance with the established canons. However, despite all our scientific knowledge, the Human-Form started deteriorating and the quartz elements failed to block this decline. We therefore decided on cloning it. This, however, did not work either owing to the corrosive action of this dense reality. We then divided the Human-Form in a masculine and feminine part to create the condition for its continuity in a natural way through procreation, the union of Man and Woman to give the Human-Form all the strength for a multiple division and further dynamic and active evolution – continues the brother Seramita – that continuation would join another continuation forming no longer 50% of each one but 25% of the four halves and so on infinitely. Thus, we strengthened the Human-Form and gave it a strong, dynamic and very active continuation. We nevertheless had failed to consider that to give life to every Human-Form in gestation would also mean the division of the brothers Volunteers' Spirit-Energy (Energetic Being) into infinite parts.

We thus had created two realities, one Antimatter and the other Material. We from the Antimatter side incarnated in the dense Human-Form to study the disease of the Tera-Cell. However, along this cycle of incarnating and disincarnating, we perceived growing anomalies in the Human-Forms' evolution. Strange sensations began to affect them, and their minds kept losing the clearness they had shown during the first incarnations.

Those Humans were the first intelligent life in the planet and preceded other life forms in the Quartz-Water and the Exterior – continues explaining the brother of the Light – they began to explore the interior of the planet discovering the large subterranean caverns that later turned immense cities and important empires. Those caverns are still there holding libraries of crystal that protect the planetary and universal archives against the ambition and avarice of today's governments and religions. Only a few individuals who keep incarnating in the exterior have today astral access to this essential source of information confirming that the prosperous and advanced City of Lemuria was the place from where we brothers of the Light applied the science and technology of the universe.

The Human-Form extensively used the knowledge we brought from our planets of origin of the Secondary Dimension. Concluded the process of evolution as Tritons and Sirens dominating the subaqueous reality, it was now ready to conquer the solid reality of the exterior. There are Lemurianos still living in Submarine Cities located under the North Pole Cone but the Human-Form along with the brothers of the Light never doubted to gain and explore the surface of the planet.

203. Did they plan to leave for the surface in the shortest possible time? I asked innocently...

No – replies the brother of the Light – a slow-moving process of extensive investigation and innumerable tests, preceded by the creation of the animal kingdom, culminated in a Human-Form that would resist the density of the quartz-water. This Human-Form was strong enough to host and allow the brothers of the Light to initiate exploration of the exterior. Their investigations and findings were of great help to continue curing the Tera-Cell. Unfortunately, the Human-Form suffered distortion to the point that it tended to imitating animal forms and behaviors.

204. What is the difference then between the Human-Form of the Lemurianos and that of the exterior?

When I ask this question, we all of a sudden find ourselves in a large city built from quartz in a futurist style. Looking at the brother of the Light I understand that I am about to meet the Lemurianos. I feel great peace and harmony perceiving clear signs of a new world waiting to receive us. I comprehend that the Elder Brothers Ayaplianos are helping us activate our memory to guide us on the Path of Return toward this extraordinary and unique reality. The Great White Brotherhood is with us from this parallel reality of LIGHT and LOVE. To be one with it, we nevertheless have to leave behind the many philosophical currents we follow. We must have a free mind. Those who look for spiritual illumination must strive to vanquish the addictive forces of the exterior and connect with their inner world. This will help them prepare for the Power of Nature to clear the way to spirituality and illumination. We finally experience the Awakening of our memory and the time has come for us to act.

It is time to remember that all we dream, think, believe and conceive originates from other worlds and that Lemuria is the origin of our life as physical human beings. The memory of past lives has never abandoned us, but we still insist on turning our backs on it. The Celestial Kingdom is close. We, however, fail to connect with our innermost self by letting in much of what is vain from the exterior. With great concern, we have waited for centuries for this awakening to occur. Now is the moment for rejoicing because we have initiated the process of purification of a soul that will pass on all its divine force to the human being.

Remaining pensive, I perceive the brother of the Light saying...

This, sister, is why all human beings of this planet belong to the city of LIGHT and LOVE. However, very few preserved it in their memory because the experiences of the exterior altered the recordings of their crystals. For a long time, we brothers of the Light have been very close. Through patient psychological work, we have finally established contact with you while brothers from planets of other constellations have taken great trouble to initiate a healing process that would help you find the path of return to your origin.

We all are the Great White Brotherhood who with different grades of elevation procure not to leave a single thought-energy without a cure. We, your brothers of the Light, out of the Spiritual Reality of Antimatter-Lemur have been in permanent communication with the White Brotherhood of the planet revealing the truth of the external world. We shelter the Knowledge of the Ancient Arcana, our Spiritual Legacy. A toll of bells, though still distant, is telling you to prepare for the moment of departure. The growing call of Knowledge, Understanding and Love will touch the heart and soul of those human beings who start remembering Lemuria. The Brothers in the different grades of the electromagnetism and magnetism are their loyal collaborators in this process.

You must be aware of the illumination and divine nature of all created – proceeds the brother of the Light – everything will be as before since the truth will never change. The Great White Brotherhood will work more closely with you and reveal the knowledge to all who have awaked and are traveling the path of LIGHT and LOVE.

The human soul will no longer be a prisoner of superstitions and ignorance. The knowledge based on the foundations of the New Spiritual Age and cosmic canons so far only available for the initiated will now be for every one of you. When the brother of the Light pauses, I get a clear view of the Beings of Lemuria. They have very tall, slender and hairless bodies with blue colored skin, slanted Ayapliano eyes, long slim arms with five-finger hands and legs with five-toe feet. Wearing tight, light-colored suits, they walk in groups looking at us. I manage to distinguish males and females among them. I find myself now in a city of brilliant light and futurist architecture sheltered under an enormous quartz crystal dome of multiple colors. Are we in or outside the quartz-water? I wonder.

In fact, we are in the quartz-water but your hologram perceives it as oxygen. Since yours is not a physical presence you have no way of feeling it as such – observes the brother of the Light – on the other hand, nor is the oxygen in the exterior a part of the air you breathe but quartz-water, too, in a very light state. In reality, you also live in a bubble of watered-down quartz, which is a part of the energy bubble surrounding the Tera-Cell for its cure.

205. Is ours then not a cosmic memory?

No. Your memory reaches back to the moment of the creation of the human-form – replies the brother of the Light – while we hold the previous memory in a cryogenic state to allow you to record everything you experience without any influence from the past. We did so because thought-energy from the planets of origin was not compatible with that of the dense matter energy we had created. In other words, both matter and thought-energies had to be entirely new energies.

206. Is this the reason that we do not remember our planet of origin?

Yes, because we withheld your Cosmic Memory leaving you with a planetary memory whose origin is Lemuria – replies the brother of the Light – the day you return to this reality, you will recover your Cosmic Memory and be able to return to your origin.

207. The books say we will have to incarnate in the Interanos to form the Energetic Being (spirit). After that, we incarnate in the Elohim, Seramitas and finally in the Volunteers of the Spacecraft to become ONE and return to our origin. Does this include an incarnation in the Lemurianos?

To end the process, it is not necessary because the moment you are with the Volunteers of the Spacecraft you will be a part of the Light – observes the brother of the Light – as for the Lemurianos, they are entirely pure and authentic since the energy of planet Satien never affected them. They are the brothers who are closest to us, which means that after disincarnating they will not go to the Internal City of Atlantis but to the Internal City of Lemur where they will join us.

They will start doing so as of the Cosmic Alignment along with thought-energies from Atlantis. This is when we will start the fusion of energies to prepare for our journey of return. As you will remember, we shall first go to Venus, then to Mercury, and finally reach and continue beyond the Pineal Gland of the Sun. The Cosmic Alignment favors our passage owing to the proximity of other realities of LIGHT and LOVE.

208. Do governments and religions know about the presence of the Lemurianos?

They certainly do – affirms the brother of the Light – they have all the knowledge regarding the different realities of this planet. However, there are unwritten agreements about the non-revelation of one reality to another to secure control and manipulation of the public. Denying people's right of access to relevant information is the modern slavery practiced by those who suffering from the disease of ambition seek to control the power. Nevertheless, Free Will does exist and nothing nor anyone can enslave an individual against it. There are three ways to face this control.

Many reading these lines may consider this knowledge the channel's fantasy. Others will remain indifferent but those who see truth in this message will break the chains that so firmly have confined them to dense thought-energies. In dreams and flashes of illumination, they will begin to remember though first believing that these might be new visions to illuminate their souls. It occurs, however, that they all remember their One Origin of Lemuria – emphasizes the brother of the Light.

209. Can the Spirits of Lemurianos incarnate in human bodies and thus live in the exterior?

They did so some 180000 years ago. Nowadays, they would not consider it because they know the reality of the exterior, which their pure and elevated thought-energies would be unable to handle – observes the brother of the Light – therefore, the knowledge of the Tera-Cell they and we have is information that the other brothers provide in accordance with their particular evolution and elevation as outlined in the books.

210. Does this mean that no "Master" from Lemuria has ever enlightened us about the Path of Return?

They sometimes present themselves in humans' dreams – replies the brother of the Light – but in general, no further contact is necessary since the "Ascended Masters" of the brothers Interanos and Elohim fulfil this task in a very competent way.

211. Did you, brothers of the Light or Volunteers of the Spacecraft and the Lemurianos leave the planet for Venus, Mercury and the Sun?

The brothers Lemurianos did not. We brothers of the Light use holograms and therefore have all the knowledge of the reality of the Solar System.

212. You tell us in the fifth book that the Solar Spirit called Christ came to the third planet (on the third day) and descended to hell leaving us a message of LIGHT and LOVE. Who is Christ? Is he a brother of the Light?

No, he is not – replies the brother of the Light – Christ is the Thought-Energy of a Cosmic Spirit. There was no figure or being that would represent it but the Christian Philosophy that descended illuminating the mind of Joshua Emmanuel. This philosophy originates from planet Kryon. You certainly remember that in the second book, we mention this event indicating that some 150000 years ago, the Interstellar Cosmic Confederation sent out a vast number of thought-energies (souls) from other realities that incarnated in the human-form on planet Tera advancing your evolution and elevation.

Joshua Emmanuel represented this thought-energy (soul). Transmitting it, he left it as a legacy to humans of the Western world and as vivid proof of continuity and correlation in a universe where everything has its place and function. Order is essential. Without it, EL SER UNO would sink into an abyss of imbalance and chaos.

213. Nowadays, channels are receiving messages from Kryon...Does it mean that their thought-energy (soul) is a part of the Christian Philosophy?

We have to clarify – says the brother of the Light – that the Christian Philosophy is neither exclusive to a channel nor to Cristian Religion but a message of LIGHT and LOVE, that general religious belief in the planet has embraced. It therefore goes beyond the teachings of Joshua

Emmanuel (Jesus) whom Christianity considers the only son of a God that holds all the truth. Both West and East have adopted the word of Christ calling it Love to God, Fraternity, Love for your fellow human, etc. as the fundament of their teachings ignoring that Christ is not a character but universal and cosmic belief, teaching and philosophy.

> ***Christ:*** From the Greek Christos and Hebrew Mashiach or Messiah meaning chosen by God but also the Savior of humanity, the Incarnated Word and only son of God. Theology studies the divine nature of Jesus Christ according to the gospel and other scriptures of the New Testament.
> The Hebrew concept of anointing or enthroning originates from the ancient belief that the act bestows special or even supernatural abilities on a person when performed by a divine authority. In ancient Israel, this procedure used to confer on somebody the authority to fill an important post in public service. However, the term Christ did not only refer to the priests as the intermediaries between God and humanity but also to theocratic kings who thus gained the dignity of priesthood. Later on, this practice included prophets and patriarchs. Nevertheless, during the transformation of the messianic concept, the term Christ only corresponded to the savior of the Hebrew nation.
> In the New Testament, the term Christ turns a common and Christian name. In these cases, it appeared alone, with or without the definite article, and associated to other terms or names. The Old Testament announced Christ as the savior of humanity sent by God whom their followers consider the incarnated son of God while to orthodox and reformist Jews and the Islam, he had just been a great prophet or preacher and founder of Christianity (Wikipedia).

214. Why do Lemurianos have a blue-colored skin?

Their blue-colored skin is one of the particular characteristics they developed in the seas – observes the brother of the Light – as in your case, climate and diet affect the skin color. The blue pigmentation is the result of a plankton and algae diet but also of quartz crystal radiation.

215. What is the Society of Lemuria like?

They lead family lives as you do but men and women establish relationships by affinity of Thought-Energies, Colors and Rhythm rather than through physical attraction and passion – replies the brother of the Light – thus they are restoring the energy that the brothers Volunteers had to divide when creating them. Unlike you who continue dispersing those energies and still have to go through a process of preparation at the Internal City of Atlantis, they already are on the path of return through strong and ever-growing spirits. The Society of Lemuria is orderly and dynamic. Individuals develop fast and from their childhood on their extremely active planetary memory allows them to remember who they are.

216. Does this mean that they have recovered all their memory?

The moment their souls incarnated in the physical form; their planetary memory had become active. After disincarnating and joining us, they will recover their cosmic memory.

217. Will this process conclude during the 7 Thousand Years of the Cosmic Alignment?

Yes – says the brother of the light – because the Cosmic Alignment is the frequency they need to complete it.

218. Is there any particular reason for your having revealed the existence of the brothers Siren-Lemurianos only in this sixth and last book?

The reason is that, unlike you as related in the previous books, they preserved the pureness of their origin, avoided distortion and remained unaffected by the disease of planet Satien. Without ever having met them, you keep their memory from legends of a remote past when they had started an evolutionary process of their own. However, a number of advanced channels well ahead of their times received our message as related in the six books EL SER UNO. On purpose, the books EL SER UNO transmit this message in a general way, thus allowing you to retrieve particular events from your planetary memory. On avoiding going into details, we wanted you to understand that to overcome amnesia you must activate your memory gradually.

These books are an introduction to others you will receive with the passing of time. We have to do it this way so that events flourish in a correct and consecutive manner from your memory. Such is the case nowadays of the Lemurianos' formerly unseparated and finned legs who developed bodies in accordance with those of the Universal-Ayapliano species. Having preserved the pureness of their Energetic Being, they need no further preparation for their return.

219. Will we someday meet the Lemurianos?

Yes, but not in a physical encounter. You will be able to contact their incarnated or disincarnated spirits after you reach the vibration frequency that they command. Consequently, you will only meet them in the Antimatter Reality. However, during the next 200 years, the brothers will appear before you and find a way to give you the knowledge of the Ayapliana presence you need.

220. Does the city of Lemuria resemble our cities with their buildings, schools, libraries, different professions etc.? Are there children, adolescents, adults and seniors?

In a way, it is similar but with some important differences – observes the brother Seramita – the spirits of very young children, for example, already have a degree of wisdom and knowledge of their planetary origin. They never fail to remember their past lives and always are the continuity of their former selves. Nevertheless, Lemurianos also are subject to the process of disincarnating and rebirth, since their physical bodies, though free of many forms of disease; finally tend to succumb to prolonged exhaustion. When disincarnating, their Energetic Being returns to Lemur and either stays with the brothers of the Light or goes to the Antimatter City of Atlantis to continue studying until it incarnates again. Why would they need schools or libraries when the knowledge has long been a part of their spirit? What they have to do, however, is the common work of continuing the studies of the quartz-water's material and antimatter realities.

221. What was life at Lemuria like when we lived there?

Once created, the human-form's evolution was such that we considered it apt to live in the quartz-water as well as in the atmosphere of the exterior – comments the brother of the Light – after dividing the new species into male and female individuals, we procured to have them adjust to the conditions of the exterior by sheltering them under a dome of quartz energy, which they could not leave nor would anyone from the outside have access to it. This is what you remember as the "Paradise".

Both male and female individuals turned out perfect sharing the responsibility of a life in community and the brothers of the Light therefore incarnated in them. Science, technology and the arts developed magnificently and in accordance with our canons in this exterior City of Lemuria located in an area not far from the North Pole that you call Greenland.

Such was the development that we as incarnated in human beings (you) started building cities to the image of our origin. All of them counted with the protection of the quartz crystal domes, for we could not risk direct contact with the exterior. Great advance in science and technology conquered disease and allowed us to build interplanetary spacecraft to visit the planets of the Solar system under the protection of the bubble-spheres of our habitat. The moon became a crystal of wisdom because it refracted the colors of the solar energy turning it into what you call Manna of the Gods to nurture all human beings. You settled on Mars and the Moon, studied Venus and Mercury while the Star Sun turned the creator of matter. Knowledge grew every day; however, there was a moment when it ceased advancing...

While groups of individuals visited the exterior protected by their bubble-spheres, we had planned to send out a number of settlers to live in this adverse reality under a process of gradual adjustments. We were aware of the extreme conditions outside after extensive testing with animal species.

Several of those species had a promising evolution; others could not take the atmosphere and succumbed. Insects proved to be the most resistant. After millions of years of evolution, we concluded that the human-form was prepared to leave the quartz crystal domes and settle in the exterior.

A large number of Lemuriano families volunteered, male-form and female, guided by us brothers of the Light who would help them and their brothers of the Light incarnated in them advance on this monumental experiment of evolution. At this point, we decided to withdraw the Cosmic Memory from the incarnated brothers-volunteers to help them concentrate on building a vast planetary memory. Once concluded the investigation about the cure of the Tera-Cell, they would recover their Cosmic Memory.

In the first departures from the Dome-City of Lemuria, there was no change. However, when the human-forms started passing from one dome to another, they were gradually adjusting to the conditions of the exterior and finally breathing its air. Their minds and bodies were functioning normally. After winning the exterior, those communities occupied appropriate habitats but thousands of years elapsed until the human-form entirely adjusted to the particular conditions of the planet's exterior.

Many individuals of the new generations turned explorers who more and more distant from the City of Lemuria were studying elements of their environment. These humans, descendants of Lemurianos, had only a remote memory of their origin and Lemuria where they took on the human-form. All they truly remember are the accumulated true-to-life experiences after their ancestors first set a foot on the exterior. Nevertheless, in a way they felt they long before had enjoyed a habitat resembling a paradise when compared to their now still inhospitable surroundings.

Having the human-form developed in the exterior in accordance with the established canons pleased the brothers of the Light. However, there was something important that they still had to consider, Food. Before, the human- form's diet consisted in nutrients from the Dome-City of Lemuria that we, brothers of the Light had provided. So far, Lemurianos-Humans had not tasted any food from the plant kingdom and we had no idea how their bodies and minds would react. Our only reference were the animals that continued their evolution feeding on plants and other animals.

The last stage of the experiment was therefore that these human-forms would have to live on the provisions of the exterior entirely. Consequently, they (and the incarnated brothers of the Light) started spreading and establishing colonies in different places. These communities succeeded on adjusting to and developing in Greenland. From there, the human-forms, very tall hairless individuals with bigger hearts and lungs but smaller feet and hands, sharper eyesight and better hearing conquered planet Earth. They continued communicating through telepathy for not having a voice yet and had full knowledge of the environment from their studies during the process of adjustment. During the establishment of those colonies that took thousands of years and further course of evolution the human-forms, however, began to show symptoms of decline. Their minds were losing agility and correct understanding. Telepathy started failing and their thinking slowed with phases of amnesia. The descendants of the human-forms were no longer perfect because they not only suffered mental but also physical anguish due to the deterioration of their organs. Deficiencies in their diet caused cell damage and drastically reduced a former life span of thousands of years.

The human-form was sick. For the first time we knew what distortion can do. This anomaly allowed us to discover that the energy of the Satien fragment was responsible for the intoxication of soil, plants, food, animals and the human-form despite all the precautions we had taken. While the human-forms in these times formed family clans that, when growing, set out to gain new territory to cover their needs, the brothers Lemurianos-Volunteers embarked on colonizing the planet descending from Greenland to areas of warmer climates where using their vast knowledge, they also formed communities of family clans to continue their evolution.

Even so, they were ill. They started producing guttural sounds to communicate imitating animals but these sounds allowed them to create a language. We brothers of the Light and the brothers Lemurianos lost communication with them since the disease of Distortion they suffered impeded mental contact. We only could appear before them in our bubble-sphere-spacecraft but soon learned that they would not understand from where we came nor whom we are. So, some started worshipping us as gods.

222. Were we then traveling the Solar System? Why did we visit Mars or the Moon?

Millions of years back in time, the Interstellar Cosmic Confederation intercepted seven Planet-Cells of the Primary Dimension contaminated by the Satien fragments – observes the brother of the Light – from the books, we know the sad history of this planet. To heal those sick cells, the Confederation sent the Ayaplianos-Volunteers of the Secondary Dimension of Alpha Centauri and the Pleiades. Their Bubble-Sphere-Spacecraft divided among the sick planet-cells and we brothers of the Light made the Solar System of the Tera-Cell our habitat since, in some way, the Satien fragment seemed to have contaminated all the planets of the System.

To conduct the healing process, we had to use the human-forms – explains the brother of the Light – once incarnated, we traveled to change toxic and lethal for sound elements in the planet-cells' atmosphere. To protect the Tera-Cell against toxic gases emanating from Mars, the Confederation created the Moon. This artificial crystal satellite blocked the gases transforming them into sound light to illuminate Tera, which thus would nurture itself with solar energy, restore its colors and finally cure its contaminated soil.

223. Does this mean that we traveled the Solar System healing Planet-Cells?

Indeed, we brothers of the Light, incarnated in the human-form, were in charge of healing the Solar System. Nowadays the elements of those gases are no longer toxic and their energy does not affect Tera as it did in the past. A recent lunar eclipse impeded gases from the Mars-Cell to reach Tera directly – affirms the brother of the Light – while remaining between Tera and Mars, the Moon showed a red color. This is a cosmic phenomenon but, in reality, the Confederation chose this position to protect Tera against any external interference. The Moon is a huge artificial crystal that refracts the Mars rays deviating them toward the universe.

224. Is the Moon a spacecraft as some writers say?

It is no spacecraft but a Space Station – clarifies the brother of the Light – in charge of control and maintenance, the brothers Interanos of Atlantida visit it regularly. The Moon is a sphere hosting a large city whose inhabitants run the space station. Thus, the brothers Interanos continue healing the Solar System, which still presents harmful cinnabar element.

225. Was the withdrawal of our Cosmic Memory actually necessary? If you allowed us to preserve it, we would remember our true origin and life in this reality perhaps be not as complicated as it is now.

Yes – explains the brother Seramita – it was indeed necessary because suffering from the disease of Distortion that is AMBITION the incarnated brothers of the Light were not to have the Cosmic Knowledge. We knew that the contaminating Reptilian energy would make them use it in the wrong way since it already now controls and manipulates incarnated souls. Can you imagine how would it be if they had the Universal Knowledge? – says the brother of the Light – souls that are awakening are going to regain that Knowledge, however, not when incarnated in the human-form in the exterior but when entering the Internal City after they disincarnate.

When your souls reach the frequency of nine, we take it that they have awaked after actively working their inner senses and will therefore conceive and gestate their Baby-Spirit. As of the fifth grade (month) of gestation, they will be ready to enter the Internal City and complete the recovery of their PLANETARY MEMORY. This means that they will not only recall past lives but also have full knowledge of the planet's history. While completing the nine grades of gestation, they prepare their energy for accessing the city of LIGHT and LOVE of Lemur from where it is going to emanate as an ENERGETIC BEING. This is when we your brothers of the Light will give you back the COSMIC MEMORY indispensable for your embarking on the journey toward Venus, Mercury and final return through the Pineal Gland of the Star Sun to your origin, the Secondary Dimension.

226. None of today's channels appears to know the History of the Planet. What seems to be the reason that you do not transmit it via channeling?

In fact, we do not – replies the brother Seramita – knowing that the Reptilian Force is after ancestral secrets and when finding an ancient revelation would hide it from the public and thus continue their control and manipulation. The ancestral wisdom they are seeking remains buried deep inside the planet and we shall never give the Reptilian Force a chance to discover it since Knowledge is Power. For that reason, we shall only consider souls that have the merit for it when coming to the Internal City.

227. I appreciate – I said to the brothers – very much your enlightening us about the founding ages of *LEMUR, LEMURIA, ATLANTIS and ATLANTIDA.*

These ages are as follows – replies the brother of the Light:

LEMUR – 600 million years
LEMURIA – 300 million years
ATLANTIS – 180000 years
ATLANTIDA – 60000 years

228. Why did you found Atlantis?

We founded the Antimatter Internal City of Atlantis to receive distorted thought-energies (souls) of the human-form from the exterior, which could not return to Lemur for having suffered contamination –

replies the brother Seramita – Atlantis is where we started the process of healing and incarnating again these energies until their complete cure. We gradually adjusted the operation of the city in accordance with the frequency grades of thought-energies (souls) we were receiving.

The Internal City of Atlantis allowed us to communicate with you, which without the treatment of recovery had been impossible before. What happened was that when disincarnating the soul's thought-energy found shelter in other beings' brains with equal frequency. This was how it resisted to fading away. We, however, had offered the souls the shelter of the Internal City, the brain of the planet, and thus created the electromagnetism, which you termed Hell, Purgatory and Heaven as representing the different grades of the energy. This gave us a chance for an in-depth-study of Distortion and for your recovery. With the turn of its axis, the Time Clock (Sandglass) of planet Earth is now in a vertical position downing all the distorted energy, as sand running in a sandglass, toward the Internal City of Atlantis, which after processing and recycling will have it incarnate for further evolution and elevation. Every 28 years, the Time Clock turns again to restart this procedure but every time there is less sand that is, ill negative thought-energies keep reducing until they eventually will vanish from the face of the Earth. This is the Internal City of Atlantis' extraordinary performance of recycling and transmuting souls.

229. When did you found Atlantida?

Atlantida: From the Ancient Greek Atlantis nesos or Island of Atlas, is the name of a mythical island that appears in the dialogues by the Greek philosopher Plato between Timeo and Critias. According to Plato, the island's geographic position is opposite the Columns of Hercules. He depicted it as being larger than Libya and Asia together and a naval power that 9000 years before the appearance of the Hellenic legislator Solon had conquered a major part of Europe and Africa. The hypothesis is that a Pre-Hellenic Athens fought and stopped it. After that, a violent earthquake and deluge during one day and one night caused it to disappear in the ocean.

Plato's description of supposedly true events led to numerous hypotheses, particularly during Romanticism in the second half of the 19th century about its location. Nowadays, the belief is that Plato's narrative holds important anachronisms raising serious doubts about the very existence of the island. Even so, investigators tend to admit that a huge natural disaster may have inspired the creation of the myth.
As a favorite of Poseidon, the island of Atlantida held abundant natural resources such as for instance copper core minerals of the mountain that the Atlantes considered more valuable than gold. There were extensive woods, numerous animal species, both free and domestic as well as a great variety of plants.
Justice and virtue were undisputed qualities of any Atlantida government. However, when the divine nature of Poseidon's descendants started declining, arrogance and the ambition of power turned the Atlantes' dominating characteristics. According to Timeo, their policy of expansion led them to control the population of Libya and Europe until Tirrenia. Nevertheless, forces of Athens defeated them after they tried dominating Greece and Egypt. Critias points out that the gods were about to punish the Atlantes for their arrogance but his narrative halts where Zeus and the other gods gather to determine the type of punishment. Presumptions are that the punishment, in fact, were the earthquake and deluge as mentioned earlier that made Atlantida vanish during a terrifying cataclysm in just one day and one night (Dictionary of Esotericism).

There is some truth in this narrative – observes the brother Seramita – in reality, there have been three Atlantidas. Historians only refer to the third Atlantida built by warriors and conquerors, descendants of the human-form, in the Mediterranean Sea some 25000 years ago. This, however, is not the authentic Atlantida. The real one is located in what is today South America.

The builders of this authentic City of Atlantida were the direct descendants of the Lemurianos who leaving Greenland did not head for the Mediterranean but traveled south founding cities on their way. The construction of this Atlantida some 60000 years ago was a process that started in what today is Mexico and extended to Central America, and the countries of South America today known as Ecuador, Colombia, Peru (Cusco), Bolivia (Titicaca Lake), Southern Brazil, Northern Argentina, Uruguay, Paraguay and Northern Chile.

In that time, the Incas named that zone: El Tahuantinsuyo – proceeds the brother Seramita – those Lemurianos had reached full development of their mental faculties. Although they still suffered from distortion without recalling their origin, using abilities and experience, their knowledge of the planet multiplied. This City of Atlantida therefore had a high reputation of cultural, scientific and technological advance, particularly in medicine. People from all over the planet came to visit it or to stay.

We brothers Ayaplianos were always very close to protect the people of Atlantida against any possible serious threat – emphasizes the brother of the Light – in fact, the Internal City of Atlantis, at all times, had been formally responsible for them. The brothers Interanos, Elohim and Seramitas have been and will be their guardians forever the way they always had been the guardians of their souls. Usual contacts were with spiritually advanced Lemurianos in the form of holograms transmitting them the knowledge that they gradually assimilated.

This way, the Lemurianos kept learning and developing for thousands of years and many gaining the orally transmitted Knowledge of the Ancestors. Atlantida continued prosperous and relatively free of ambition. In other words, the human-form of those times was broadminded and the disease of ambition seemed to have failed to affect individuals seriously. Through our teachings, we therefore could help them preserve the energy of their souls pure and elevated. The ATLANTES of Atlantida turned an immense hope for the future.

The disease of distortion-ambition is under control but obviously without a cure as evolution shows – reminds the brother of the Light – some of their descendants incarnated with the virus of ambition and started using the knowledge they received for personal benefit by controlling and failing to transmit it to others. Consequently, the Lemuriano human-form fell gravely ill triggering great suffering. We no longer could communicate with them and only assist their disincarnated souls when entering the Internal City of Atlantis. Similar happened in the Mediterranean Sea with humans abusing of other humans by using extreme ambition, avarice and violence. The inevitable occurred with an enormous amount of sick energy causing devastating earthquakes, hurricanes and floods that buried Atlantida. The Gulf of Mexico collapsed and Central America's geography suffered total transformation. South America was no exception as terrifying tsunamis flooded a part of the continent while new landmasses emerged. Many of today's islands of the area formed during those times. Atlantida fell apart sinking its parts into the deep of the Atlantic Ocean. New rivers and lakes emerged. The face of Earth would never again be what it was.

This first Atlantida remains buried underneath the countries mentioned earlier. Many years later, explorers from other parts of the planet settled in the area founding the second City of Atlantida. They carried the knowledge of their ancestors about a City, blessed by the gods of the Titicaca Lake that once had prospered in that area. Legends about this event never ended.

You managed to discover and open this dimensional Passage in 2004. We will use it to free the souls of Atlantida that had waited for this moment to incarnate and anticipate the beginning of the Cosmic Alignment, which would help them transcend to LIGHT and LOVE. This is why we have been working for some 180000 years with you and never stopped. Now, we are succeeding to free many of you from the virus of ambition and that an ever-growing portion of the population has already conquered the disease – emphasizes the brother of the Light – this time, we did succeed because you are going to join us again, with pure hearts and souls and we are ready to meet you.

230. Where is the third Atlantida then?

You are because you have been building this third Atlantida over the second one – replies the brother of the Light – nevertheless, the millennial arcana of Ancient Atlantida continue hidden underneath those countries of South America. You are the incarnated Atlantes who ever since lived true-to-life experiences on Earth after you left Lemuria and now are on the Path of Return. The Atlantes therefore never vanished and just continue with what they had left uncomplete.

When we say that you are the Atlantes, we not only refer to the inhabitants of North, Central and South America that is to those who incarnated and lived in these areas. Atlantes are the souls of all human beings everywhere in this planet. They are who incarnate over and again in the exterior suffering from distortion and the disease of Ambition, those who started and continue awaking to walk the Path of Return toward Lemuria.

231. How can we from the exterior help the Internal City recycle and transmute souls?

You are already helping – observes the brother of the Light – because human beings who awake by activating their memory are elevating the frequency of their energy and that of their environment and thus of the entire planet. Remember that the electromagnetism will directly benefit from your lasting endeavor as those higher incarnated or disincarnated thought-energies are going to purify and transmute the negativity of zones one, two and three when passing through them. An example on a larger scale would be your Solar System where the Asteroid Belt works as a filter letting pass only the souls that are ready for it.

232. Does this mean that zones one, two and three of the electromagnetism keep dense souls from reaching grades that are more elevated?

That is correct because those dense thought-energies (souls) represent enormous opaque crystals without light that heavily weigh on the electromagnetism of these zones – replies the brother Seramita – instead, elevated souls carry tiny crystals that easily pass dense and heavy thought-energies. These will be the thoughts for July 7th, 2014. The union of millions of individuals will help us free of those heavy energies and allow many confined souls to transmute with a chance to incarnate and keep on with their process of evolution and elevation.

233. Why – I ask thoughtfully – do those souls remain trapped in zones one, two and three?

These are elementary and inappropriately worked thought-energies that you are trying to remove from your Subconscious. Similar occurs with the Planet-Earth-Brain – observes the brother of the Light – the Subconscious of the planet filled with ill negative thought-energies dwells in the lowest grades of the electromagnetism. The reptilian force takes there advantage for control and seeks flooding the zones with those energies in a way to make them impenetrable for anybody. Which means no other thing than leaving the planet in total darkness. We, under no circumstances, will tolerate such barbarism. The brothers of the Internal City and we brothers of the Light have therefore a standing compromise to free the planet of these extremely harmful energies.

234. There is so much we still have to learn!! – I exclaim with emphasis.

Indeed, there remains much to do – agrees the brother Seramita –. However, you are going to recover full memory of everything when coming to the Internal City. Meanwhile, we keep sending you information to nurture your incarnated and disincarnated souls with Knowledge, Understanding and Love.

235. Having now completed the six books, will there be more information from your side? – I ask while looking at them.

Yes. We shall not cease transmitting – says the brother of the Light – other interlocutors will continue our work to make the information available to every one of you. After these six books, you will continue writing – assures the brother Seramita – there will be other books to have the Knowledge and the Awakening of Conscience flourish in humans' souls.

236. Below, brothers, you will find letters addressed to EL SER UNO. Those we have selected are from persons who experience extrasensory phenomena in their dreams they do not understand. What explanation could we give them to help?

These as so many other persons who have visions in their dreams but are unable to understand them are without the KNOWLEDGE that these visions represent experiences that their memory carries from lives at Lemuria, origin of your material reality on the planet – observes the brother of the Light.

READERS' LETTERS

- Can someone help me? Something extraordinary happens with me. I do not only feel having left my body but also turned a fast-traveling blue light that takes me to a blue-colored world full of white light without a body just as in my case and with other beings moving in an equal manner. Please, help me understand this experience that makes me lose my mind but feel happy and not want to miss anymore.

- I am aware that many people have similar experiences. It is necessary that they learn how to control them, which they however cannot do alone. Many of us feel misunderstood when showing such sensibility or going through certain events that others do not. I therefore sincerely hope to be able to share those experiences with you. I know paranormal phenomena; even have had near-death experiences and have a very lively imagination often hard to control. Nevertheless, believing in certain things that produce visions and sensations I fail to control, makes me feel sick. The resulting imbalance and stress take all day to overcome but then everything comes back.

- Good morning, brothers. I hope you had a good night's rest. I am writing you about something interesting that happened to me today. I dreamed that I went for a trip presumably to the Marcahuasi plateau east of Lima (Peru) where I had been shortly before and plan to return on July 6th, 2014. All of a sudden, I felt my mind disconnect from my body and open my eyes in another body, which I perceived as light and subtle. I found myself in a place full of green vegetation surrounded by plantations. Someone by my side whom I could hardly see with my eyesight trying to adjust to the environment made mental contact saying – we are here – Afterwards, two persons with what seemed to me greenish skin color spoke right into my ear asking: brother atanita, are you alright? I told them yes. However, the answer did not come out in words but as rare vibrating sounds. I then went for a walk to have a look at the surroundings. The person who was talking to me in my mind suggested that I should drink a blue-colored liquid that would make me know the truth about the planet and myself but might scare me and even be a shock to my new body. Asked if I would have to take the liquid right away the person said that there was no hurry for being this my first trip. After that, I found myself again in my body getting off the bus and, feeling deeply touched, I woke up.

- I am very thankful to EL SER UNO for bringing fresh air to my life since I felt extremely suffocated by the Catholic Church. From childhood on, I have lived too many strange events, some of rare beauty but others highly scaring such as levitation, seeing my family and I descend a gigantic sphere of light on us, and a number of other occurrences for which I have no explanation until today. May the Universe and our Lord bless you forever!

- How are you? While studying the French Revolution at university the "coincidence" between the date of this historical event and that of the Cosmic Alignment greatly surprised me. I find it unbelievable (though not really) that the revolution (July 14th, 1789 /1+7+8+9 = 25 = 2+5 =7) starts only seven days after the beginning of the Cosmic Alignment as announced by EL SER UNO. As we know, the revolution occurred at a moment when the population realized that taking political action it could change politics, institutions, beliefs etc. History considers the French Revolution the most important event of the Occident for having changed more situations than any other before. It began with the removal of the monarchy and the Catholic Church and was the beginning of a new world order. Another coincidence appears to be that it occurred during the movement of Illustration or ENLIGHTENMENT. Enlightenment would be illumination that is what occurs now with so much information available to wake and illuminate us. In fact, many are awakening through the knowledge that you transmit. However, I ask myself how we can be so oblivious of all that we had been fighting for in those times and repeat the mistakes we made. The more I read about the French Revolution the clearer it appears that now all this is happening again as if in a pre-established program.

- Five years ago, I applied for a job at a cosmetology center that was looking for a therapist. To my surprise, during the interview they asked me for a demonstration of my physical therapy. When I was in the middle of concentration, a man with a white beard handed me a lilac or light lilac color light to use it on the patient who seemed to have a problem with the heart chakra. Recently, this man appeared in a dream passing me that light, which this time was of brilliant white color. I very much appreciate your enlightening me about the symbolism. With love and thanks for the message of your books.

- Dear *Ser Uno*, I just want to say how thankful I am for the knowledge, understanding and love that you are transmitting. In a very particular way, I feel you closer than ever to me and with extraordinary clearness. On May 5th and 6th, 2014, I had this wonderful experience that makes me feel you so close and I see you...I was in a state of plenitude because I received immense tenderness, love and much, much energy and light. Enormous flashes of light in front of my face, spirals of energy and images. It was overwhelming. It is so extraordinary that I find it hard to put into words what I see and forever will feel inside myself. Light, Love and Blessings for you, Brothers...

You must never forget that you are BEINGS of LIGHT, who came to this planet from a reality of the future, the Secondary Dimension – proceeds the brother of the Light – you all carry the inborn faculties of the Ayapliana Species. Therefore, what you consider special are "natural" abilities in the universe since the species always uses all of its brain capacity. What happened to you is that after losing your Cosmic Memory, your seven Inner Senses slowed, and you started relying on your External Senses.

These letters clearly show that your souls are victims of oblivion. You have to comprehend the origin of those experiences you deem special and make you feel illuminated, chosen by the universe, God or even think not to belong to this planet and that you therefore are superior to others. Once you are aware you will no longer let your Ego carry you away believing that you are beings of other realities or planets who came to fulfill some tasks assigned by the Interstellar Cosmic Confederation.

You call those experiences Extrasensory Phenomena but, in reality, you must understand and treat them as feelings emerging from the soul and the spirit but always in context with your Inner Senses. When Human Beings awake with their Inner Senses beginning to flourish, they have to assimilate these Phenomena with their Soul and Spirit to keep the Ego or distorted emotions from arousing. Thus, they avoid boasting of something that in fact everyone has.

It takes humility and maturity to accept the origin of these phenomena as only then you will be able to control your Ego and the emotions they produce in your soul. Therefore, reading the books will help you sort out thought-energies in your mind and make you feel certain from where you came, whom you are and where you are heading. Recalling your origin and accepting it means centering on its context with the universe. There was never anyone "special" in the universe. Since your minds do not have a clear vision of the past, your Egos tend to make up beings with superior faculties using them afterwards for personal benefit and power...

We all have been listening in silence. The brother of the Light proceeds to covers us with his LIGHT and LOVE, the presence of which I feel intensely. When looking at my right, I see two planets Earth in the distance...one of it weak and almost without Light, the other brilliant full of life and colors...this must be Tera, I think to myself – the luminous and hoped for Earth that waits for us to arrive – we are trying to build it with thoughts, love and the LIGHT our hearts and souls irradiate. The world, however, continues dejected and we are responsible for it because the emotions of our egotism have made us what we are. We therefore must strive for the Awakening and Growth of our Conscience. To work, spirituality claims our unconditional compromise and its fulfillment – concludes the brother of the Light. After these words, I understand that our dialog has ended. When looking at every one of them, I feel great love in my soul. I hardly can put into words my feelings of joyfulness but also of sadness for not knowing if I would meet or communicate with them again. I realize that there is no way to tell how long it will take to walk the path of return but firmly believe that it is not impossible to succeed. The Awakening of millions of souls is already occurring, but we all know that we must keep the strength to persist. Feeling an indescribable force inside and a beam of light invading me, I perceive the immenseness of all and our being a part of it. With this in mind, I turn to the brothers saying:

"All I wish to say on behalf of humanity without feeling sure, if I have the right – THANK YOU BROTHERS – for the Dedication, Patience and Love during your work with us. I thank you, our Creator, for this life of plenitude that only you have the love to give me. THANK YOU for guiding us on the Path of Return. THANK YOU for the Knowledge that you have transmitted to understand our reality. THANK YOU for always being close helping us walk through life. THANK YOU for teaching us to live a joyful and peaceful life. THANK YOU for favoring the union of all human beings. THANK YOU for making us open our minds and activate our memory. THANK YOU for giving our soul the strength to continue, without fear, realizing the work with our inner senses. THANK YOU for teaching us about Forgiveness.

THANK YOU AGAIN, BROTHERS". I remain in silence knowing that we are about to say good-bye. They give me the look of love I always feel and I instantly understand that they will forever be close because they are our brothers, sisters, fathers and mothers. WE SHALL NEVER BE ALONE. The brothers nod in agreement and the brother of the Light addresses me saying:

"Spirituality means that you have the true key that opens the door to the Divine essence of the Being. The name of the key is "Authenticity". Being authentic throughout this reality of existence makes it easier for the soul to use the inner senses extolling their deeds, actions and thoughts. "Authenticity" is a divine gift and the language of the human soul. Its secret is that it opens all the doors to LIGHT and LOVE. "Authenticity" makes you listen and see with your heart and soul the Divine essence, the energy of life and existence. It is the source of natural, spontaneous and eternal existence. Life becomes TO BE and so authentic that with every breath you take you will have full conscience of your Divine Inner Self that lives deep inside EL SER UNO".

To our children, brothers and sisters

Many are the hardships you have gone through but here you are with us!! Not for an instant, we have abandoned you. We have always been close. Now you will keep on walking the path of return for having advanced on the cure of yourselves and of your habitat, the planet. You are the beloved children of the universe taking with you the knowledge to nurture the source of life, the One Origin of LIGHT and LOVE.

The message of these books will reach all those who have already advanced on the path of return. Many of you still embrace enchanting mysticism and romanticism yielding to the temptation of fantasy. The books EL SER UNO will be of help whenever a person needs a clearer vision to be able to face sometimes very tough realities. Not all are ready to accept listening to details of a displeasing past or facing unworked emotions from the subconscious.

This is the last of the books EL SER UNO, however, the message of their knowledge will continue. Their teachings will allow certain cerebral circuits to open favoring the process of the AWAKENING of CONSCIENCE. The course lying ahead is often hard in this dense reality and claims sacrifice. Instead of counting on words of magic or miracles, the truth you seek is inside your souls and hearts.

Therefore, brothers and sisters do not desist. Do not let dejection or the lack of belief win but keep in search of LIGHT and LOVE deeply rooted in your souls, ready to turn a reality. Be patient and listen to your inner voice.

The discussion about truth will never end. The controlled, manipulated or even false truth frequently does not allow you to see or feel through true-to-life experience the sincerity and integrity that live in all of you. The inner voice and your divine essence are still dormant thus blocking the sublime manifestation of their infinite nature. You have stopped taking a cosmic breath and a rush of impotence has cut off the reconciling and divine message.

You will never find spirituality in reading or listening to chants of celestial glory. Spirituality is in the essence of your being, in your divine self, in your cultural advance and in the thoughts of your mind. It listens, sees, perceives, learns and wakes dormant thoughts whose dreams and illusions do not let them progress because of weakness and guilt.

To walk the spiritual way does not depend on theoretic but on practical knowledge for people to see and feel and not consider themselves superior but to raise the quality of their and other brothers' spirituality. The accumulation of knowledge is of no use if you do not know how to employ it. It would be as if you created an expectation without turning it a productive reality. Walking the path of spirituality means to create better living conditions every day regarding health, work, well-being, joyfulness, harmony and peace. Spiritual knowledge is a tool every wayfarer should have to be successful in this life.

Brothers, generosity and compassion are the prelude of Love. They are essential qualities in a life based on comprehension, harmony and spirituality. It is the spiritual practice that will take all those guided by the illumination of their Being to the origin of the teaching of fraternity. Compassion frees you from suffering.

Oh, Humans!! Your dormant energy fails to awake to reality because it is a prisoner of its dreams. Wake up to see and feel the universal union connect with the Energy Centers of the Cosmos. Wake from ambition, avarice and ill negative emotions that make you forget the essence of the soul and everything that illuminates the truth. This is why the DNA of your hearts and souls continue in the darkness of treason, ignorance and blindness. Ill and disconnected from the eternal source you fail to see the light, the infinite essence of love and the perfection of the Universal Mind.

The reality of the Cosmos functions as a compass showing you the correct path to reach the origin of the memory. The silence of the soul will take you to ever-shining, brilliant and clarifying lights. Move freely in the inner silence of wisdom evoking sublime moments during which equanimity will grant you the primacy and virtues of solar and cosmic beings whose conscience disperses in the unity of life.

Brothers, may LIGHT and LOVE accompany and guide you on the path to infinite Knowledge, Understanding and Love!! WE LOVE YOU VERY MUCH AND ARE AWAITING YOU. RETURN TO ETERNAL LIGHT AND LOVE!!...

WITHOUT KNOWLEDGE, I DO NOT LIVE
WITHOUT UNDERSTANDING, I DO NOT EXIST
WITHOUT LOVE, I AM NOT

EL SER UNO

FRANCA CANONICO DE SCHRAMM became a channel for the Masters of Orion, Alpha Centaury and the Pleiades who started preparing her for this communication when she was 33 years old. This preparation culminated in 2002 when she started channeling the Knowledge of EL SER UNO in six books dictated via telepathy by the Elder Brothers Ayaplianos of the Sixth, Seventh, Eighth and Ninth Dimension of the Universe. EL SER UNO is a Philosophical, Psychologic and Spiritual knowledge.

Made in the USA
Monee, IL
18 May 2022